BEST SPORTS STORIES 1987

Edited and Published by

The Sporting News

President and Chief Executive Officer
RICHARD WATERS

Editor
TOM BARNIDGE

Director of Books and Periodicals
RON SMITH

Published in the United States by THE SPORTING NEWS Publishing Co., 1212 North Lindbergh Boulevard, St. Louis, Missouri 63132.

Library of Congress Catalog Card Number: 45-35124

ISSN: 0067-6292
ISBN: 0-89204-243-5
10 9 8 7 6 5 4 3 2 1

First Edition

Table of Contents

The Prize-Winning Stories

Other Stories

The Prize-Winning Photographs

Other Photographs

The Prize-Winning Color Photograph
Look Out Below

by Ken Geiger of the Dallas Morning News. The winning color photograph, which appears on the front cover, shows Detroit Tigers catcher Lance Parrish tumbling over a railing during a game against the Texas Rangers in Arlington, Tex. Copyright © 1986, the Dallas Morning News.

Back-Cover Photograph
A Head Case

by Howard Lipin of the San Diego Union. Boise State basketball player Arnell Jones finds himself in an awkward position during a 1986 game against San Diego State. Copyright © 1986, Howard Lipin, the San Diego Union.

PREFACE

The road to the top of the 1986 sports world ended in New York. At least that's the feeling one gets when recalling the major occurrences of a year gone by. But sports fans in Boston, Denver, Anaheim, Houston and Louisville had few complaints and Joe Paterno and his Penn State Nittany Lions certainly gave State College, Pa., football fans a season worth remembering.

New Yorkers, however, long will cherish 1986 as the year of the Mets and Giants. The Mets, who brawled their way through the regular season while running away from the rest of the National League East Division field, survived a stubborn Houston Astros test in the League Championship Series and then came back from the brink of elimination in Game 6 of the World Series against the Boston Red Sox to become champions of the baseball world. The Giants, led by the strong right arm of quarterback Phil Simms, the running of back Joe Morris and the fierce defensive play of linebacker Lawrence Taylor, rolled through the regular season and playoffs before recording a January 1987 Super Bowl victory over the Denver Broncos.

But those two stories were just the tip of the sports iceberg. In baseball, Roger Clemens dazzled Boston fans with his Cy Young Award-winning performance and added a 20-strikeout masterpiece to the sport's record books. Atlanta's Bob Horner snatched his piece of baseball history by rocketing four home runs in one game. In basketball, the Boston Celtics added another National Basketball Association championship banner to their already-crowded rafters and the Louisville Cardinals became kings of the college world by winning the NCAA Tournament championship. And pro golf fans will relish the memory of the master, Jack Nicklaus, donning the prized green jacket, again, in the twilight of his fabled career.

Wherever the action, *they* were there. "They" refers to the men and women who put as much effort into their pursuit of the perfect story or picture as athletes put into their search for excellence. The competition is fierce and the results gratifying. Those who chronicled the 1986 sports world for newspapers and magazines throughout the country continued to move toward the lofty goal of perfection, taking their readers behind the scenes for insight and perspective on the personalities and events that made the year memorable.

The Sporting News is proud to present a small sprinkling of those memories in the 43rd edition of *Best Sports Stories*, the anthology that honors the year's top writers and photographers. TSN is editing and publishing its fifth edition of the anthology, which traces its roots to 1944 and the efforts of Irving Marsh and Edward Ehre. The contest to select winners and contributors attracted hundreds of newspaper and magazine entries. It was open to writers and photographers throughout the country and accepted only stories and pictures that were published in 1986. Serving as judges for the fifth straight year was a panel of five teachers from the University of Missouri, home of one of the world's most-respected journalism education programs. They are:

Brian Brooks, the *St. Louis Post-Dispatch* Distinguished Professor of Journalism at the University of Missouri and managing editor of the *Columbia Missourian*, a student and faculty-run newspaper that serves the city of Columbia, Mo.

George Kennedy, associate dean of the University of Missouri's School of Journalism.

Bill Kuykendall, associate professor and director of the University of Missouri's photojournalism sequence.

Daryl Moen, a professor in the University of Missouri School of Journalism's news-editorial sequence.

Byron Scott, a Meredith Professor of Magazine Journalism and the University of Missouri's service journalism program director.

Those five judges can attest to the agonizing problems that arise when you sort through hundreds of creative, well-written stories in search of the *four* that deserve special recognition. Likewise, the selection process for *three* pictures. But, after painstakingly considering the merits of each entry, the judges chose the following winners, each of whom receives a $500 prize:

WRITING

Reporting	Ron Cook	Pittsburgh Press
Feature	William Gildea	Washington Post
Commentary	John Feinstein	Washington Post
Magazine	David DeVoss	Los Angeles Times Magazine

PHOTOGRAPHY

Color	Ken Geiger	Dallas Morning News
B&W Action	William Johnson	Bucks County Courier Times
B&W Feature	Louis DeLuca	Dallas Times Herald

It also was difficult to weed the selection list to the choice stories that would appear in this book. By no means are the stories and photos that follow the winning selections losers. They are, rather, a tribute to the sports journalism profession, which seems to get stronger every year. All of the *Best Sports Stories* contributors are providing an entertaining look at the 1986 sports year, as seen through the eyes and lenses of those who were there.

Best Feature Story

Donovan Still Casts A Big Shadow

PRO FOOTBALL

By *William Gildea*

From the Washington Post
Copyright © 1986, the Washington Post

Growing up in Baltimore in the '50s, we knew these were the best of times: We had good food on the table (it has always been important there which butcher to use and where to get the crabs), a grass lot to play on, The Diner where we ate the fries and dreamed American dreams and, most of all, the Colts. Our beloved Colts. On a Sunday at 2 o'clock in the stadium, the roar would swallow the introductions: Gino Marchetti, Art Donovan, Big Daddy Lipscomb . . . One after the other. (To say nothing of Unitas.) They were the greatest. You can argue, but they were.

You know the rest, and you don't know the rest.

Unitas let his crew cut grow, Marchetti went into hamburgers, Big Daddy died, The Diner (the real one) was torn down, the Colts were taken to Indianapolis. Most of it figured: The trolley barn is Johnny's Auto Body and Fender, and Sam and Elmer's barber shop (What a duo! One tall and bald, one short and round. They did a soft-shoe and had a calendar girl over the cash register)—Sam and Elmer's . . . vacant. But the Colts move?

"I says, you're nuts, they're never gonna leave. First thing I know, I was watchin' TV, the 11 o'clock news and they have the Orioles packin' up in Miami and comin' north, and the next thing I know I see a Mayflower van and it's snowin'. Well, I said, it don't snow in Miami. I think, hey, maybe I better change the brand I'm drinkin' here.

"No, they were talkin' about the Colts, movin' out. In the dead of the night. They rode off into the dark, into the dead of night."

Art Donovan, old No. 70, is talking about his Colts as he drives his Chevy truck past Sam and Elmer's empty storefront, past what was the trolley barn, less than a mile from where The Diner was. Art Donovan—constant in a world of turmoil, adopted Baltimorean and civic bedrock.

"Little Arthur" of the Bronx, son of the boxing referee, Art Donovan, "Big Arthur," the third man in the ring for 18 of Joe Louis' fights, including the 1938 rematch with Max Schmeling. "Little Arthur" was the kid on the subway from the Bronx who carried his father's small bag with his gray referee's uniform in it downtown to him on fight nights. Then, grown up to be one of the Colts (champions in 1958 and 1959) and their "Magnificent Seven" (Unitas, Lenny Moore, Raymond Berry, Jim Parker, Marchetti, Weeb Ewbank and Donovan).

And today, at 62, in what he calls his "twilight years," marking his third epoch as an '80s media figure who has spawned a cult on David Letterman and another of squealy teen-age girls who saw him as "a big cutie"—a 325-pound crew-cut dumpling—diving into the goal-line pileup of hot dogs on the recent Maryland State Lottery "Instant Baseball Game" commercial that, as a lottery official put it, "sold out almost instantly."

Maybe there'll be another game with Donovan because Donovan'll be around. He has always been around. Owner of a tennis and swim club, into the empty pool of which he once slipped and dropped 23 feet—no joke, he didn't crack the pool bottom, like some say, he lay in agony for an hour until someone found him in a broken heap. A bushwhacked blimp.

And a beer salesman. Schlitz. A man made for Miller Lite who has always drunk Schlitz, 12 to 18 cans a night. (And 20 to 30 hot dogs a sitting.) He doesn't need the money, he just likes the beer. That's why he goes to these liquor stores, pushing the brand he has drunk forever. Twenty-one years he owned a liquor store—that's where he made his big money. Until, near the end, he was stuck up five times in a month. Once, a man aimed a shotgun at him. "It felt like I was lookin' through the Lincoln Tunnel."

Now, among all else, he's a two-days-a-week salesman who can get a proprietor's attention even when he's only semi-serious.

"Where's the Schlitz?"

"Where's the Schlitz? It's in the back."

"You told me you were goin' to put it up front."

"Well, do you want me personally to put it up front?"

"I'll put it up front . . ."

This is how much he likes Schlitz: "I went to California with my wife and we drove 11 hours up to Reno and I couldn't find Schlitz in Reno. You know what I did? I drove all the way around Lake Tahoe to California and they had Schlitz. I bought myself a case. Then I come out and a kid wants to start a fight with me. I said, I think I'm a little too big for you. 'Nobody's too big for me.' He said I had him blocked in, and I didn't. I got out of the car. I said, 'Let's think this over.' I called him a name and then I left."

Now, he has parked his truck and is walking down the sidewalk to Jim Parker's liquor store. Jim Parker, one of the "Magnificent Seven," old No. 77. From behind, Donovan's form fills the horizon, shoulders sloping like mountains under a tan raincoat. Like that bent-edged, black-and-white photo of him, taken from behind, leaving the stadium in the twilight, the shoulders then covered by a cape with a Colt on the back. Art Donovan, Gladiator. On the corner, youths gape. He's walking right at them.

"Hey, you're . . ."

"It is. It is!"

"ARTIE!"

"Hiya, fellas." Said in a faint New York rasp, a big man with a little wave, reaching a new generation.

★   ★   ★

He never sought fame. He understands it to be not of merit but accident. Three times it has happened. Every Bronx kid knew his old man. Then, himself, a giant who trod the earth, the old Colts' fun guy with a knack for knowing which direction a play was heading, then trundling laterally from his defensive tackle slot in plenty of time to stuff it. He made it to the pro football Hall of Fame. And now . . . Now . . .

"Now, my picture's all over the place with this lottery. We go to all these liquor stores and my picture's on the door—they got glasses drawn on 'em, they got cigars stuck in my mouth. . . .

"Is this going to be my claim to fame? Eating hot dogs? Seventy-two times I had to bite into the hot dog to do that commercial. Yeah, they made 72 takes. I kept biting. Cold hot dogs. Seventy-two bites."

How did fame strike again? First, by luck, NFL Films included him in a show on the golden age of pro football. Somebody from the Letterman show saw it. Then an agent in Atlanta saw Donovan and put him on a lecture circuit. Then somebody else called about the lottery commercial. Then Schlitz called. "I can't say no," he says.

He was happy the way it was. He's happy now. He'll be happy. "I have no ax to grind. I was lucky. I played. How many guys play high school, college football never play pro football? I wouldn't want to go back over my life. I've done it all. I wouldn't have wanted to miss the Marine Corps. I wouldn't have wanted to miss the war. I wouldn't have missed college. Or playin' for the Colts. I got all the money I need. Five children. I got a truck. I have no regrets whatsoever."

Donovan and Parker. Behemoths. Parker embraces the visitor he calls "Fatso Fogarty." Parker's hair is gray and he smokes a pipe, lights it frequently. He pushes his glasses back up the bridge of his nose after every guffaw. In the center of the floor, next to the Billy Dee Williams' Colt 45 poster, Parker tells about an old awards banquet: "We were up on the stage. The man was introducing us. He said, 'Art Donovan.' He stood right like this. He said, 'Jim Parker.' We stood like this. 'Big Daddy Lipscomb.' He stood up. BAMMMM! The damn stage fell. Everybody went into the basement."

They laugh so hard their bellies almost bump. What more can a man ask? They have their memories, and they still have each other.

★   ★   ★

Donovan's voice echoes through the big, 120-year-old, empty house of the Valley Country Club that he has owned since 1955. He's talking on the phone, in the kitchen. A serious-looking man who speaks softly is with him, holding a football and getting Donovan to sign it. The man is Jim Mutscheller, the tight end of the championship teams who caught the pass from Unitas that took the ball to the Giants' 1-yard line in overtime of the game that ushered in the modern era of pro football—"The Greatest Game Ever Played," 1958 in Yankee Stadium.

Mutscheller gathered in an unconsciously daring Unitas pass into the flat that caused coach Weeb Ewbank's heart to quake. Now, Mutscheller says he's going up the road to get Tom Matte's autograph on the ball, and Donovan says Ordell Braase is coming by. They've never drifted apart; it's just that someone's taken their team away.

In the bar, three generations of Donovans are on the walls. His grandfather, Mike Donovan, fought in the Civil War at age 15—his medals are up there—before he became the middleweight boxing champion. ("Ahhh, he must have been some tough guy," says the grandson.) Mike Donovan taught prizefighting at the New York Athletic Club, where he worked for 40 years. He was succeeded by "Big Arthur," boxing instructor there for 55 years. There's "Big Arthur," pictured with "Little Arthur" at the Colts' training camp. "Big Arthur" ("the toughest man I ever met in my life") lived to be 90, well after he had seen his son play on the two title teams. "Big Arthur" is just out of that picture of "Little Arthur" and Richard Nixon in the locker room after the 1959 title game in Baltimore, this time an easier (31-16) victory against the Giants.

"I wanted to get my father in the picture with the vice president, but he was too busy talkin' to the mayor of New York. The mayor, Wagner, he's askin' my father what's he doin' here, and my father's tellin' him I play with the Colts."

And Nixon?

"He asked me what I was gonna do with the money."

He got almost $5,000 that day. That was a lot. He had grown up in the Bronx with few material goods but 14 cousins within a two-block radius. He had been born in his grandmother's house and raised for several years, with his sister, in a small apartment on 202nd street. "When I was 7, my father started makin' a little money and we got high class and moved two streets up to the Grand Concourse." He went to church and school at St. Philip Neri, and when he started getting big, his mother sent him up to the brothers' school, Mount St. Michael. When Donovan came onto the Yankee Stadium field for The Game in 1958 he heard a guy in the stands yell, "Ya better be better than you were at Mount St. Michael."

He was just "Big Arthur's" kid then. "Big Arthur," who was never so presumptuous on the day of a fight to take his bag with his ref's stuff (the pants, shirt, boxing shoes, bow tie) when he went to work at the New York A.C. The way it would work was, the afternoon of the fight somebody from the boxing commission would call him over at the N.Y.A.C. and tell him he'd be working that night, and then "Big Arthur" would call home. "Mary, would you get the bag ready?" Every time. "Little Arthur" would take the bag to 50th Street and meet his father outside the Garden, or Yankee Stadium or the Polo Grounds.

They met again, "Big Arthur" and "Little Arthur," by accident, during the war, on Guam. "Big Arthur" had volunteered, even though he was in his 50s, and worked in USO sports tours. There, one day on Guam, this big troop came walking down the road. By God, it was—could it have been anyone else? For then, he was big—"Little Arthur!"

"So then," says Donovan, "they dropped the bomb and we all went home."

It was the beginning of his second epoch, highlights of which hang on the bar walls: a plaque certifying that Art Donovan has crossed the Arctic Circle, his wife, Dottie, with Pope John, a football from Colt Corral No. 5, a Boston College Hall of Fame plaque, a plaque on the retirement of No. 70 on September 16, 1962, the "Magnificent Seven" portrait. A yellowed newspaper story titled: "Donovan Goes on Forever."

★   ★   ★

Jim Wertz comes in. He works for Schlitz and he'll go around with Donovan this day to six liquor stores. This is only Donovan's ninth day on the job. Gotta get the product moving. Donovan likes to say, "I drink more than they sell."

He drives his truck. "I just got that script about that movie down in Beaumont. I'm going to be in a movie. The big stars of it, evidently, are Bubba Smith, Dick Butkus and Alex Karras. But the script doesn't say what I'm supposed to do. I guess drink. . . ."

"Hey, Unitas lives right there. See where that white thing is. That's a church. He lives in the next big house. You gotta go up Mount Kilimanjaro. You get nosebleed goin' up there."

He pulls into a shopping center parking lot and he's talking about Marchetti. "Ooooh," Donovan goes. "He never said anything. Played alongside him for 10 years and he never said anything. The only thing he ever asked me was, what was the defense. I said, 'For cripes sakes.' We were in the same formation, a 4-3, 99 percent of the time. We never blitzed. They figured we should put pressure on the passer without the blitz, and we didn't want to blitz because we figured we were all doin' our job. Gino, he never said boo.

"The only guy who used to scream and holler all the time was (Bill) Pellington. Crazy. But tough. You know he played five plays with a broken arm?"

Into Padonia Liquors. A customer does a double take.

"Hittin' anybody recently?" Donovan says to the man behind the counter.

The man behind the counter is Jim Wertz's brother, Charlie. Artie Donovan's Baltimore is a metro village, where everybody knows everybody and a good half must be related.

Outside, he points to a restaurant. "Up there is where I used to have my radio show. They must have had 500 people in this place, listening to this goofy radio show. Braase and I were on it.

"On my radio show, Miller was the sponsor. And I'd say, 'Give me another Miller.' And I'd open a can of Schlitz. The liquor store here, they used to send me up 12 cans of Schlitz on the house so I could drink the Schlitz."

He's driving along, remembering Big Daddy, 6-feet-6, who instituted the practice of helping up a player after he had tackled him. Some players and coaches would tell Daddy to "leave the guy alone, leave him down on the ground. But he'd tackle the guy, he'd pick him up. He figured that would get him some publicity. But none of us worried too much about publicity. We knew how good we were. The way you knew how good you were or not—don't let anybody kid you —is the guy you played against. He could tell you whether you were good, bad or indifferent. . . .

"Fifty-eight. They say it was the greatest game ever played. I don't think it was. But if they say it was, who am I to say no? The greatest game was the '58 game here in Baltimore against the 49ers. They were beatin' us, 27-3, at halftime and we come out in the second half and we absolutely annihilated them. I mean, annihilated them. Unitas and Berry and Moore and (Alan) Ameche, our offensive line, they just killed 'em. In fact, I'd only get on the field to block for the extra points. I'd say to Leo Nomellini, 'You comin', Leo?' That's how I knew if he was goin' to rush. And he'd say, 'Hell no, it's all over now.' So you knew, he was just going to lean on you. But if he was to say, 'Yeah I'm comin',' watch out, here they come. . . ."

Everybody in the stadium screaming. . . .

Jim Wertz: "Greatest fans in the world."

"They were. They were wild. I'm tellin' you, they were wild. This town, in 1955 till when I got through, this town was so wild that ladies use to knit us sweaters for your kids, hats. . . ."

★   ★   ★

Into Fink's Discount Liquors. Big Donovan. Small Wertz. Bernie Fink says, "Now I know what they mean by the odd couple." Commotion. A customer talking to Donovan, Wertz talking to Fink—Baltimore talk (the old guys, who they married, how they're still there). Like in "Diner."

Next stop: Pinehurst Gourmet & Spirit Shoppe. The proprietor with the handlebar mustache, who's the brother of a guy at Eddie's Super Market, one of the next stops, remembers Donovan from the days he was starting out, with a distributor. "He came in one day, when he was playing for the Colts, and I think we needed a case of Dewar's scotch. It came packed in a wooden case, with metal bands around it. He came in with it in one hand, like this. 'Here's your case of scotch.' Carried it like a little parcel."

Over to Anthony and Sal's, Donovan's old place. On the way: "Right down here, we lived together. (Don) Shula, I and Pellington. You know, in the years when you got hurt and there was a timeout charged against you, we had three guys on the sidelines walk up and down with Weeb—it was Shula, (Carl) Taseff and (Bert) Rechichar. And if somebody got hurt they'd run out on the field and drag 'im off so we wouldn't get charged a timeout. God's honest truth. 'Go get 'im.' Guy have a broken leg, they'd pull him off the field. . . .

"There's Anthony." He's wearing an Orioles cap.

"Hey, Anthony, got my picture hangin' up here?"

In back is a deli with meats and salads and slaw and cakes. Everybody's getting a sandwich to go, everybody but Donovan. He eats only one meal, around dinnertime. Wertz: "The one meal he eats is unbelievable. Twenty-five, 30 hot dogs. He'll take two hot dogs, two rolls. He'll take one hot dog out of the other roll and put the two hot dogs in one roll."

To Eddie's, on Roland Avenue. It's Donovan's town he's driving through, but it could have been otherwise. "In '54, I went up to New York to take the exam to go on the New York police department. They were going to let me come down here and play football for six months and go back and be a cop. Two of my uncles were inspectors and detectives and three other men who lived in my neighborhood were all big shots in the department.

"I would only have stayed a uniformed policeman for about six months and then I would have got into the detective bureau. But in the meantime, I got a job working here with Schenley. So I said, 'Well, this is it.' I got married. We bought the club. I'm not blowing my own horn or anything, but I'm a big fish in a small pond. Everybody knows me. Where in New York, all my next door neighbors didn't know I played for the Colts. They don't give a damn in New York."

★   ★   ★

Outside a drugstore next to Eddie's, a man calls, over his shoulder, "Who's that guy blocking the doorway? Looks like an old football player." The cashier tells Donovan she'd been out to his club for a wedding reception and he knows her father's cousin, no less. Her husband used to be the radio engineer for the Colts games, way back, "when the guys sat out there and froze to death. Now they sit in a booth."

In Eddie's, at the meat department, Donovan orders liverwurst to take home. On the sidewalk, he says, "So I'm walkin' out without payin' for the meat. Way to be a salesman."

Past Pimlico race track and on to Jim Parker's. Above Parker's door is the "Magnificent Seven." Above the counter, his hightop cleats and Colts helmet, white with the blue horseshoes on the sides, everything dusty. Since 1967 they've hung there.

"Hey, I don't have that picture," says Donovan. "Is that us with the Giants?"

"This is the only man I know," says Parker, pointing his pipe toward Donovan, "who's got a million dollars and is too poor to have somebody to paint his pool. He got into the pool, fell off the ladder, buried down there. Couldn't get up and couldn't get out. They had to call the fire truck to pull 'im out."

"I'm serious," says Donovan. "The guy says, 'You think you can go up the ladder?' I says, 'I just came down on it.'

"They took my kneecap out. I broke all my ribs. I broke my wrist and my elbow. They got me to the hospital and they put me on the table and the table's too small. I fell off the table."

A man wants Donovan's autograph and he wants Donovan to draw a little star next to his signature. "Aren't you a Hall of Famer?" "Yeah." "Can I shake your hand?" "Yes sir." "Hey, don't break it." Big Parker shoos the man with, "You got everything. First time in your life you ever saw two Hall of Famers in one store."

★   ★   ★

"I'm on the plane with Lenny (Moore)," says Donovan to Parker, "and he's readin' the Bible. Lenny Moore on the plane readin' the Bible! Says he's a born-again Christian."

"He learned it from me," says Parker. "He said, 'Why're you so happy all the time?' I said, 'I'm a born-again Christian.' He said, 'But you're still sellin' this.' I said, 'Makes no difference.' "

"You don't drink?" asks Donovan.

"No."

"You still lie, though."

They laugh.

Driving home, Donovan says, "So many great players. . . . And the guys you didn't hear about, they were great, too. Like Alex Sandusky. Alex Karras called me, first time I ever talked to him. I said, 'We often talk about you, Alex.' Alex Sandusky and me. He said, 'You know, you were on your way out when I started, but Shula told me to watch all your movies, the way you played.' He said, 'As far as I'm concerned, you were the best.' Now he didn't have to say that because he was a good football player himself."

Pulling in the long driveway, where his big brick home sits next to the even bigger clubhouse, Donovan remembers. He's late for his 10-year-old's car pool. But then he knows his wife, Dottie, his long love and partner in the club, without whom he's made no decision and without whom life could not be this way, he knows Dottie's picked up the kids. He knows this because when he rounds the bend, her new creamy 420 Mercedes SEL—"$46,000"—is in the driveway. She likes the Mercedes; give him the truck.

"I'll be around," he says.

With a limp not from football but the fall into the empty pool, he heads inside, walking off as he had in his cape Sunday afternoons in the dusk at the stadium, unmistakable as ever from behind with the shoulders and the crew cut, walking away from us again but never, never out of our lives.

Judge's Comments

So many stories about our athletic heroes are as superficial as a handshake. The handshake may be a momentary thrill for the fan, but wouldn't it be better to get to spend some time with the hero? Time, not in an interview room but with the heroes in their own environment, seeing them as they really live.

That's not possible, of course, so William Gildea does it for us. You don't have to be a former Baltimore Colt fan to be interested in tackle Art Donovan, a man bigger than life, a 325-pound refrigerator before his time.

By taking us into Donovan's neighborhood, Gildea lets us see the aging, interesting, funny fellow in his own environment, at ease despite a reporter at his side. Because Gildea captures the scenes, the sights and sounds, the camaraderie between Donovan and the boys in the neighborhood so well, we all are at his side.

The story has its moments of humor: Donovan once fell 23 feet to the bottom of his empty pool. *". . . no joke, he didn't crack the pool bottom, like some say, he lay in agony for an hour until someone found him in a broken heap. A bushwhacked blimp."*

We hear the exchange between Donovan and Jim Parker, one of his fellow offensive linemen who lives in the same area. Johnny Unitas and Tom Matte are nearby. *"They've never drifted apart; it's just that someone's taken their team away."*

Best Action Photo
A Situation Well in Hand

by William Johnson of the Bucks County Courier Times. Johnson exploited his knowledge of the game, his camera skills and his best instincts to capture Roynell Young's end zone interception of a Los Angeles Rams pass in a game with the Philadelphia Eagles. The simple background emphasizes the clutching arms which highlight the action, hide the faces of all but Young and lead the viewer's eye to the ball. Copyright © 1986, William Johnson, Bucks County Courier Times.

Best Feature Photo
Autograph Seekers

by Louis DeLuca of the Dallas Times Herald. The sharpest shooters not only search endlessly for action shots, but scour the sidelines and stands for highly prized surprises. DeLuca caught these young worshipful Texas Rangers fans eyeing rookie slugger Pete Incaviglia in the Arlington Stadium dugout. The star-struck stares and baseball proffered for autographing hint at why so many devote so much time, money and dreams to the pursuit of sports. Copyright © 1986, Louis DeLuca, Dallas Times Herald.

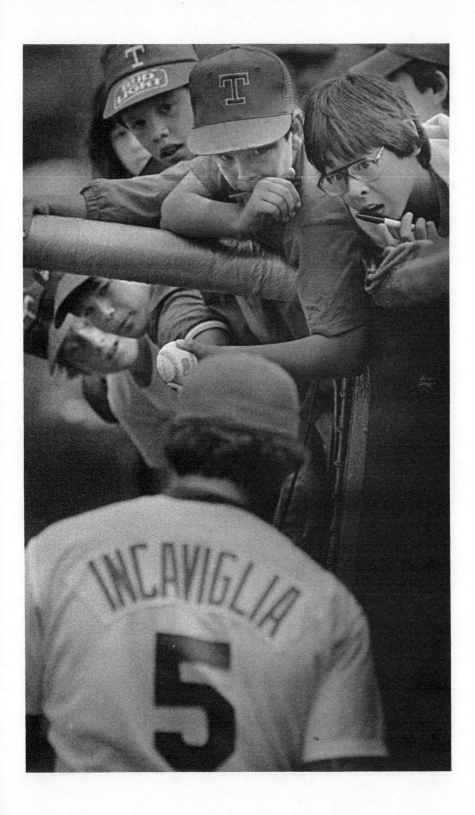

Best Magazine Story

Edwin Tapia Gets His Chance With Dodgers

BASEBALL

By *David DeVoss*

From the Los Angeles Times Magazine
Copyright © 1986, Los Angeles Times

Los Angeles Dodgers scout Ralph Avila shifts the Land Rover into four-wheel drive and fishtails through the spume of a mountain stream. Behind him lie five hours of hot dust and jungle. Ahead looms the jagged cordillera that forms the Dominican Republic's border with Haiti.

Avila's destination is La Meseta, a torpid Dominican village of 30 families that bureaucrats back in Santo Domingo prefer to overlook. The town has no paved streets, plumbing or electricity. Its sole civic improvement is a rock-strewn baseball diamond. In a farming community without irrigation or fertilizer, that field is arguably La Meseta's most fertile plot of ground, for it has produced Edwin Aquino Tapia, a young pitcher whose power and poise remind Dodger scouts of Sandy Koufax.

"This boy can throw 86 mph and he's only 20," Avila yells as palm fronds rake the roof of the lurching car. "He's already got the strength of a major-leaguer. Just think what he'll do once Larry Sherry and Johnny Podres get hold of him. In three years I bet he'll be throwing 90 mph."

Tapia had been seen several months before by Dodgers scout Eleodoro Arias at a semipro game in the Dominican city of San Juan. "It was the ninth inning of a lopsided game, and all the other scouts had gone home," Avila, a Cuban, says with a wink. "We've been in contact ever since, and Eleodoro says the boy's amazing. I think we're the first baseball scouts ever to make it all the way to this village."

Pascual Aquino, his wife, Damiana Tapia, their 10 children and the family burro all are on hand to greet Avila. At 6-foot-3 and 181 pounds, Edwin is not hard to spot. On this scrubby plateau, deep within the island of Hispaniola, only the banana trees are taller than he. The boy is all ankles and arms, a jungle sprout with the fingers of a concert pianist. "Edwin began playing ball when he was 12 right out there," his 56-year-old father says proudly, waving his sweat-stained fedora toward a fallow bean field. "We should be getting some rain," he sighs, surveying a distant stand of withered corn. "It's going to be awfully dry come summer."

Inside the Aquino's small clapboard home, chairs are gathered around a homemade table that Avila quickly covers with glossy brochures. For Edwin and his parents, it's like a sneak preview of heaven.

"This is the pool where Jackie Robinson used to swim," Avila says, "and these are our classrooms. Just look at that dining room. A lot of clubs put their rookies in motels and give 'em $10 for meal money, but at Dodgertown, Edwin eats with (Fernando) Valenzuela and sleeps in a room identical to Pedro Guerrero's. And if he's fortunate," Avila says, pointing to a picture of a sellout crowd in Dodger Stadium on a smogless day, "this is where he'll be working in a few years.

"Some second-division club may offer you a bigger bonus, but if you sign with them, remember that the only money you'll ever get is your salary," Avila explains to the rookie. "Players earn extra for getting to the playoffs and the World Series. You want Edwin to get that playoff money, don't you?" he asks, turning back to the parents. "Well, he's got the opportunity with the Dodgers because we're always pennant contenders."

"The life of a professional ball player isn't easy," Avila says, and heads nod in agreement. "Joaquin Andujar is a millionaire today, but he had to suffer first. You don't make a great deal of money your first three years."

"I understand," Edwin's father says. "But there's nothing to be afraid of in the U.S. I'm just happy he's got a chance to travel away from here."

"There's a lot of temptation in the U.S.," Avila says with a sigh and a slight uplift of eyes. "Cars are very important up there, and Edwin will want a Chevrolet. But he can't afford to play around if he wants to be a success."

"*Exactamente,*" says Damiana with a stern look at her son. "No fantasies now!" she says in mock reproof.

"Edwin, do you want to be a star?" Avila asks.

"*Si, senor.*"

"Well, then give me three years of sacrifice. Practice eight hours a day. Go back home and rest at night. You have the skills to earn $80,000 in three to four years, and if you work hard, I think you will."

Outside the house, a neighbor squats in the shade, preening his fighting cock. Children scamper through the swirling smoke from a cooking fire. Inside, Avila takes a yellow player contract from his briefcase, pushes his Dodgers cap back off his forehead and hands a pen to the parents. In return for their signatures, the family receives a $4,000 bonus, almost three times their annual income. Avila gains a pitcher whose earned-run average over the last 60 innings of semi-pro ball is 0.61.

"Before this moment Edwin has been part of your family," Avila says, snapping his briefcase closed. "But from now on," he says, turning to the bashful rookie "you're part of mine, too. When you arrive at spring training, I'll be buying the clothes and providing food." He slaps the boy benevolently on the shoulder. "From now on I'm your father, your priest and your benefactor."

★   ★   ★

Forty years ago, U.S. baseball had only one Latin American starting regularly—shortstop Gil Torres of the Washington Senators. Today, Latinos account for more than 10 percent of the 650 major-league players. The percentage is even higher in the minor leagues, where one of every six players claims *beisbol* as his profession. No team has been more active than the Dodgers in recruiting Latin players. From the headwaters of the Amazon to the Mexican border, 16 scouts constantly look for talent. The results of their efforts will be seen this week when spring training begins at Vero Beach, Fla. Ten Latin veterans will suit up in Dodger blue, four more than a decade ago. They will be joined by 30 Spanish-speaking minor-leaguers and rookies, the newest of whom, Edwin Tapia, didn't even own a baseball glove until two years ago.

In the business of baseball, where young talent is the most valuable commodity, the Dominican Republic is a mother lode of promising rookies. Though the country's population is only 6.2 million, 36 Dominicans play major-league baseball. Canada, by comparison, which has two baseball franchises and a population of 24.3 million, currently can muster only one major-leaguer—Pittsburgh Pirates outfielder Doug Frobel.

San Pedro de Macoris, a sugar-mill town of 123,000, 40 miles east of Santo Domingo, has become the most important city in the hemisphere for professional baseball. Over the past 15 years, 270 *Macoristas* have made it to the major leagues. A dozen are currently playing in the majors—including Pedro Guerrero and Mariano Duncan of the Dodgers—with 140 more on U.S. minor-league teams. If the Dodgers had played the Toronto Blue Jays in last year's World Series, 12 percent of the players would have been Dominicans, and 10 percent would have called San Pedro home.

"We look for talent wherever we can find it," says Dodgers executive vice president Fred Claire, "but there's no question the best place to start looking is in the Dominican Republic."

Baseball was brought to the Dominican Republic by U.S. Marines, who occupied the country from 1916 to 1924. One of the biggest fans was Gen. Rafael Trujillo, a dictator who owned the Dominican League's Escojido baseball team. Trujillo dominated Dominican politics and sports for more than 30 years, but in 1959, when Fidel Castro's guerrillas came down from the Sierra Maestra in nearby Cuba, Trujillo began to worry. Some advisers suggested it might be time for a democratic election. Instead, Trujillo defoliated large stretches of the country's Central Cordillera, figuring that the easiest way to defuse an insurgency was to deny it a place to hide.

The tactic halted communism's march through the Antilles, but it was hell on agriculture. The coffee and tobacco industries declined rapidly, but Trujillo told his people to look on the bright side. Turn those leached swatches of mountainside into baseball fields, he said, and the government would provide the Louisville Sluggers. Free baseball equipment was an offer few villages could refuse.

The Dominican passion for baseball continues. The climate allows the game to be played year-round, and with a 25 percent unemployment rate, there is plenty of time for the jobless to work on their screwball. Between sugar-cane harvests in the rural areas, boys pass the days hitting cloth-bound rocks with appropriately sized tree limbs. "Everyone around here plays baseball," laughs Pascual Aquino. "There's nothing else to do. We play for fun, not for money."

According to Dominican Baseball Commissioner Reynaldo Bisono, tens of thousands of baseball games are played throughout the Dominican Republic every Sunday. San Pedro de Macoris alone has more than 200 teams. Baseball is more than the national pastime, Bisono explains. "It is part of our national identity. In your country, people make heroes out of politicians. Down here we admire a good shortstop."

Bisono may be guilty of understatement. Inside most *campesino* homes, a picture of the local baseball team hangs beside that of Jesus Christ. At the Gomez Patino Hospital in Santo Domingo, male newborns are identified not by blue booties but by tiny baseball uniforms.

Dominicans take baseball seriously, but on the field it is still very much a game. There is no exploding scoreboard or AstroTurf at Santo Domingo's Quisqueya Stadium. The infield, like a comfortable toupee, has precise dimensions but is a bit ragged around the edge. The fans that pack the 16,000-seat stadium might raise a few eyebrows at Dodger Stadium—if they could afford a ticket. They suck on lollipops, slurp *pina coladas,* dance to marimba music between innings and embrace the closest stranger at the drop of a sacrifice bunt.

Quisqueya may be the best place in the hemisphere to watch baseball. Indeed, one can pass a pleasant afternoon without watching the game at all. The atmosphere is a blend of Rio Carnaval, the Circus Circus casino and the deciding game of the World Series. Icy beer, barbecued chicken and chunks of three varieties of cheese are available. Rum at $1.15 a bottle comes in plastic flasks bearing the invitation to "pour in a little rum and give flavor to your emotions."

Vendors not only allow you to run up a tab but they also return periodically with fresh ice and the latest odds offered by bookies who cruise "Wall Street"—the nickname given to the uppermost tier of the grandstand.

The carnival atmosphere ends abruptly at the box seats behind home plate, which are reserved for major-league scouts. There is little eating or drinking here. In this part of the grandstand, baseball is serious business. Scouts are speculators in baseball futures, a risky enterprise since only 3 percent of the players signed ever reach the big leagues.

It is twilight in Santo Domingo, and Quisqueya is packed with fans who have come for the Dominican League's All-Star Game. Behind the plate, the scouts' conversation turns on the cost of signing players, both here and in the United States. "Personally, I like to sign 'em right out of high school," says Larry Himes, scouting director for the California Angels. "I tell the guy who wants to play baseball not to waste his time in college."

"We've had good luck with college players," counters Al Campanis, Dodgers vice president and director of player personnel. "At least their adjustment is easier. The players from down here have tremendous problems with the language and food (in the United States). We've had a couple of great prospects who just got homesick and quit."

A sharply hit line drive momentarily stops conversation. "Not a bad swing," Campanis muses as the Licey Tiger runner scrambles back to first base.

"I might sign a senior but not a college junior," Himes continues. "It can cost an additional $70,000 to sign a junior who has the option to complete his senior year. A senior can't bargain; if he wants to play ball, he signs. It's all a question of leverage."

"Every year the bonus goes up $25,000," sighs the Phillies' Joe McDonald, waving away a vendor determined to peddle yucca croquettes. "Who knows where it's going to end?"

Though it often seems a contentious business based on salary arbitration, American baseball actually is tightly regulated. Twice each year, amateurs become eligible for the draft. From that pool of eligible talent, 26 teams select in turn—the club with the worst record choosing first. A prospect who believes a club's offer is inadequate can put himself back in the pool, hoping to receive a more generous offer from another club in a subsequent draft. But it is a risky ploy, and with first-round bonuses currently averaging from $80,000 to $100,000, most elect to sign.

Latin America, in contrast, is a huge supermarket of talent where every player age 17 and over is a free agent. In the Dominican Republic, where supply is greater than demand, bonuses run from $3,000 to $5,000. The prospect of signing a player at a fraction of the U.S. price is so attractive that 16 teams spend between $30,000 and $50,000 a year on Dominican baseball academies designed to spot, evaluate and improve potential major-leaguers.

The country-club atmosphere uniting baseball's franchise owners in the United States does nothing to mellow the competition between their scouts in Latin America. The Houston Astros screen prospects at a guarded sugar mill. With the help of Dominican-born, former San Francisco Giants pitcher Juan Marichal, Oakland was able to locate its school inside the Santo Domingo Navy Yard.

Some clubs have tried to hide talented prospects. Three years ago, the Dodgers, Cardinals and Blue Jays—all of whom had more talent than they could sign—got help from Domingo Monchine Pichardo, owner of the Dominican League's Licey Tigers, who put 186 players on his active roster, temporarily denying other major-league scouts access to them. Since it's not fair to take a player out of the open market without offering him the security of a contract, professional baseball now requires a player be signed or released within 30 days of entering an academy. Last October, when Pirates scout Pablo Cruz heard that the Yankees were hiding an outstanding left-handed pitcher for more than two months, he marched into the Yankees' academy and signed him.

Avila keeps the competitive edge sharp by distributing 20,000 baseball caps throughout the Caribbean Basin every year. "You've got to keep the doctors, judges and police chiefs on your side in Latin America," he says. "If they were to start advising young players to sign with St. Louis or Pittsburgh, the Dodgers would be dead down here.

"Recently, the Royals tried to steal a player from me," Avila confides. "I offered $5,000, and they came in with a $10,000 bonus. He signed with the Dodgers anyway. I'd been talking to the boy since he was 14 and once had given his father some money when he lost his job."

A foreman in a Miami sheet-metal shop by day, Avila was managing a semipro Cuban team in Florida when the Dodgers noticed his ability to evaluate young ball players. He scouted two years for free and in 1970 moved to the Dominican Republic to direct Latin American scouting. Since then he has signed 100 players; 10 of them, including Dodgers shortstop Mariano Duncan, have reached the majors. As a baseball scout, Avila has only one peer—74-year-old Howie Haak, the Pirate of the Caribbean.

A Palm Springs resident who has roamed the Caribbean for 29 years, Haak plays Long John Silver to Avila's Capt. Smollett. While Avila keeps dietary charts, gives inspirational lectures and monitors church attendance, Haak hobbles between playing fields looking for "fast sumbitches who can score from second on a single."

"I give 'em less than their worth in the U.S. but more than they could ever earn down here," Haak rasps. "Three thousand tops with a $7,500 bonus if they make the Pirates. That's like spitting out the window if you can get a major-leaguer for $10,000."

Haak's unconventional approach has produced 60 major-league

players. Haak proteges such as Manny Sanguillen, Rennie Stennett, Julian Javier (later traded to the Cardinals), Al McBean, Omar Moreno and Angel Mangual made the Pirates a frequent pennant contender from 1958 to 1983. "I signed Manny Giron out of Panama, and boy, that rascal could throw," he remembers. "He lived in a hut right on the ocean with his father, who was a fisherman. When I came for the signature, I had to pull the old man down from a coconut tree."

Haak attributes his success to one simple rule: "I go for the mothers."

"Back in 1973, I almost lost Miguel Dilone, a 17-year-old kid, when Cardinal scout Roberto Diaz kidnaped him out of school," Haak says as he walks across the Quisqueya infield to the boisterous dugout of the Santiago Aguilas. "The kid was 17, but the Cardinals grabbed the father and got his signature. I went for the mother. She was crying, 'Where's my little boy,' and I told her, 'Hell, lady, I want him, too.' It took me a year, but I raised the ante $4,000 and finally got him."

★   ★   ★

Located on the outskirts of San Pedro de Macoris in the shadow of a rusting sugar mill, the Dodger academy is both baseball camp and finishing school. Since its founding six years ago, more than 4,000 Dominicans have received tryouts. Three times a week, young hopefuls from the provinces are invited to join the 40 athletes in residence for a tryout. Those who can run 60 yards in under seven seconds, hit a curve ball and throw with some power are offered a month's room and board and a chance to make the rookie squad. One measure of the academy's standards is that 200 of its rejects have been signed by other major-league clubs.

"A lot of players arrive here with style but no strength," says Avila. "We feed them plenty of meat and vitamins and see if they can develop their skills on the ball field and make progress at the nightly English class. If their attitude is positive and they learn from their mistakes, there's a chance they'll eventually be asked to join the Dodger family."

School starts at 10 a.m. at the Dodgers' academy, when uniformed rookies and teen-agers seeking tryouts form a thin blue line. At 10:01, inspection begins when Avila strides across the infield.

"Spring training will be starting soon, and that means working harder," he says to the milling teens. "I have a small trophy here for Rolando Bell, who is a good example of what I mean by hard work," he says as he straps a Japanese watch on the young outfielder's wrist. "It's not expensive, but at least it's gold."

By 10:10 the sweat is starting to flow. While Avila times new arrivals for speed, four assistant coaches hit ground balls, try to improve a second baseman's double-play pivot, and loft fungoes to outfielders who glide around cow paddies. As the morning passes, other teens filter through the coconut groves to test themselves, mostly unsuccessfully, against Avila's stopwatch.

"None of this batch will ever amount to anything," he mutters, but when one boy in a U.S.A. for AFRICA T-shirt asks for a second chance, Avila smiles encouragement.

The morning, like every other, is devoted to fundamentals monotonously repeated beneath the white glare of a cloudless sky. One youth has trouble bunting; another winces at the sight of a curve. Both receive attention.

"Chico Fernandez (a former Brooklyn Dodger from Cuba) used to say the baseball field is a factory, but I feel differently," Avila says as a self-proclaimed pitcher warms up. "Baseball is my religion, and this field is my church. And out there . . . out there are my disciples."

The Dodgers' interest in Latino recruiting has not resulted by accident. Los Angeles was the first team to broadcast its games in Spanish. Thirty Mexican radio stations rebroadcast every game pitched by Fernando Valenzuela. That Campanis, manager Tom Lasorda, the team trainer and three of the five pitching coaches speak Spanish aids in recruiting. In all, 28 people in the Dodgers' organization are fluent in Spanish. The team's image is especially strong in the Dominican Republic, where the Licey Tigers under Dodgers' management won seven Dominican League championships and four All-Caribbean titles over a 12-year period.

The race for Latin talent is not just a public-relations battle. To a large extent, a team's ability to compete for a pennant today is determined by its scouting organization in Latin America. Though Latins are free agents, they cannot be freely signed. The number of aliens allowed into big-league farm systems is strictly regulated. Each club has a quota, but unlike the player draft, which favors the perennially weak, the distribution of minor-league visas is determined by the commissioner of baseball, who must balance the individual demands of 26 teams against government pressures to limit the number of foreigners playing America's summer game.

In the early 1970s, the Immigration and Naturalization Service and the Department of Labor suddenly realized that the national pastime was moving offshore. Baseballs were stitched in Haiti; Japan was promoting the aluminum bat. A growing percentage of baseball gloves was coming from Taiwan. As for players, Americans weren't being forced out of baseball, but their abilities were being challenged. Half of the starting lineup of the 1971 world champion Pittsburgh Pirates hailed from Latin America. Cincinnati's strongest hitter in the 1972 World Series was not Pete Rose but Tony Perez from Camaguey, Cuba. In 1973, a quota was imposed.

A major-league team's quota results from bargaining with the commissioner's office. It can be increased by a trade in which a Latin player is acquired, or reduced arbitrarily if the club, as is the case with some American League teams, shows no real interest in adding Latinos to its roster. Pittsburgh can import 31 Latinos, while the Dodgers are limited to 24. The Angels, who entered the Latin American recruiting scramble late and don't have an academy, would like to have 22 visas but must settle for a quota of 18. Ironically, Toronto, which can find no Canadian players worthy of a uniform, has 39 Latinos under contract. Montreal, which has a quota of only eight, does not aggressively push for a larger number because Latins often have difficulty adjusting to Quebec's French-speaking culture.

Though the number of foreign players allowed into the U.S. rookie and minor leagues is limited to 526 (major-leaguers receive H-1 visas and are not included under the quota), baseball remains sensitive to the ethnic question. "We don't discuss this issue," says George Pfister, an administrator in the baseball commissioner's office in charge of labor and immigration matters. "If some teams had their way, they'd be signing 50 or 60 Latins, but now they realize they can't go whole hog."

★   ★   ★

It is midway through the third inning of a practice game with the St. Louis academy at the seaside town of Boca Chica, and Edwin Tapia is throwing nothing but strikes. Dressed in a blue *guayabera*, Al Campanis paces the dugout assessing his new acquisition. "It's not what you see but what you think you'll see. That's my philosophy of scouting," he says rhetorically.

"Well," Avila says, "what do you think you're seeing?"

"I like him even better than your report," Campanis grins. "He's still a baby, but will you look at that delivery? Wait till we get some milk in him at Vero Beach."

Two fastballs and a curve send the Cardinal batter corkscrewing into the dust for the third out. Tapia ambles into the dugout, and Campanis shakes his hand. "He's got fingers just like Koufax," Campanis announces, pulling the lanky rookie down beside him on the bench.

"You're a little bit skinny," says Campanis, massaging the rookie's shoulder. "Don't you eat meat?"

"Plenty of meat," Tapia ventures. "Desserts, too. My mother does great things with coconut."

Campanis smiles and settles back on the bench, his arm around the rookie's shoulders. "The Dominicans are great people," he says, despite the return of one who just struck out. "Always respect your parents and remember to go to church."

"I guess I may have missed a few Sundays," Tapia admits sheepishly, picking up his glove for a return trip to the mound.

"It's important you go to church," Campanis warns. "And don't put rum in your Coke. Better still, just stick to milk. You have what it takes to become a star."

"Gracias," says Tapia, turning to leave, but Campanis is still holding on.

"Son," he whispers paternally. "Say, *'Gracias, Senor Campanis.'* "

Judge's Comments

You don't have to be a baseball fan to enjoy this article. You don't even have to be interested in sports. But the strength of David DeVoss's article is that it's about human beings—a designation we all have in common.

Too often in sportswriting this human aspect is lost. Edwin Tapia exists in the Dominican Republic, in La Meseta, in his clapboard house and as a member of the family that gathers around a rude table there, looking at the scout's glossy brochures *(". . . a sneak preview of heaven.")*. Too soon he will be portrayed in print as a statistic in Dodger blue and white. If he succeeds, he will ascend to an even more cardboard portrayal, that of sports hero.

This article is one of several outstanding ones in this year's magazine competition attempting to penetrate the personalities and motivations of athletes. Perhaps because Edwin Tapia is just beginning, has yet to learn the protective cliches of sports language, DeVoss has succeeded. *("Edwin, do you want to be a star?'* Avila asks. *Si senor.' ")*. Readers also get insights into the other characters in the drama, particularly the competitive, stopwatch-clutching scouts. *("The country-club atmosphere uniting baseball's franchise owners in the United States does nothing to mellow the competition between their scouts in Latin America.")*

Instead of relying on creative flash, DeVoss combines a more-or-less straight writing style with keen observation *("Inside most campesino homes, a picture of the local baseball team hangs beside that of Jesus Christ.")* and an ear for dialogue. This is appropriate for this type of story, but does not eliminate the opportunity for an occasional simile *("The infield, like a comfortable toupee, has precise dimensions, but is a bit ragged around the edge")*.

Best Commentary Story

For Driesell,
A Sad Farewell

COLLEGE BASKETBALL

By *John Feinstein*

From the Washington Post
Copyright © 1986, the Washington Post

He never had The Moment. Most men who are as successful as Lefty Driesell was as a basketball coach have one memory that clearly outshines all the others, one of such unadulterated joy that everything after that may be sweet but somehow never the same.

Lefty had moments. He did, finally, win the ACC tournament in 1984. He did beat Dean in the Dean Dome in as improbable a comeback as one is likely to see. He whipped UCLA in a double-overtime game that defied belief and shook his fist to the heavens over and over when the deed was done.

But there was never the national championship or even a trip to the Final Four. He was involved in what may have been the greatest college basketball game ever played. And lost. He had Dean Smith and North Carolina down and almost out with the entire country watching when he went for his 500th career win and called a bad timeout and lost. He ended up winning No. 500 against Towson State.

To some, he was overbearing, overrated and obnoxious. He had to have his foot surgically removed from his mouth more times than can be counted. But in truth, those who came to know Lefty came to understand one thing about him: There is no malice in the man, no real meanness. All he ever has wanted from life is the love of his family and The Moment. He always has had the former. He hasn't quite achieved the latter.

★   ★   ★

To those of us who have spent time with him, whether it be on the receiving end of a screaming 7 a.m. phone call or the laughing end of a post-midnight "Aah can coach" diatribe, the finale Wednesday morning was a sad one. There was no escaping the irony of the quiet emptiness of Cole Field House as he and his family exited. This was a building he had given life for 17 years. He had filled it and kept it jumping and, in many ways, had owned it. They cheered him, occasionally booed him, often doubted him, but never deserted him.

As he walked back through that tunnel and into the bright sunshine of a cool fall morning, more than one reporter cried. Yes, cried. Fact is, Lefty made plenty of mistakes, but he never tried to hurt anyone. Usually, the one hurt most by his mistakes was Charles Grice Driesell.

If you cried when Hamlet died in Horatio's arms, why wouldn't you cry when Lefty fell on his sword in Cole Field House Wednesday? After all, Hamlet was at least as foolish in his own way as Lefty. In truth, Lefty is Shakespearean in many ways. Always, he was tragically flawed, whether it was calling time out at just the wrong moment or saying the wrong thing at the wrong time. But if Lear was not evil in being deceived by his two oldest daughters, was Lefty evil because his basketball players failed him as human beings?

Others, who were here when Lefty arrived in a town devoid of big-time basketball, have talked at length about what he did for basketball here. It is all true. One could argue for hours about his coaching ability. Was he overrated as a recruiter and underrated as a coach? Did he lose control on the bench in the clutch? All moot. If John Lucas makes two free throws with the score North Carolina State 101, Maryland 100 with nine seconds left in overtime back in 1974, does Maryland—instead of N.C. State—go on to be national champion? If Moses Malone doesn't turn pro in 1975. . . .

The ifs don't matter now. What matters are the memories. Some of us remember the phone calls. There was one in 1980 after a long story praising then Notre Dame rookie football coach Gerry Faust. The story had glorified Faust for being different from dour predecessor Dan Devine, for being bubbly and personable, and for riding around campus in a golf cart on the morning of his first game in order to greet alumni and fans.

"Why'd you go and write that stuff about that guy when he's only coached one damn game? Dan Devine won a national championship out there, won all those games and you writin' this guy is Knute Rockne."

"What have you got against Gerry Faust?"

"Nothin', but I got plenty against you."

Three years went by and Faust lost and lost. The phone rang again, another early morning call. "Aah got a question." "Yeah." "Yo' buddy Faust still ridin' around out there in a golf cart, or he get himself an armored tank?"

★   ★   ★

There is still a little tingle every time the old field house looms on trips to College Park. It always conjures up remembrances of those cold winter nights when one would walk into the old place and feel it rocking with anticipation. Lefty vs. Dean; Lefty vs. Norman; Lefty vs. the old alma mater; Lefty vs. The World. He took them all on, never backing down, never making excuses when his team wasn't quite as talented as he would have liked.

And when he didn't win, he always went out kicking and screaming and vowing to come back. And, one way or the other, he always did come back. Lefty was like one of those trick candles: You keep thinking you have blown it out and then it flickers back to life, stronger than ever.

Now, Maryland has blown him out and blown him away—at least for now. All the stories, all the mistakes, all the laughs and there is one Lefty memory that won't go away. It was on Halloween night, three years ago. It was cold and rainy and Lefty was making a recruiting visit in Anacostia. A reporter, working on a magazine piece, trailed in Lefty's wake. As he walked toward the apartment building where the would-be Terrapin lived, a group of kids, none more than 10 years old, raced up waving paper bags.

"Trick or treat," they yelled.

Lefty had no treats, and the only tricks on his mind were those that competitors might play on him to steal the 6-foot-9 youngster who waited inside. "Aah ain't got no candy," he said, reaching into a pocket. He pulled out his money clip and began peeling off bills. One bill after another came off the clip and went into the brown bags. Finally, there was no money left.

The kids moved on. So did Lefty. "I hope," he said, "I didn't have any big bills in there."

It was the ending of the magazine story back then. It is the end of this story now. Because the bottom line is the same: Whatever else one says about Lefty, he would give away his last dollar without knowing it.

You can cry for someone like that. Especially when he has never had The Moment.

Maybe, someday he will. A lot of us will cheer then.

Judge's Comments

Lost in the aftermath of the Len Bias affair was the story of the demise of his coach, Lefty Driesell. That may sound like a ridiculous statement given the extensive coverage the event received in the press. But John Feinstein takes the story a giant step beyond the rest with his commentary on Driesell.

Feinstein recounts the public Driesell (*"To some he was overbearing, overrated and obnoxious"*) but goes beyond that to show his readers a side of Driesell often ignored.

Feinstein recounts the story of one Halloween night when Lefty was on a recruiting visit. Outside the home of a 6-foot-9 prospect, Driesell was besieged by a group of kids, none older than 10, shouting "Trick or treat." The coach had no candy but proceeded to reach into his pockets and peel off dollar bills for the children. One after another went into brown bags until there was no money left.

That simple story tells the reader much about the kind of person Driesell is.

Feinstein's theme throughout is that Driesell was a winner—a coach with more than 500 wins—yet never really had the great moment every coach dreams of. He never won a national championship or even took his team to the Final Four. As Feinstein writes, Driesell never had The Moment.

It's tough to generate a lot of sympathy for those wrapped up in a scandal such as the one at Maryland. It's also tough to generate a lot of sympathy for Driesell. But Feinstein reminds us that people—indeed, real people—were hurt in myriad ways by the Len Bias affair. Bias was not the only one to suffer.

Best Reporting Story

Alcohol: Sports' Deadliest Drug

GENERAL

By *Ron Cook*

From the Pittsburgh Press
Copyright © 1986, the Pittsburgh Press

(Editors note: The first, third and fifth installments of Cook's six-part series, "Alcohol: Sports' Deadliest Drug," is reprinted here. The segments excluded were "Hitting Bottom," an expose of Los Angeles Dodgers pitcher Bob Welch's alcohol problems; "Patients Treated, Not Cured," an up-close look at an alcohol rehabilitation center in Wickenburg, Ariz., and "Breweries Create Strange Bedfellows," an examination of the special relationship between beer manufacturers and professional sports.)

Legal but Lethal

Whitey Herzog thought he was funny when he offered his method of dealing with losing streaks: "Get drunk."

Paul Waner thought he was funny when asked how he could hit after drinking sprees: "I see three baseballs, but I only swing at the middle one."

John Riggins thought he was funny when, in a drunken stupor, he fell asleep on the floor during a speech by Vice President George Bush and told Supreme Court Justice Sandra Day O'Connor, "Loosen up, Sandy baby."

They were right.

They were funny and people laughed.

But no one should have been laughing.

Alcohol has destroyed more lives and careers than illegal drugs have or probably will.

Alcohol problems strike doctors and lawyers, bankers and pilots, journalists and insurance salesmen. And they strike sports stars:

• Former Detroit Tigers first baseman Norm Cash drowned in Lake Michigan October 11 after falling from a boat dock while he was drunk.

• Former Philadelphia Flyers goaltender Pelle Lindbergh was killed in November 1985 when he drove his Porsche into a wall while he was drunk.

• Former Pittsburgh Penguins General Manager Aldege "Baz" Bastien was killed March 14, 1983, when he drove his car into the rear of a motorcycle while he was drunk.

• Former Pittsburgh Steelers defensive lineman Gabe Rivera was paralyzed for life in an October 1983 automobile accident, which, he said, "could have been caused by my drinking."

• Former Los Angeles Rams linebacker Mike Reilly killed a man in August 1982 while he was driving drunk.

• Edmonton Oilers forward Craig MacTavish killed a woman in January 1984 while he was driving drunk.

• Former Penguins captain Mike Bullard's car struck two women and sent both to the hospital with multiple injuries in January 1985 while he was driving drunk.

• Pirates Manager Jim Leyland, Chicago Bears Coach Mike Ditka and Atlanta Braves General Manager Bobby Cox are only a few who have been caught driving while under the influence of alcohol. Leyland and Ditka were convicted of DWI charges, Cox has a January 15 court hearing.

• Los Angeles Dodgers pitcher Bob Welch, Texas Rangers catcher Darrell Porter and former University of North Carolina basketball star Phil Ford are only a few who have received treatment for alcohol dependency.

"Alcohol is the most abused drug in baseball and society," Porter said.

"Alcohol is the devil," said Don Newcombe, a former National League Most Valuable Player and Cy Young Award winner whose career was shortened by alcoholism.

"Ninety-nine percent of the problems in this country—well, at least 95 percent of the problems—start with alcohol," Newcombe said. "Trouble in the community, trouble in the schools. . . . My Lord, kids start drinking so young these days. I've seen Little League games turn into beer parties. Kids are taught they have a right to use alcohol.

"How do you stop it? You can't. It's legal. If you're of age, you can walk into a liquor store and buy it. People accept that. Police accept that. Everyone accepts that.

"Alcohol is the culprit, but we can't get America to admit it."

*   *   *

Dr. Harry Edwards, a sports sociologist at the University of California-Berkeley, is among those leading a campaign to get professional sports to recognize alcohol as a drug and alcoholism as a primary disease.

He said he fights a losing battle.

"Alcohol is the most devastating drug in society, nicotine aside, but it doesn't receive the attention. We're so accustomed to it that it has a low media priority.

"But cocaine? That makes for darn good headlines."

Alcohol is treated differently than cocaine because:

• It is legal.

That is at the crux of the drinking problem in sports.

Although pro leagues have taken admirable stands against illegal drug use, they say they are powerless to control alcohol abuse.

"We do not combine the issues at all," Baseball Commissioner Peter Ueberroth said. "One is against the law, the engine of crime in our society. The other is legal in this country. Those people who want to mix the two and treat them the same, I think, are missing the point."

• It is easily accessible.

Hotel bars, restaurants, liquor stores and the pub down the street sell alcohol to anyone of age.

Athletes usually do not have to search for it or buy it. Beer is provided, at the club's expense, in most professional locker rooms, although it is prohibited in National Football League locker rooms.

"Having beer in the clubhouse was a perfect setup for an alcoholic," Welch wrote in his autobiography, "Five O'Clock Comes Early." "I would always slip a couple of cans inside my coat for the hotel room or the drive home from the ball park."

• It is socially acceptable.

Dr. Abraham Twerski, founder and medical director of Gateway Rehabilitation Center in Beaver County, received an invitation to a program honoring the release of the book, "Addictions in the Jewish Community."

At the bottom of the announcement: "Wine reception to follow."

"Can you believe that? Wine at a reception for a book on addictions?" Twerski asked, waving his arms.

"It's not just a matter of alcohol being legal. It's desirable. We want it to be a part of our lives.

"I defy you to throw a party or banquet without a cocktail hour. I mean, even the president of the United States gets on television and toasts over alcohol. . . ."

• It is pushed on consumers through advertising.

Edwards said alcohol use "has been institutionalized into our work.

"After a hard day on the job or on the playing field, it's Miller Time, right?

"That advertising—that association of alcohol with a good time with the fellows—makes it very easy to take a drink. After one takes care of the serious business of the job, the chances are very good he'll take a drink."

Estimates on the number of problem drinkers vary.

"I've seen estimates of 12 million alcoholics in America, but I think that's a gross underestimation," Twerski said. "I'd say there are well over 20 million people who have a drinking problem or have had some negative effects from drinking. Closer to 10 percent of our population is the truth."

Estimates of athletes with a drinking problem range from 12 percent to 15 percent by Newcombe to 35 percent by Ryne Duren, who, like Newcombe, is a former baseball star and recovering alcoholic who has dedicated his life to fighting alcoholism in sports.

"I think the numbers underestimate the problem," said Pittsburgh native Sam McDowell, another former baseball star, who is a recovering alcoholic and an addiction counselor for the Pirates and Texas Rangers.

"There probably aren't as many guys who drink as there used to be, but that doesn't mean there's any less of a problem. There is far more addiction now than ever."

★   ★   ★

Alcohol and sports have been linked for decades.

Drinking stories are legendary, from the antics of Babe Ruth to the escapades of Bobby Layne to the night moves of Kenny Stabler, who said he used to study his playbook by the light of the jukebox.

Drinking is traditional and macho.

Sports are traditional and macho.

Hence, a perfect marriage: drinking and sports.

"Drinking was my way of confirming my manhood," San Francisco Giants pitcher Vida Blue said. "Turning 21, being able to walk into a bar and say, 'Give me a shot,' man, that was a great feeling."

"The guys used to tease me when I drank milk after games," said Mike Marshall, a former Cy Young Award winner with the Dodgers. " 'You're a sissy,' they would say. 'Aren't you a man? Can't you drink beer?'

"My response always was, 'You prove you're macho your way and I'll do it my way. I'll pitch in 100 games a year and we'll see who's macho. My macho is on the field.'

"Macho isn't sitting in a bar, drinking half a dozen beers."

"People who brag about being able to drink the most should not brag," said Pat Mellody, executive director of The Meadows, a substance-abuse treatment center in Wickenburg, Ariz.

"They have the disease," Mellody said. "They are addicted. People can't use a large quantity of anything without becoming addicted. The definition of addiction is a development of a tolerance."

Marshall was somewhat of an exception in sports.

A trained physiologist, he had a thorough understanding of alcohol's effects on the body. He also had the conviction to go his own way.

Many athletes do not share that courage. They yield to peer pressure, the urge to fit in, to be one of the boys.

"I was as clean-cut a kid as you'll ever see," Porter said. "But when I got to pro ball, I got to struggling. That's when the other guys would say, 'C'mon, forget about it. Let's go out and get drunk tonight. Let's blow it off for one night and relax.'

"Finally, that got to me. I thought, what the heck? I'm going out with 'em. I had always been taught that athletes don't drink and smoke, that the stuff is bad for you. But my first thought was: 'Hey, people lied to me! Golly, this stuff makes me feel good.' "

Athletes often turn to alcohol for reasons other than a macho image and peer pressure:

- Boredom.

"People think baseball is more glamorous than it is," Dodgers third baseman Bill Madlock said. "You're on the road a lot. You're lonely. You're looking for something to happen and there's nothing there but alcohol. . . . Unless you want to do drugs."

"Athletes buy cars, they buy stereos, they get a new condo," Edwards said, "but then they realize that music is just music and a car is just a car and a condo is just a condo. So then someone comes along and says 'I can liberate you in your mind, have a drink, snort some coke.'

"It's a way to fill the void."

- Stress.

"People in sports are highly visible and vulnerable to criticism," said Kevin Ringhofer, a training specialist at the Hazelden Foundation, a treatment center in Center City, Minn.

"If I make a mistake in my work, the boss calls me in and only the two of us know. But when an athlete makes a mistake, everyone knows. And I'm not just talking about pro athletes. It's the same for high school and college kids who are playing before their friends and teammates.

"There's also the continual need to improve one's skills. We've all heard the statement that an athlete is only as good as his last game. Whatever level he's at, he's always asked to do more. That's pressure. . . . "

- Escape.

Joe Arnold, successful baseball coach at the University of Florida, said he drank because he "wanted the reward of feeling good that alcohol gave me."

Arnold is a recovering alcoholic.

"The thing you have to remember is that reward is only temporary. When you wake up in the morning, the same problems are still going to be there. Everything will still be the same except the headache is worse."

★   ★   ★

Athletes are supposed to know better.

They, more than many others, have been taught the value of proper training and conditioning. They are well paid to be in peak condition.

The negative affects of alcohol on the body have been well documented.

The more a person drinks, the more chance he has of developing liver hepatitis. Worse, cirrhosis of the liver often develops, resulting in the loss of liver cells that are not regenerated. This can lead to death.

Brain cells also are destroyed when a person drinks to excess. Doctors estimate as many as 10,000 are destroyed with every drink. This occurs because alcohol keeps oxygen from moving readily to the brain. It also is what causes blackouts.

So why do athletes abuse alcohol?

Why, for that matter, do they do drugs?

Why do they risk everything?

Why do they drink and drive when the risks thereof have been graphically portrayed?

"It's because they think they're invincible," Edwards said. "We all have that characteristic, a tremendous capacity for saying it always happens to the other guy.

"When an athlete looks at Pelle Lindbergh or Len Bias or Don Rogers, he rationalizes: 'Those guys made a mistake. They took too much. They got bad stuff. I don't drink that much. My body physiology is different than his was. . . .'

"There's always a way to rationalize to stay on the positive side of the fence."

The sense of security is particularly strong among athletes.

Many have been coddled, treated as if they are special because of their ability to excel in sports. Not just by their parents and friends, but by their coaches and teachers.

As Edwards said, "The athlete figures: 'If I get caught with cocaine or if I get caught drinking and driving, somebody will take care of it. Somebody always took care of my grades. Somebody always took care of the traffic tickets. Somebody always took care of the misdemeanor. Somebody is always there to pick up the pieces. So why worry?' "

Athletes know no limits on the playing field, which is one reason they succeed. Unfortunately, that attitude can carry over to their lifestyles. When it does—when an athlete plays hard and lives hard—chemical dependency often follows.

"Tell an athlete he can't do something—I don't care what it is—and he'll go down dying trying to prove you wrong," Houston Astros third baseman Phil Garner said. "If you tell him he can't drink. . . ."

That also is why it is difficult for an athlete to seek help for an addiction.

Alcoholism is an incurable disease but can be treated and kept in remission. But for that to happen, the victim must face up to the problem and admit he is powerless to control the substance. To most, that is tantamount to admitting failure.

"Do you know how tough it is to say, 'I surrender. I recognize I've lost control'?" Twerski said.

"The bigger your image, the bigger your ego, the harder it is to admit the problem. If a pitcher can throw a baseball 100 miles per hour within a millimeter of where he wants it to go, if he has that kind of control, how does he admit he doesn't have control over himself?"

Newcombe appreciates that difficulty.

He won the MVP and Cy Young awards in 1956 and was kicked out of baseball four years later because, as he said, "no one wanted a damn drunk on their team."

"I'll take this paper and you tell me the traits you associate with an alcoholic," Newcombe said. "Drunk? Bum? Cheat? Guttersnipe? Wife beater? Child rapist? Liar? Atheist? Agnostic?"

Newcombe studied the list with a sad look—equal parts shame, guilt and pain.

"I was most of those things when I was drunk," he said, softly. "People said I was out of my mind for telling the public I was a drunk. I was vilified.

"How many other people will admit it, particularly after all the publicity about the drug trials in Pittsburgh last year? It's really tough now because of that. That drove people underground. They're too afraid to talk about their problems.

"That's what we're up against—getting people to face up to the problem. That's why I only see the problem getting worse unless our attitude toward it changes."

★   ★   ★

What is the solution?

There is none, Edwards said, sadly.

"Eradication of alcoholism in sports and society is out of the question. Alcohol is legal. It's society-wide. It's subsidized and taxed. No sir, we're going to have to live with that.

"All we can really hope to do is manage the situation. The message we have to give to people is if you can't abstain from alcohol, use it in moderation. We have to educate with an eye toward control and management."

Education. That is the watchword.

"Everyone needs to be better informed—the players, the teams, the public," McDowell said.

"The players need to know just what alcohol does to the body. They still think of it as a harmless substance. But I guarantee you if every person saw graphically and dramatically what alcohol addiction does to you, no one, with the exception of those people who are born with the addiction, would ever drink again. . . .

"The teams need to know what alcohol leads to. They think a player goes from diapers to drugs. They don't realize that he goes from diapers to alcohol to drugs. Alcohol is a step in the process. . . .

"The public needs to know what alcoholism is. It is a physical disease that results in a chemical change in the brain. Yet, alcoholics are scorned and publicly ridiculed. Why? Would you ridicule someone with heart disease and diabetes?"

Ueberroth said he is optimistic about the future.

"I think the education process is working. I don't think there have been too many incidents in baseball recently. In a sport that has a tradition of drinking I think that's progress. And I think you're going to see more progress."

Edwards said he does not share that rosy outlook.

"I saw (NFL Commissioner) Pete Rozelle and Peter Ueberroth on TV, and they were saying we've turned the corner on drugs (including alcohol), that we just about have this thing licked. That is a joke. They haven't the foggiest notion of what they're talking about. Nothing could be further from the truth. What they say is great for the public relations, but it isn't true. . . .

"The worst is yet to come. We should brace ourselves for a good deal more."

Wrecking a Dream

Gabe Rivera, Mike Bullard and Jim Rooker drank, drove and wrecked.

They did not think it could happen to them. They thought these accidents only happened to the other guy.

Bullard and Rooker were lucky. They got second chances.

Rivera did not. He will live the rest of his life in a wheelchair.

"When I was growing up, no one really said too much about drinking and driving," Rivera said. "Now, that's all you hear.

"That's good. There's so much information around, you should know what's going on. You should know the consequences *before* something happens instead of having to wait until after it happens. Like I did."

★   ★   ★

Rivera, a former Steelers defensive lineman, spends his days at his home in Fort Worth, Tex., or at his parents' home in San Antonio, Tex.

The future depresses him, the past haunts him.

"The people at the bar said I was close to normal when I left that night," Rivera said. "Not noticeably drunk. Not noticeably anything. I can't say one way or the other because I don't remember. I might have been drunk. . . .

"Just thinking about it now, it could have been that way. I'll never know. But something must have been wrong. I have something wrong with me now, don't I? That (drinking) could have been the whole thing, the reason for my accident."

October 20, 1983.

The Steelers were 5-2, coming off a 44-17 victory against the Cleveland Browns and preparing for a game at Seattle. Rivera, the team's No. 1 draft choice that season, endured a rugged practice, then stopped at Julian's, a North Side tavern, on his way home to the North Hills.

Jim Julian, owner of the pub, estimated Rivera arrived about 6 p.m. and left shortly before 8:30 p.m. Friends drinking with Rivera estimated he had four or five draft beers.

"He was an absolute gentleman, real nice to the rest of the customers," Julian said then.

Had someone of Rivera's size (6-2, 285) been drunk, Julian said, "You can bet I would have noticed."

"At the time, I didn't think the drinking was a big factor, but it could have been," Rivera said.

"I was drinking, but I wasn't doing anything else to counteract the drinking. I was coming off a hard workout and my system probably was drained. I was just trying to revitalize my body. All I drank was beer. I just stopped off for a few...."

Rivera was injured in a head-on crash at 8:55 p.m. on Babcock Boulevard near the intersection with Three Degree Road in Ross Township. His 280-ZX crossed the center line of the rain-slickened highway and collided with a car driven by Allen Watts of Ross Township.

Watts was not seriously injured. Rivera, who was thrown from the rear window of his car, received fractured ribs, a punctured lung and a crushed right shoulder blade. His spinal cord also was crushed, leaving him paralyzed from the chest down.

Rivera was charged with drunken and reckless driving and speeding. The speed limit at the crash site is 35 mph; Rivera's car made 90-foot skid marks.

Later, District Attorney Bob Colville dropped the drunken-driving charge because prosecuting Rivera "would be futile and even a little cruel....

"Mr. Rivera has had an awful ordeal. The law cannot punish him any more than he's already punished himself....

"I'm sure that after all he's gone through, Mr. Rivera understands the consequences of drinking while driving."

Rivera understands.

"It's pretty hard to tell someone what to do," he said. "The only thing you can do is show them what can happen. Show them the effects. It's bad. The consequences are bad.

"Usually, people drink with other people. Someone else can take the step forward, to tell a person to stop drinking or not to drive. But it's hard to do that. You're always afraid the person who is drinking won't like that. And that's true because your natural tendency when you're drinking is to say, 'I can take care of myself. I'm all right.'

"If you could just hold off your pride a little. When you start drinking alcohol, your pride comes out a little more. That's the hardest part to overcome."

Rivera was asked if he is bitter about not getting a second chance.

"My second chance is living . . . getting the chance to know my son (Timmy, who was born less than a month after the accident).

"From what I hear, it was 50-50 for me. My family told me I could have gone either way. But I lived. I'm lucky that way. . . .

"There are times I look back and think what if? Not much, but I do. When I'm feeling down, I'll say, 'Why this? Why me? Why couldn't it be someone else?' Then, I think it's better me than someone close to me.

"It was tougher in the beginning. It was just a lot different for me, being so young. Everything was going the right way for me as far as my goals in football were concerned. But it changed. It just changed.

"It took me a while to realize the situation, that asking why this and why that isn't going to change it. I'm in the situation I'm in and I have to live with it."

Rivera returned to Texas in mid-August after spending nine months in China, searching for a miracle cure for his paralysis. He said he is trying to live a normal life. He talked of getting a job, perhaps in computers or electronic assembly.

"If I could do it all over again, things would be different, I'm sure of that," Rivera said.

"But I can't do things over again. It doesn't work that way."

                    ★   ★   ★

Former Penguins captain Mike Bullard was drunk, behind the wheel, driving home from an impromptu going-away party for teammates Andy Brickley and Bruce Crowder, who had been demoted to the minor leagues. His car struck two women as they crossed a street in Mt. Lebanon, sending both to St. Clair Hospital with multiple injuries.

That was 22 months ago. Bullard still cringes when he remembers.

"That woke me up. That was the big thing. . . . Sometimes people need something to wake them up."

Bullard was 20 when he joined the Penguins in 1981 and discovered fame and fortune.

The combination, he said, could have been deadly.

"The big thing is the amount of free time you have. It's particularly bad, say, if you're staying with three or four guys. Guys don't go home after practice to watch soap operas. It's not like being married and going home to your family and relaxing.

"You end up spending most of your time in the bars. You go out with the guys for a couple of beers and that turns into a couple more beers. Then, you've got a problem.

"And the money? One day, you're in college or junior hockey making $90 a week. The next day, you're making $100,000. You're not used to having that kind of money and you don't know what to do with it. So you go out and tell yourself, 'I've got $300 in my pocket. I'll spend it tonight and get more out of the bank tomorrow.' Then, you do the same thing the next night."

Bullard—who was traded to the Calgary Flames November 12 after Penguins Coach Bob Berry questioned his work ethic, threw him out of practice and stripped him of his captaincy a day earlier —said he was a big drinker early in his career.

He said it was not until he was married in August 1984 that he began to watch his drinking habits.

"Getting married is the best thing that ever happened to me. It changed my life. I was a pretty heavy drinker, but my wife put me in line. She tells me when I have to slow down. It's been a big help. She just says, 'You can't keep going like this. Look at what it's doing to you. You'll be burned out within four years.'

"It's true. My first couple of years in the league, I was wild. But as you get older you get smarter. You realize you can't take it like you used to. Your body can't take it. And it's hard to get motivated after you've been drinking. Your play suffers. Eventually, you have to look in the mirror and say to yourself, 'Holy, geez, I'm not going to be here much longer if I keep this up.' "

Bullard said he was not thinking about those things on the night of January 31, 1985. He was commiserating with friends, Brickley and Crowder.

Things got out of hand. Bullard should not have driven home, but he did. His automobile struck Marion Spahn and Dolores Molinaro.

Spahn said she received five fractured ribs and Molinaro's leg was fractured. Molinaro declined to comment on the accident.

"He (Bullard) was very nice after it happened," Spahn said. "I didn't know he was drunk at the time, but I was in such pain I don't even remember what he looked like.

"I do remember him bending over me and asking if there was anything he could do. I just told him, 'You've already done it. You hit me. I need a doctor now.' "

Bullard said the accident "screwed up my whole mind. For two weeks after that I didn't know if I was coming or going. It wrecked my play on ice. . . .

"But I was lucky. I could have killed someone."

Bullard was convicted of drunken driving and given one year probation May 31, 1985. He was accepted into the Accelerated Rehabilative Disposition Program for first-time offenders. After completing a year of safe-driving classes, charges were dropped against him in October.

"You look at the other people in the class and think to yourself, 'Do I belong here?' " Bullard said. "But it doesn't matter because I made a mistake and I was there.

"It was important to me to come back. I had something to prove to myself, that I could bounce back and not go into a shell. I had to prove something to my wife and parents. My parents live thousands of miles away, but they still had to read about it. It hurt them and hurt my wife. That was tough for me to live with. . . .

"I feel great now. I'm really enjoying life. My first couple of years in the league, I couldn't handle it (alcohol). Now, I can. It's a great feeling."

Bullard still drinks, he said, because "I'm part of the team and you want to keep the team together."

As recently as March, the Penguins suspended him for one game for missing curfew after a 4-3 loss to the Montreal Canadiens. It was not his first curfew violation.

Bullard said he no longer drinks and drives. His accident, and the death of Philadelphia Flyers goaltender Pelle Lindbergh, convinced him of the dangers.

Lindbergh was killed November 10, 1985, when he drove his Porsche into a wall. His blood alcohol content was twice the legal limit.

"I can't take the chance of something similar ever happening to me again," Bullard said. "It won't happen again. I won't let it happen."

Alcohol long has been the drug of choice in hockey, Bullard said. Kids are taught that drinking is a tradition, the thing to do after practice or games. If those same kids see what alcohol abuse can lead to. . . .

"I don't think there's any doubt that's happening now," Bullard said. "I see the problems lessening unbelievably.

"In the old days, veterans used to go to the bar every day. It was automatic, and they'd ask the young guys to go with them. What were you supposed to say? 'No, I'm not going.' You looked bad if you did that. At that stage of your career, that's the last thing you wanted. You wanted to get in good with the vets. What they did, you did.

"Now, it's different. It's not the same with the younger guys coming in. Jobs are on the line. The athletes are in far better shape. There are conditioning coaches telling you what you can and can't eat and drink. The knowledge is unbelievable.

"You have to remember there are a lot of smart kids coming into hockey today. More and more are coming from the colleges instead of quitting school after grade 10 to play hockey. That's made a big difference."

★   ★   ★

Pirates announcer Jim Rooker nearly killed himself in an automobile accident.

Rooker said he rammed his car into a tree on his way home to Library after a night of drinking in September 1977. He escaped with a broken right arm, bumps and bruises.

"I'm not a saint," Rooker said, "but I don't drink like I used to. I've toned it down. A certain amount of maturity has set in. At least now I recognize when I'm doing something wrong, when I shouldn't get into my car. . . ."

Rooker remembers the first time he met Don Newcombe, a former National League Most Valuable Player and Cy Young Award winner.

Alcohol shortened Newcombe's career and nearly killed him. He used to visit major-league camps to tell his story.

"I knew he was talking about people like me, but it didn't make any difference," Rooker said. "I'd look around at the guys I had a drink with the night before and we'd laugh under our breath. It was a big joke."

Rooker was young at the time, a big-league pitcher. He played 13 seasons with the Detroit Tigers, Kansas City Royals and Pirates, finishing with a 103-109 record.

"I was a starting pitcher and a starting pitcher has the best schedule of any athlete in sports because he knows he's only going to pitch one day in every five. I knew I would get bombed twice every week—after the games the two nights I pitched. There were times I'd blow it out so much after a game that I'd be so sick the next day I could hardly run."

Alcohol was part of Rooker's life for as long as he can remember.

He said he started drinking in the seventh grade. He said he and his buddies would steal alcohol from the liquor store and drink Old Crow and 7-Up.

"I grew up in Southern California. We were wild out there. I'm lucky I didn't go down the tubes. I know a lot of people who did."

Baseball's lifestyle contributed to Rooker's drinking. He was young, handsome and engaging with free time and money in his pocket.

"In this business you think drinking is part of the game. People don't say, 'Hi, how are you doing?' They say, 'Hey, let's go get a drink.' You've got to know how to control it. Many times, you don't.

"There's no question you want to be accepted by the other guys. I remember when I was a young kid in the Detroit organization and I was called up to pitch in an exhibition game. Afterward, Al Kaline, Don Wert, Hank Aguirre and, I think, Dick McAuliffe asked me out for a few drinks. If you're me, you don't say no. So I tried to impress them. They probably only had two drinks, but I was drinking a lot. I even offered to buy them drinks. But instead of impressing them I probably turned them off. . . .

"It's easy to say you drink because you're pressured into it. But the truth is most of us like the image of being macho. It comes down to who can drink the most. Some guys want to show off a little. I was like that. Then, once the alcohol gets into your system, it knocks down all barriers. You'll do anything and say anything."

Rooker admitted his accident did not slow his drinking.

"You would think that would be a deterrent for me, but it wasn't. You might say you'll never drink again, but you're lying to yourself. It happens. You go out for a drink, then someone buys you one. You start to feel good after two or three so it becomes six or seven. The bartender is making them so good you don't even know they've hit you until it's too late. By then, you're back in the jackpot."

Rooker was stopped by Pittsburgh police for running a red light early one morning in 1983. When he failed to produce identification, he was taken to the police station, where he refused a Breathalyzer test. He lost his driver's license for one year.

Rooker said that incident shook him. He said he learned his lesson.

He is 44. He said he wants to live to see 45.

"Don't drink and drive," Rooker said. "It's just not worth it."

NFL Trying to Address Problem

World Series Most Valuable Player Ray Knight fought back tears in the New York Mets' champagne-sodden clubhouse—not from the ecstasy of a world championship, seventh-game victory against the Boston Red Sox, but from the sting of champagne teammates poured on his head.

Keith Hernandez gulped giant swallows of champagne and told a national television audience he would have drowned his sorrows in Budweiser if the Mets had not staged their Game 6 ninth-inning, two-out, two-strike comeback.

Ron Darling, Rick Aguilera and a few teammates toasted the victory on the pitching mound long after the final out had been recorded.

Baseball's liberal stance toward alcohol use was beamed into America's living rooms from Shea Stadium.

It not only was the celebration that offended the folks who are trying to control alcohol abuse in America. It also was the potential repercussion of that celebration.

Millions of teen-agers watched. Experts said it is difficult to imagine them not being influenced by their heroes' behavior.

"It's reinforcement," said Kevin Ringhofer, a training specialist at the Hazelden Foundation, an alcohol-abuse treatment center in

Center City, Minn. "We are all taught very early that it's very acceptable to use alcohol."

"I call it mind control," said Sam McDowell, a former major-league pitching star, recovering alcoholic and addiction counselor for the Pirates and Texas Rangers. "Those celebrations, the pervasive nature of today's advertisements on television. . . . A young kid thinks he has to drink in order to meet a young lady or be a successful athlete."

Conspicuous by his presence amid the revelry was baseball Commissioner Peter Ueberroth, who presented the championship trophy to Mets Manager Davey Johnson.

Ueberroth has taken a tough position against drug abuse but has not included alcohol as a drug.

That is why his oft-quoted pronouncement last summer—"We've basically surrounded the (drug) problem and I don't think you're going to see any baseball players having a problem this year"—was received with skepticism and criticism.

"That's a bunch of garbage," said Don Newcombe, a former National League Most Valuable Player and Cy Young Award winner whose career was shortened by alcoholism.

"Alcohol is here. It always was here and always will be here. It's a legal poison. What the commissioner should say is there are no more illegal drugs in baseball."

"Hey, my doctor tells me a drug is a drug is a drug," said San Francisco Giants pitcher Vida Blue, a recovering alcoholic and drug abuser. "Alcohol is a drug and it leads to other things. You go from drinking to cigarettes to marijuana to cocaine to whatever. . . .

"The commissioner is naive. He says he's cleaned up drugs in baseball, but to do that he has to take beer out of the clubhouse. And he can't have beer commercials on baseball's radio and television broadcasts. But that's not going to happen, and I understand why.

"Why do you think you see a Marlboro Man in every stadium instead of a fan-o-gram scoreboard or something like that? You can see the big letters on the sign: 'The surgeon general has found cigarette smoking to be harmful to your health.' So why is it there? Why are the beer signs there?

"Because they pay the bills."

Ueberroth disagreed.

"People who say such things don't know what they're talking about. I'm not going to get into a debate with people who are misinformed. If they want to say alcohol is more dangerous than drugs ever have been and ever will be and blah, blah, blah, that's fine. That's just somebody's statement and it's woefully inaccurate."

Ueberroth said he differentiates between alcohol and drugs because one is legal and the other illegal, "the engine of crime in our country."

That philosophy is shared by commissioners of other sports, who have done little to combat alcohol problems. Their problem, they say, is: How do we control use of a substance that is legal and socially acceptable?

Only the National Football League has addressed the alcohol issue. And, as Steelers President Dan Rooney said, "We (NFL leaders) haven't done enough."

At least, NFL Commissioner Pete Rozelle included alcohol in his drug proposal:

"The league takes the position that although alcohol use is legal in society and will not be a prohibited substance under this program, it is without question the most abused drug in our sport. If urinalysis reveals an unusually high concentration of alcohol or a player becomes involved in a case of serious misuse of alcohol, including violations of the law while intoxicated, he will be subject to the treatment procedures of this program in addition to whatever legal action the commissioner might deem appropriate."

Although the plan was declared invalid by arbitrator Richard Kasher because it violated the league's collective bargaining agreement with the players, Rozelle is expected to push for a similar plan in a new basic agreement after the season.

Major-league baseball, the National Basketball Association and the National Hockey League have no such clause relating to alcohol in their drug packages.

Rozelle also has demonstrated he will not tolerate alcohol-related offenses. He suspended Los Angeles Rams linebacker Mike Reilly for the 1983 season after Reilly was convicted of felony vehicular manslaughter, driving while intoxicated.

Commissioners of other sports have done less.

NHL Commissioner John Ziegler, for example, did not punish then Boston Bruins forward Craig MacTavish, who was convicted of vehicular manslaughter in 1984. MacTavish was imprisoned for one year.

Ueberroth said he would be reluctant to impose punishment on players who committed alcohol-related offenses, although he would consider each case individually.

"We have laws to cover those offenses," Ueberroth said. "I feel as if those laws are adequate."

The NFL also is the only one of the four professional leagues in question to ban alcoholic beverages in its locker rooms. That includes champagne during championship celebrations.

"We have fined teams significant numbers of dollars for that offense," NFL Executive Director Don Weiss said. "The Denver Broncos were fined $10,000 one year. We just don't feel beer or champagne is appropriate in that setting."

The other leagues leave locker room control to the discretion of the clubs.

Pirates management, for example, allows beer in the clubhouse.

"It's in there consciously, not by mistake," President Mac Prine said. "Our experience is that these men are adults and they'll drink responsibly."

"Most of my guys don't stay long in the clubhouse," Manager Jim Leyland said. "I wish they did. In the old days, we'd sit around talking baseball until 2 or 3 o'clock in the morning. Now, the guys are off and gone."

Penguins management does not permit beer in the locker room or on team buses or flights but provides a room at the Civic Arena where the players and their families can eat and drink after a game.

"I think it's a good policy," General Manager Eddie Johnston said. "If you provide the players with beer in the locker room right after the game, while their adrenaline is still high, it would be easy for them to suck down two or three in a hurry. This way, they get a chance to cool down a little and relax. By the time they meet their families, they're not likely to want to drink as much."

Johnston said he has seen "lots of guys get into the firewater and drink themselves out of the game."

He said that explains why he has placed more of an emphasis on alcohol-related problems than have many of his colleagues. He said that explains why he insists the Penguins' first-year players live with a family instead of on their own or with teammates.

"I think if you stay with a family, you're going to have respect for those people," Johnston said. "You're not going to come home dead drunk every night. Now if you're on your own and the only thing you have to answer to is the alarm clock in the morning. . . .

"You don't realize the temptations these young guys face. They're single, good-looking, making huge money, away from home on their own for the first time, women chasing after them. They think it's Christmas every day.

"The thing they have to remember is they have an image to maintain for kids. If they're out falling down drunk, they're an embarrassment to themselves, their families and the organization."

The Pirates also have spent considerable time and money on educating players about the evils of alcohol and drugs. One significant step was the hiring of McDowell to work in their minor-league system.

"Sam has been there. He can talk in terms those kids understand," Prine said.

"I'm not just talking about alcohol and drugs. I'm talking about everything—their financial affairs, the language, their dress, you name it. They're going through a growing-up process and we're trying to help."

"I think the whole education thing is working," Leyland said. "I think drinking and smoking are done less now than ever. I've never seen such a big push in this country toward physical fitness. I think we're all trying to live to be 150."

Unfortunately, some athletes still die young.

In the past 13 months, Philadelphia Flyers goaltender Pelle Lindbergh was killed while driving drunk, and University of Maryland basketball star Len Bias and Cleveland Browns safety Don Rogers died after ingesting cocaine. Their deaths are haunting proof that problems exist.

"It's sad to say, but those deaths will have more of an impact than anything we can do," NHL Security Director Frank Torpey said.

"Craig MacTavish killed someone and went to jail for a year, but he's back playing hockey (with the Edmonton Oilers). But Lindbergh, he's dead. He'll never play again no matter what happens. That has an effect on people.

"The same is true of Len Bias' death. A drug-enforcement official told me Len Bias did more for drug enforcement in one night than he did in 16 years."

It is unfortunate that it takes a tragedy to make athletes and their teams aware of the problems. Why can't something be done *before* the deaths, when it still is not too late?

"I think we all wish we had an answer to that question," said Dr. Abraham Twerski, founder and medical director of the Gateway Rehabilitation Center in Beaver County.

"Alcoholism is such an insidious disease. No one thinks about a can of beer. No one really even notices three or four cans of beer unless there's some sort of crazy behavior that follows. And if a player is really good, that crazy behavior is often overlooked. Sam McDowell used to do some crazy things, but he could still throw a fastball 100 miles per hour so he was OK.

"That's the way it is. The only thing we can confront is performance. But by then, it's often too late."

Twerski has watched people die from alcoholism. He has seen lives destroyed because of it.

"We all talk about a person hitting bottom before we can help him. The thing we have to do is raise that bottom. There has to be enough support and pressure from the employer, family and friends so that a person can raise the bottom and not be a Humpty Dumpty the rest of his life."

Judge's Comments

Sports journalists, like their colleagues covering politics or wars or entertainment, seem to feel most comfortable running in packs, chasing whatever happens to be the story of the moment. In sports, the pack has been baying on the trail of drugs for the last couple of years. The drugs of choice have been cocaine, its derivatives, and steroids.

But in journalism as in other forms of hunting, a daring soul occasionally breaks away from the pack. Ron Cook and the *Pittsburgh Press* seized on a truth that the pack has overrun in its pursuit of crack and urinalysis: Alcohol remains the *"most abused drug in baseball and society."* That assessment came from catcher and recovering alcoholic Darrell Porter.

Cook's series was originally run by the *Press* in six parts, three of which appear in *Best Sports Stories.* "Legal but Lethal", "Wrecking a Dream" and "NFL Trying to Address Problem" were the first, third and fifth installments to appear in Cook's six-part series.

The series, which was painstakingly reported and compellingly written, goes beyond the horror stories to explore the social, psychological and economic forces that make alcohol both a bigger problem and a less appealing target than the illegal drugs that have captured the attention of the sports establishment and of journalists.

Perhaps the strongest element in Cook's work is its reliance throughout on the real stories of real, identified people. There is Porter and Don Newcombe, as well as other players past and present. There is Pirates Manager Jim Leyland. There is University of Florida baseball coach Joe Arnold. And there is Bubba Smith, who quit the lucrative and popular Miller Lite commercials because he decided it was wrong to help sell alcohol to kids.

Cook's series is a winner because it is ahead of the pack.

King of the Sports Page

GENERAL

By *Rick Reilly*

From Sports Illustrated
Copyright © 1986, Sports Illustrated

The thing about Jim Murray is that he lived "happily," but somebody ran off with his "ever after." It's like the guy who's ahead all night at poker and then ends up bumming cab money home. Or the champ who's untouched for 14 rounds and then gets KO'd by a pool-hall left you could see coming from Toledo.

Murray is a 750-word column, and 600 of those are laughs and toasts. How many sportswriters do you know who once tossed them back with Bogie? Wined and dined Marilyn Monroe? Got mail from Brando? How many ever got mentioned in a governor's state of the state address? Flew in Air Force One?

How big is Murray? One time he couldn't make an awards dinner so he had a sub—Bob Hope.

Murray may be the most famous sportswriter in history. If not, he's at least in the photo. What's your favorite Murray line? At the Indy 500: "Gentlemen, start your coffins"? Or "(Rickey Henderson) has a strike zone the size of Hitler's heart"? Or that UCLA Coach John Wooden was "so square, he was divisible by four"? How many lines can you remember by any other sportswriter?

His life was all brass rails and roses—until this last bit, that is. The end is all wrong. The scripts got switched. They killed the laugh track, fired the gag writers and spliced in one of those teary endings you see at Cannes. In this one, the guy ends up with his old typewriter and some Kodaks and not much else except a job being funny four times a week.

They say that tragedy is easy and comedy is hard.

Know what's harder?

Both at once.

★   ★   ★
Murray on Large People
MERLIN OLSEN: ". . . went swimming in Loch Ness—and the monster got out."

FRANK HOWARD: ". . . so big, he wasn't born, he was founded . . . not actually a man, just an unreasonable facsimile."

BOOG POWELL: ". . . when the real Boog Powell makes . . . the Hall of Fame, they're going to make an umbrella stand out of his foot."

BILL BAIN: "Once, when an official dropped a flag and penalized the Rams for having 12 men on the field . . . two of them were Bain."

★   ★   ★

Arnold Palmer had two of them bronzed. Jack Nicklaus calls them "a breath of fresh air." Groucho Marx liked them enough to write to him. Bobby Knight once framed one, which is something like getting Billy Graham to spring for drinks.

Since 1961, a Jim Murray column in the *Los Angeles Times* has been quite often a wonderful thing. (He's carried by more than 80 newspapers today and at one time was in more than 150.) Now 66, Murray has been cranking out the best-written sports column this side (some say that side) of Red Smith. But if a Smith column was like sitting around Toots Shor and swapping stories over a few beers, a Murray column is the floor show, a setup line and a rim shot, a corner of the sports section where a fighter doesn't just get beaten up, he becomes "sort of a complicated blood clot." Where golfers are not athletes, they're "outdoor pool sharks." And where Indy is not just a dangerous car race, it's "the run for the lilies."

In press boxes Murray would mumble and fuss that he had no angle, sigh heavily and then, when he had finished his column, no matter how good it was, he would always slide back in his chair and say, "Well, fooled 'em again."

Murray must have fooled all the people all of the time, because in one stretch of 16 years he won the National Sportswriter of the Year award 14 times, including 12 years in a row. Have you ever heard of anybody winning 12 anythings in a row?

After a Lakers playoff game against the SuperSonics in 1979, Muhammad Ali ran into Murray outside the locker room and said, "Jim Murray! Jim Murray! The greatest sportswriter of all time!"

Which leaves only one question.

Was it worth it?

★   ★   ★
On Grouches
NORM VAN BROCKLIN: ". . . a guy with the nice disposition of a top sergeant whose shoes are too tight."

PAUL BROWN: ". . . treated his players as if he had bought them at auction with a ring in their noses. . . ."

CONRAD DOBLER, former guard for the St. Louis Cardinals: "To say Dobler 'plays' football is like saying the Gestapo 'played' 20 Questions."

WOODY HAYES: "Woody was consistent. Graceless in victory and graceless in defeat."

★   ★   ★

Marilyn Monroe and Murray were having dinner at a Sunset Boulevard restaurant. This was not exactly an AP news flash. Murray was *Time* magazine's Hollywood reporter from 1950 to 1953, and you could throw a bucket of birdseed in any direction at Chasen's and not hit anybody who didn't know him. He has played poker with John Wayne ("he was lousy"), kibitzed with Jack Benny (who gave him an inscribed, solid-gold money clip) and golfed with Bing Crosby (later, Crosby sent him clippings and column ideas).

On this particular night, somewhere around dessert, Monroe started looking as if she'd swallowed her napkin.

"What's wrong?" Murray asked.

"Jim," she said, "would you mind if I left with someone else?"

"Not as long as you introduce me."

"OK." She waved to a man across the room, who, sheepishly, made his way to the table.

"Jim, I would like you to meet Joe DiMaggio."

Not bad company for a kid who came up through the Depression in his grandfather's standing-room-only house in Hartford, Conn., where, at various times, the roster consisted of himself, his two sisters, his divorced father, his grandparents, two cousins and two uncles, including, of course, Uncle Ed, the one who cheated at dice, a man so bored by work that "he couldn't even stand to watch" people work.

For his part, Murray liked to write, and his first critical success was a 50-word essay on his handpicked American League all-star team. For winning the contest, he received a razor. He was 10.

Murray devoured any book featuring European history, and so, after graduating from Trinity College in Hartford and working a city-side stint at the *New Haven Register,* it is no wonder that when a real war came along and history was being made, he wanted to see it up close. But as a youth, he had had rheumatic fever, and that made him 4-F. He was so disappointed that he wouldn't be seeing Europe that he took the first and farthest-going train out to see distant parts of his own country. Besides, "I wanted to be as far away as I could when the casualties started coming in," he says. "I didn't want any mothers leaning out the window and saying: 'Here's my son with a sleeve where his arm used to be. What's the Murray boy doing walking around like that?' "

The train was bound for Los Angeles, where Murray talked his way into a job as a reporter and eventually became a rewrite man for the Hearst-owned L.A. *Examiner.* Those were gory, glory days for Murray. "There was seldom a dull moment," he wrote in "The Best of Jim Murray." "And if there were, the front page of the *Examiner* never admitted it."

He specialized in murders. He wrote, ". . . we slept with our socks on, like firemen waiting for that next alarm." But Murray never could get used to the blood. Once he covered a story about a little girl who was run over by a truck and lost a leg. Murray took the $8 he had left from his $38 paycheck and bought her an armful of toys.

That figured. Murray always was a sucker for a pretty face. And in those days, in a town with pink stucco houses and restaurants shaped like brown derbies, every nightclub window was filled with pretty faces. One night, Murray and a cohort were entertaining two of them when Jim went to call his best friend. The friend had good news.

"You know that girl over at the Five Seventy Five Club that you're always saying melts your heart? The one who plays the piano?"

"Yeah, so?" Murray said.

"If you can get over here in the next five minutes, she said she'd like to meet you."

Murray threw $2 on the table, grabbed his coat and headed for the door. Outside, his nightclub buddy caught up with him.

"I'm coming, too," he said.

"Why?" Murray asked.

"Because those two girls were mad enough to kill one of us, and it wasn't going to be you."

Murray married the girl at the piano, Gerry Brown, and theirs was a 38-year date. Folks say you've never seen two people carry on so. The Murrays appeared to be happiest at the piano, with Gerry playing (she was an accomplished pianist) and Jim belting out maudlin Irish songs. "If the phone rang at two in the morning, you knew who it was," says Tom McEwen of the *Tampa Tribune*. "It was the Murrays saying, 'All right, what do you want to hear?' And you'd say, 'Well, whatever you feel like.' And Murray would break into *Galway Bay.*"

Murray longed to be a foreign correspondent—"and wear a trench coat and carry a Luger"—but when *Time* called with $7,000 a year, he took it. Over the years he worked on a dozen cover stories on such subjects as Mario Lanza, the Duke, Betty Hutton and Marlon Brando.

"You'd go knock on Brando's door," Murray says, "and you'd knock and you'd knock for an hour and he'd never answer it. But as soon as you walked away, he'd fling it open and cackle like a rooster."

Humphrey Bogart became a friend, too. "He was the kind of guy who'd get nasty after a couple of drinks. What's the old line? 'A couple of drinks and Bogart thinks he's Bogart.' That's how he was. . . . But I remember when he was dying, his wife, Lauren Bacall, would allow him only one drink a day, and if I was coming over he'd wait, because he knew I'd have it with him."

When a sports assignment in Los Angeles came up at *Time*, Murray got it—by default. His proclivity for sports was so strong that, in

1953, when Henry Luce decided to launch a sports magazine, Murray was asked to help start it up. He did, and a year later *Sports Illustrated* was in print. Although Murray did return to *Time* for a while, he eventually became SI's West Coast correspondent. In 1961 he jumped to the L.A. *Times,* where he was ready to take on the daily world of sports. Unfortunately, that world was not ready to take him on.

★ ★ ★

Letter From a Rookie's Wife

Dearest Darling:

How are you? . . . I am working now at the Bon Ton Grill. . . . All the fellows from the box works ask for you and say, 'Boy, I bet if that old husband of yours could only see you in them net stockings he'd bat a thousand. . . .'

The other night was election night and the bar had to be closed; so I had the whole gang over to our house. . . . The party wasn't as noisy as the papers said. . . . I didn't see why the police came. . . .

I sure want you to meet Cesar (a new roomer). . . . (He) feels terrible he had to take this long business trip just the time you come home. . . . He'll come back. He has to; he has the car.

Faithfully yours, Cuddles.

★ ★ ★

Back in 1961, before the Computer Age, writers on the road would type hard copy and Western Union would wire it to the home papers. Except for Murray's stuff. The guys from Western Union would come back to Jim looking befuddled.

"Hey, Murray," they would ask, "you *sure* you want to say this?"

Says Murray, "I think they kept waiting for 'and then, his bat flashing in the sun, the Bambino belted a four-ply swat,' and it never came."

What came instead were one-line snapshots that a hundred fulminations couldn't top. Elgin Baylor was "as unstoppable as a woman's tears." Dodgers Manager Walt Alston would "order corn on the cob in a Paris restaurant."

It was the kind of stuff that the guy with a stopwatch hanging from his neck hated, but almost everybody else liked—especially women. "I love your column," one female fan wrote him, "even when I don't know what you're talking about."

Murray became nearly as famous as his subjects. Once, during a tournament, Arnold Palmer's golf ball rolled into a gully, leaving him an impossible shot out of a thicket. Just then he saw Murray in the gallery. "Well," Palmer said, "you're always writing about Hogan. What would Hogan do in a situation like this?"

Said Murray, "Hogan wouldn't *be* in a situation like that."

In 1969 Texas and Arkansas met in Fayetteville in a classic battle for number one, a football game attended by President Nixon. After the game Murray was slammed into a chain link fence by a Secret Service man who apparently thought Murray looked suspicious. Murray found himself a foot off the ground, suspended only by his collar. Just then, Nixon walked by.

"How ya' doin', Jim?" Nixon said.

"I'd be better," Murray said, "if you could get this monkey to put me down."

★   ★   ★

On Cities

 LONG BEACH: "The seaport of Iowa . . . a city which, rumor has it, was settled by a slow leak in Des Moines."

SAN FRANCISCO: ". . . it's not a town, it's a no-host cocktail party. If it were human, it'd be W.C. Fields. It has a nice, even climate. It's always winter."

CINCINNATI: "They still haven't finished the freeway outside the ball park . . . it's Kentucky's turn to use the cement mixer."

ST. LOUIS: ". . . had a bond issue recently and the local papers campaigned for it on a slogan 'Progress or Decay,' and decay won in a landslide."

OAKLAND: ". . . is this kind of town: You have to pay 50 cents to go from Oakland to San Francisco. *Coming* to Oakland from San Francisco is free."

THE TWIN CITIES: ". . . didn't like each other and from what I could see I didn't blame either of them."

BALTIMORE: ". . . a guy just standing on a corner with no place to go and rain dripping off his hat. Baltimore's a great place if you're a crab."

LOS ANGELES: ". . . underpoliced and oversexed."

★   ★   ★

Murray and nuclear waste dumps have a lot in common. Everybody likes them until one shows up in the backyard.

Take the state of Iowa. When the University of Iowa got stuck on its ear in the Rose Bowl this year, Murray felt for the visiting vanquished:

". . . I mean, you're going to have to start covering your eyes when these guys come to town in the family Winnebago with their pacemakers and the chicken salad. . . . They're going home, so to speak, with a deed to the Brooklyn Bridge and a watch that loses an hour a day and turns green on their arm."

That ruffled Iowans so much that two weeks later Governor Terry Branstad began his state of the state message (as if he didn't have more pressing issues) with a comment for Murray: "Jim, we're proud to be Iowans. . . ." the governor said. "We're tough and we're coming back."

No, no, no, Governor! You're taking it all wrong. To have your nose tweaked by Murray is to be hockey-pucked by Don Rickles. Look on it as privilege. You're one of the lucky ones. Some people roast celebs. Murray roasts America. He has zinged and zapped every place from Detroit (". . . should be left on the doorstep for the

Salvation Army), to Munich, West Germany ("Akron with a crew-cut!").

In fact, Murray maintains Spokane once got to feeling neglected and wrote in asking for the treatment. Always helpful, Murray wrote: "The trouble with Spokane . . . is that there's nothing to do after 10 o'clock. In the morning. But it's a nice place to have breakfast."

Besides, if Murray had dropped dead as thousands have asked him to, sports wouldn't be the same. He has championed dozens of causes, many as stark as black and white, and they've made a difference in the nation's landscape. It was Murray's badgering of the Masters, for instance, that helped that tournament change its Caucasians-only stance: "It would be nice to have a black American at Augusta in something other than a coverall. . . ."

He was incredulous that Satchel Paige was having difficulty being inducted into the Hall of Fame: "Either let him in the front of the Hall—or move the damn thing to Mississippi."

He championed the cause of the beleaguered, retired Joe Louis: "As an economic entity, Joe Louis disappeared into a hole years ago and pulled it in after him. He cannot tunnel out in his lifetime. He owes the United States more than some European allies."

Crazy, isn't it? For a man who is half blind, Murray sure could see.

★ ★ ★

I lost an old friend the other day. He was blue-eyed, impish, he cried a lot with me, laughed a lot with me, saw a great many things with me. . . .

He had a pretty exciting life. He saw Babe Ruth hit a home run when we were both 12 years old. He saw Willie Mays steal second base. . . . He saw Rocky Marciano get up. . . . You see, the friend I lost was my eye. . . .

July 1, 1979

★ ★ ★

The beginning of the end announced itself one morning in Miami, three days before the 1979 Super Bowl, in the form of Dallas Cowboys linebacker Thomas (Hollywood) Henderson.

"Funny how dusty the air is in Miami," Murray told Henderson. "Been like this all week."

"What do you mean, Jim?" Henderson said. "It's as clear as a bell out."

The retina in Murray's left eye had become detached—and that was his good eye. The right one had carried a cataract since 1978, leaving him only peripheral vision. Now both eyes were out and Murray was legally blind. Over the next year five operations on the left retina could not restore it.

"At that point, I did not care," Murray says. "I would like to have died, actually. When you're blind, there's no quality to life."

★   ★   ★

I guess I would like to see a Reggie Jackson with the count 3 and 2 and the Series on the line, guessing fastball. . . . Rod Carew with men on first and second and no place to put him, and the pitcher wishing he were standing in the rain someplace. . . . Muhammad Ali giving a recital, a ballet, not a fight. Also, to be sure, I'd like to see a sky full of stars, moonlight on the water, and yes, the tips of a royal flush peeking out as I fan out a poker hand. . . . Come to think of it, I'm lucky. I saw all of those things. I see them yet.

★   ★   ★

Funny, he didn't feel lucky, even as sympathies stacked up in his hospital room. Once, when Murray had just come out of surgery, and was not allowed visitors or phone calls, the phone did a funny thing. It rang anyway.

"Hello?"

"Hello, Jim? You OK?"

"How'd you get through?"

"Persistence."

Reggie Jackson does, after all, have a heart.

As for Murray, he had lost his and it wasn't until six months later that he got it back. Unable to see the keys on a typewriter, he began to use a tape recorder. Writing a column with only the sound of your voice is something like assembling a 1932 Ford roadster wearing boxing gloves. "It wasn't very good," Murray says. "But to me, it was a hell of an achievement."

With no chance to repair the left eye, doctors in December 1979 decided to remove the cataract from his right. That worked until the retina detached from it, too. Retinas 2, Murray 0. The right retina was finally repaired on January 18, 1982, and Murray's vision, albeit tunneled, one-dimensional and precarious, came back.

Who knew that there would be times when he wished it hadn't?

★   ★   ★

To my three sons, Ted, Tony, and Ricky, who have never read my columns and doubtless won't read this book, and my daughter, Pammy, who won't, either. To their mother, Gerry, who not only read it, but, bless her, laughed at all the jokes.

The Best of Jim Murray
Dedication, 1965

★   ★   ★

Rearing teen-agers in the late '60s and early '70s was a bitch, though the Murrays seemed to have done OK. Tony pitched for Cal and, at one time, had scouts bird-dogging his games. Ted and Pam were good kids, and Ricky, the baby, was a delight. "He could play the piano like an angel," Murray says.

His father got him a job in the nuts-and-bolts end of the *Times,* and everything seemed fine. Many were the days Ricky would call his dad and laugh it up about that day's column.

"I don't know what happened," Murray says. "Dedication is hard on the marriage, hard on the family life. Maybe it was the column. Maybe it was the Malibu beach scene. Maybe it was all of it."

In the early evening of June 6, 1982, Jim and Gerry came home to find a business card sticking out of the door. It was from the county coroner.

CALL RE: CASE NO. 82-7193.

Case No. 82-7193 was better known as Ricky, age 29, dead from an overdose.

"I think about it all the time," Murray says, fingering that card, wrinkled from the years it has been in his wallet. "I don't know if I should say this, but it was always easy for me, the column. It's not like I spent long, long hours on it. I had plenty of time to be with my family. . . . But I don't know. You lose a son and you think, 'Was I a lousy father?' But then, when you're a semifamous father, that's another load to bear."

There was one load yet to go.

★   ★   ★

It wasn't supposed to be this way. I was supposed to die first. . . . I had my speech all ready. I was going to look into her brown eyes and tell her something I should have long ago. I was going to tell her: "It was a privilege just to have known you."

I never got to say it. But it was too true.

April 3, 1984

★   ★   ★

Toward the end, because of the treatments, Gerry wore a wig. One day, on the way to Palm Springs, they stopped at a coffee shop and, for some reason, she wanted a milkshake, the first she'd had since high school. They sat there and had a few laughs. And when they'd stopped laughing, Gerry tipped her wig cockeyed for a few more laughs.

Two nights later, she got up in the middle of the night and fell; she faded into a coma and stayed there from January through March.

Four times a week, Murray would write his column, get an interview at lunch and then spend the rest of the time at the hospital at Gerry's bedside. Sitting down at the typewriter with sorrow staring back at him was de rigueur for Murray. Through Ricky, through blindness, through Gerry, the show went on.

"I have sat down and attempted humor with a broken heart," he says. "I've sat down and attempted humor with every possible facet of my life in utter chaos. . . . *Carmen* was announced. *Carmen* will be sung."

What was hard was trying to write over those infernal voices, trying to forget the doctor's voice on the phone. The first X-rays showed the cancer hadn't spread. But there had been a mix-up at the radiology clinic, just like in the movies. What in fact had happened was just the opposite. "Sorry," the doctor said. "The cancer has metastasized."

The cancer has *metastasized*.

"The most terrible collection of syllables in the language," Murray says.

Gerry died on April 1.

That figures. You write punch lines your whole life and then the last joke is on you.

★   ★   ★

Writing a column is like riding a tiger. You don't want to stay on, but you don't want to get off either.

March 12, 1961

★   ★   ★

Not 10 minutes down the hill from Murray's house is the Hotel Bel-Air, where a famous low-calorie beer company is holding a dinner for the stars of its next 60-second sports celluloid extravaganza. Murray is invited, so he arranges for a ride (he can't drive at night) and makes an appearance. What the hell, as Murray says, might be a column in it.

Walking in, Murray turns heads. For some in the sports world, seeing Murray come into a room without a guide is sufficient reason for a celebratory dinner. "How ya' feelin', Jim?" asks Red Auerbach. "How you makin' out, Jim?" asks Bob Lanier. "Everything OK with you, Jim?" asks Bob Uecker.

Over in the corner, Boog Powell cannot quite get up the courage to say hello. "I haven't ever met him," says Powell, "but I've been reading his stuff for many years. And he's written about me, I don't know, half a dozen times, but I've seen him in a locker room only twice. He's a great man. I'm one of his biggest fans."

This is how it is now for Murray. He is in that the-legend-walks-and-talks-and-eats-breakfast stage. The last King of Sportswriting, boys, sitting right over there.

But Murray the writer has seldom seemed younger. He was named the nation's best columnist for 1984 by the Associated Press Sports Editors. Odds are that Murray will go on winning awards three years after he is buried.

Why he has never been awarded the Pulitzer Prize is an unsolved mystery. Then again, only three sportswriters have won it—Red Smith, Dave Anderson and Arthur Daley—and all three worked for *The New York Times.* "If Murray worked for the *Times,*" says Dan Jenkins, author of *Semi-Tough,* "he'd already have three."

Murray doesn't care. "Gerry's gone. So what?"

He missed her. "I'll be watching TV once in awhile and I'll see somebody we knew and I'll say, "Gerry, come take a look at . . .' And then I'll catch myself."

Two years after Gerry died, friends are still telling him: "Why don't you move out of that house? It'll help you to forget." And he answers, " 'Cause I don't want to forget."

So he fills his days at home, in a house that is far too big for him, the lights always turned on low. He's a steel ball in a giant pinball machine, banging around off the walls, nothing much in the refrigerator, stacks of books and untended mail cluttering up the counter space. No room in the house really means much to him anymore except the corner of a small downstairs bedroom where he writes his column by the light of a lamp and a window. It strained his eyes to make out the tiny print on his portable computer, so someone hooked up a magnifying monitor. It is chilling to watch him with his back to the door, his shoulders hunched over an eerie green light, writing jokes for the greater Los Angeles area.

And Murray never misses a column. "What else would I do?" he says.

A tour of the house is really more of a tour of Gerry—here we are at the Masters, at Pebble Beach, at the Dunes, at Madison Square Garden—until you arrive at a 3 X 5 on the piano.

"This is my favorite," he says. "I don't know if she'd like it or not. But I like it. Look at those eyes. Look at them. There's just no jealousy in those eyes."

He fingers the frame, clears his throat.

"The final curtain is pretty bad, isn't it? The last scene, the last act, is pretty bad." Pause.

"Put it this way," he says. "It'll never sell in Dubuque."

You laugh. But Murray doesn't. He just smiles.

Fooled 'em again.

No. 1 on the Hit Parade

by Dave Bauman of the Riverside Press Enterprise. New England Patriots General Manager Patrick Sullivan feels the force of Matt Millen's powerful right hand while walking to the locker room after the Pats' NFL playoff win over the Los Angeles Raiders. The Raiders claimed Sullivan had been heckling them the entire game from the sideline and Millen decided to take action when a post-game shouting match developed. Copyright © 1986, The Press-Enterprise.

Read My Lips

by Paula Nelson of the Dallas Morning News. Kansas player Ron Kellogg seems to be taking his frustrations out on the basketball after being whistled for a foul in a 1986 NCAA tournament game. Copyright © 1986, The Dallas Morning News.

The McMahon Mystique

PRO FOOTBALL

By *Phil Hersh*

From the Chicago Tribune
Copyright © 1986, Chicago Tribune

What does it all add up to, this combination of simulated Charles Bronson, simulated Sid Vicious, simulated James Dean and simulated Ward Cleaver?

Where is it that he came from, this athlete with such a cosmic comprehension of his sport that he must have played in another place, presumably on another planet, before he landed here? Through the looking glass to that wonderland, is there a man of many dimensions or an Alice made 10 feet tall, with one dimension skewed by trick mirrors?

Why is it he can be rude, crude and lewd and have it pooh-poohed, even in polite society?

When was it that he got this distaste for losing, a man who has almost never lost, yet becomes intemperate about even the thought of it?

Who is this Jim McMahon, a character—what a *character,* chuckle, chuckle—or a series of characters? Is he simply role-playing with the cameras and the good times rolling?

"Nobody knows what I'm like," McMahon says, "and that's the way I want it. I want to keep them guessing."

Is it an act? Is he an actor? Does it make a difference?

★　　　★　　　★

We want our sports heroes to let their actions speak louder than words, yet are oddly uncomfortable if those actions fall outside conventional ethics. We want them to be like Homeric heroes, whose predetermined essence governs their existence, leaving us no surprise. We want them to be complete conceptions, not something in the process of being. It is hard to understand a piece of work in progress.

And Jim McMahon is nothing, if not a piece of work.

A television reporter approaches the quarterback in the locker room at Soldier Field after he has made his triumphal return as a starter in early December. With the lights on and camera rolling, he asks McMahon what he has done to pass the time on the sidelines. With a wild-eyed look, the quarterback holds up a copy of a skin magazine that makes *Penthouse* look like *National Geographic.*

"McMahon is the only person in the world who can honestly say, 'I don't care what other people think about me, I'm going to enjoy life and do what I want,' " says Don Plater, McMahon's best friend and former teammate both at Brigham Young University and briefly with the Bears.

"If people remember me as a good person, I'll be happy," McMahon says. "And if they don't, I'll be happy, because you can't please everybody."

Unless, that is, they are all children, whose demands are so much simpler. Invite McMahon into a roomful of kids, and they will immediately be crawling all over him or playing catch with him or getting his autograph. "My little kids could tell he had a big heart," says orthopedic surgeon Brent Pratley of Provo, Utah, whose words were echoed by a dozen others.

"The only time I've ever seen him open up is with children," said Carl Severe, in whose house McMahon lived during his last months at Brigham Young. "He doesn't relate well to adults."

A friend recalled watching McMahon lovingly exhort a 4-year-old boy to eat his vegetables. And yet he needs no urging to behave like the eggplant that ate Chicago.

McMahon's wife, Nancy, once said to her husband, "Your kids will think you were a real weirdo."

"No," he answered, "they're going to think I was a cool dad."

One who butted heads with his teammates—and authority. One who dangled from hotel balconies hundreds of feet above the ground. One who wore sunglasses under his helmet at practice. One who let the nation watch him take a pain-killing shot on the sidelines. One who turned a bad haircut into a shaved head and then a prickly subject people talked about for weeks. One whose locker stall at Halas Hall in Lake Forest was recently decorated with pictures of his young children, Ashley and Sean, and a picture of an unidentified female breast. One who, as a child himself, was often unusually cruel to other children.

"I don't think those things are strange," he says, barely half an hour after he has explained some of those actions by saying: "I like to do strange things to see what they write about. I just like to act crazy to see what reaction I get. I laugh at myself, too, for some of the things I do."

And then when they write about it, the headstrong McMahon calls them "idiots and puppets." Only a few weeks before that outburst on a paid radio appearance, he had sat through an unpaid, lengthy interview with a combination of diffidence and courtesy, filtering his words through a mixture of beer and chewing tobacco that turned into a viscous scum when he spat it into a paper cup.

"I get a big kick out of it all," he says. "People think they have the inside story, but I'm not the person they read about or see on TV."

"Jim wants an identity not only from football," says Ernie Jacklin, his high school football coach in Utah. "He wants people to know he's an individual. I don't think it's a bit phony."

McMahon's image may have been etched in stone by his actions in and around the nationally televised Thursday night game against Minnesota in September. He spent the Sunday and Monday nights before the game in traction with muscle spasms in his back. He missed practice Tuesday and Wednesday and developed an odd leg infection Wednesday. That was enough for Mike Ditka not to let McMahon start the game, even if the quarterback hadn't infuriated the head coach by spending part of one practice talking in the stands with ABC-TV analyst Joe Namath. Some time that week, McMahon had a meeting with Ditka that was more a shouting match, with papers flying around the coach's office.

McMahon kept making his point loudly on the sidelines in Minneapolis, letting Ditka know he was ready to play. Ditka finally put him into the game in the third quarter with the Bears trailing 17-9. In the next seven minutes, the essence of McMahon came out: all the fearlessness, defiance, surpassing talent and catalytic leadership ability were on display, as if this were the microcosmic look that would make the big picture clear.

Here was McMahon in the act of self-definition. Here was a man improvising his part in a script that seemed less the work of Ditka than of Sartre. Said one of Sartre's characters in the play "No Exit": "Only actions determine intentions."

Says McMahon: "I knew what was going on, and I knew what the game plan was, and I knew what I was supposed to do, and I proved it to them that night."

His first play, called as a screen pass, turned into a 70-yard TD bomb to wide receiver Willie Gault. His second play was also a TD pass; so was his eighth. None of the touchdowns looked remotely like anything in the playbook. The Bears won 33-24. McMahon slicked some goo into his 'do and went back into the hospital for more rest.

What he had really put to bed was the modern image of a quarterback as a robot who comes to work with computer printouts and the *Wall Street Journal.* Open McMahon's briefcase, and all anyone will usually find is a sandwich. What would you expect from a man presumed to be out to lunch all the time?

"When I see him on TV, I say, 'Shoot, Jim, stop putting on a show.' That's not really him," says Norm Chow, BYU's receivers coach. "But it must be him because it has gone on so long."

"At 7 months, I began to become a brat," McMahon said in an autobiography written for English class his senior year in high school.

It wasn't long before his athletic ability became equally evident.

When McMahon's mother, tired of chasing her 2-year-old *enfant terrible* through the house, tried to stop him from tormenting his brothers by throwing little balls at him, McMahon frustrated her by catching the balls.

"When he was 2, I'd have him outside with a broomstick handle as a bat, pitching rubber balls to him, and Jimmy would hit the ball all the time," says his father, Jim Sr.

The confluence of talent and temper produced a remarkable athlete with a willful streak barely below the surface. And he was soon getting under everyone's skin.

Wrote McMahon in the section of his autobiography called "Zero to Five":

"The first few years of my life were trying times for my mother and others around me, but they seemed to handle it pretty well. If they only knew what was in store for them in the years to come."

★　　　★　　　★

Jim McMahon was born August 21, 1959, in Jersey City, the second of six children of Roberta and Jim McMahon. His parents—mother a Californian, father from Jersey City—met when they were on military duty at the 5th Army Machine Records Unit on Pershing Road in Chicago. When Jim was 3 years old, the family moved to California, staying with his maternal grandmother in Fresno until his father found a job as an accountant in San Jose.

The McMahons lived in a bungalow in an ethnically and racially mixed, lower middle-class neighborhood in San Jose within walking distance of their children's elementary, junior high and high schools. That was convenient for his mother because "I was in school as much as Jimmy was. . . . He was always in trouble." Constant rounds of recrimination and apology with school officials led them to a child psychologist, who determined McMahon was hyperactive.

McMahon, a quick learner, was soon bored with school, and his idle mind turned to mayhem. He crawled under tables and poked classmates with straight pins lifted from the teacher's desk. He threw blocks and puzzles at the other children during rest periods. He became peevish with classmates who were slower in school and was, in his own words, "the neighborhood bully." McMahon was especially fond of picking on a chubby Hawaiian boy, and he threw rocks at a little girl on crutches.

"All I ever wanted to do was recess," he says.

Recess meant sports, where McMahon didn't need to wait for his classmates because he could simply play with the older kids. In an area of California loaded with talented young athletes, McMahon was a 9-year-old starter on football and baseball teams dominated by 11- and 12-year-olds. He was one of two sophomores in 30 years to start at quarterback for Andrew Hill High School in San Jose.

His problems were with elders. Told by his mother he had to wear a belt and tuck his shirt in for elementary school, McMahon would pull off his belt and pull out his shirt when he was still close enough to home that she could see it. Slapped by a seventh-grade teacher, he slapped her back in the face. Called for a net violation in a ninth-grade volleyball game, he cursed both the referee and a teacher who tried to calm him down. Told by a college coach to run a short pass off a three-step drop, he dropped back three steps, stopped, then kept dropping back to throw the long pass he wanted. For a touchdown, of course.

"The kids loved his overall cockiness," says Rick Alves, coach and guidance counselor at Andrew Hill. "They like a guy who talks big and then can back it up. He'd do it, even if you thought he was nuts to try."

Perhaps that best explains the stunning series of injuries that began at age 6, when McMahon nearly lost an eye. He was trying to untie a shoelace with a fork, but the fork snagged and flew into his eye, damaging the retina. Surgery restored his vision to 20/200, where it remains. (Think of that irony: a quarterback who has limited sight in one eye and an almost visionary idea of the game.) The eye became extremely sensitive to light, leading McMahon to wear the sunglasses that became a trademark when he switched from a utilitarian style to the mirrored, wraparound shades he favors now.

The eye injury was merely the beginning. He severely cut a hand riding his bicycle. Sprained an ankle jumping off a fence on a short-cut to a friend's house the week before his first game at Roy (Utah) High School. Caught chicken pox while his leg was in a cast from knee surgery at Brigham Young. Broke his hand early last season. Ended 1984 after 10 games with a lacerated kidney—who ever heard of anyone getting a lacerated kidney?—that threatened his future as a professional athlete.

"McMahon does things for a thrill, but he knows where he is going. He isn't on some sort of suicide trip," says Plater, a second-year medical student at the University of Southern California whose own career was ended by a brain injury. "I just hope he can quit on his own terms."

Where he is going is always the end zone; so much the better if it means running over a defensive tackle to get there. His goal, in no uncertain terms, is winning, which sometimes leaves doctors at a loss to explain the things McMahon has done to his body and which is why Sunday's playoff game with the New York Giants will be his first. The kidney injury kept him on the sidelines for the Bears' two postseason games a year ago.

"Football is not an easy game to play," McMahon says. "It's brutal, it's a sick game, but it's fun. My wife says she doesn't worry as much about me getting hurt as she does about me throwing an interception, because she knows that makes me angrier.

"No one wants to get hurt or walk away crippled, but I'm sure that will happen, anyway. As long as I can walk out there, I will. When I came in, I wanted to last at least 15 years. Now I want to last week to week. But I don't think I'll quit. They'll have to drag me out of here."

That was apparent even as a sophomore in high school, when McMahon responded to aspersions about his guts by letting a witless assistant coach yank a dislocated shoulder back into place during a game. That macho folly obviously damaged the arm more, but it was only a minor annoyance until McMahon's junior year at Brigham Young, when he could barely lift it before a game at Hawaii. He played "on guts alone," according to Pratley, throwing 55 passes in a 34-7 BYU victory.

Bored after the game, McMahon decided to take the shortcut between his 24th-story room at a Waikiki hotel and the room a floor below where Plater, who calls himself "McMahon's better half," was studying the anatomy of a shark he had secreted in his luggage for the trip. The sore-armed quarterback simply hung from his balcony and dropped in to see Plater, who was less surprised than impressed by the way McMahon got there.

"You know how hard it is to do that?" Plater asks.

Like everyone else, Plater marveled at his friend's athletic ability and daring on the road less traveled. Jack Germaine, head coach at Andrew Hill for three decades, watched in awe as McMahon ran a two-minute offense to win his first game as a sophomore quarterback. He only wished his time with McMahon didn't seem as short, because the quarterback and his family moved to Utah before his junior year of high school.

"I cried when he left," Germaine says. "It was like finding a huge nugget while you were panning for gold and then dropping it back in the water and seeing someone else find it."

The man who picked it up, Roy High School coach Jacklin, learned he had struck it rich from McMahon's father, who had come to Utah ahead of his family. Jacklin's team was already blessed with two senior quarterbacks, but he made one a linebacker and the other a defensive back after McMahon exceeded even his father's advance billing. The only regret Jacklin has is taking a year to switch from a wishbone to an I-formation offense.

"After you watched him throw the ball once, you knew Jim was good," Jacklin says. "He had the best release I've ever seen.

"What really set him apart was his ability to lead. He never was reluctant to take charge. His greatest ability was being able to make decisions quickly. Right from the start, he was calling nearly all the plays."

But major colleges weren't calling McMahon, a small kid—he is still just 6-foot and 190 pounds—from a state with only 26 schools in the enrollment class against which Roy competed. Notre Dame, his first choice, never showed the slightest interest. He wound up going just 80 miles down the road to Brigham Young, where he set so many passing and total offense records the NCAA needed a recount before it determined the total to be 70. Or was it 71?

They would have been even greater if he had not spent a year as a backup, another splitting the starting job and a third as a redshirt. McMahon thought, with some justification, he was ready to play from the minute he put on a Brigham Young uniform, no matter eventual All-America Marc Wilson was the man ahead of him.

"The first time we met," Pratley says, "it was on the sideline at the first game of his freshman year, and I asked Jim what he did. He said, 'I'm a quarterback, but they've got this quarterback out there who can't do crap, and I should be playing.' Jim was the punter, too, and I bet him he couldn't kick the next one over 40 yards. It was raining cats and dogs, the ball was soaking wet and he kicked it 65 yards."

His end results, measured in wins and losses, were as impressive, just as they would be with the Bears. Despite having just a 3-4 record as a starter during a National Football League debut disrupted by the players' strike, McMahon was the highest-rated rookie passer in the league. In the three seasons since, he is 23-4 as a starter for a team whose back-to-back playoff trips began only when McMahon was allowed to kick-start its motor.

He kicks butts and commands the respect of his teammates on the field, especially the linemen, with whom he feels such kinship that McMahon sponsors their weekly off-the-field revels. Whether the respect brings the winning, or the winning brings the respect, is as hard to answer as why losing leaves such a bad taste in the mouth of a man who rarely has to eat his confident words.

"How can he do it?" Plater is asked.

"Why does he beat you at dominoes or cards all the time?" Plater asks, unable to answer the question without asking others. "No one knows, except that he hates to lose and does the things *he* thinks are going to make the team win."

"You see a guy that plays as hard as he plays, and it inspires you to do your job," says Bears center Jay Hilgenberg. "You know if you do, he'll make things happen."

The linemen admire McMahon for that and his defiance and his fearlessness—or, if you will, recklessness. The quarterback never shuns a challenge, whether it is blocking a linebacker or disregarding the silly play some coach sent in from the sideline, where he couldn't possibly know what was happening on the field. McMahon rolls up his short sleeves, quite literally, and gets down to the dirty work.

"Kids would follow him to the ends of the earth," says Glen Tuckett, the Brigham Young athletic director.

"Jim's idiosyncrasies pose absolutely no problem to anyone on the team," says Bears safety Gary Fencik. "What Jim has is a gun-slinger attitude—risk-oriented, not afraid to take chances. He is quicker on the draw because he has presence and vision."

It is the vision granted the Gretzkys and the Birds and the Peles, who have such a clear point of view they understand the way their games work. "He sees a picture the way a photographic shutter does," says BYU offensive coordinator Roger French. "One click, and it's recorded in his mind."

One click is all McMahon usually gave it. He didn't watch much film even at Brigham Young, finding such exercises as boring as schoolwork. What was the point, if you had the answer right the first time?

"It's hard for some people to realize, but he can look at film once and get what he needs," says BYU head coach LaVell Edwards. "He would come out to practice and yell at the prep team for not lining up exactly the way they were supposed to mimic the opponents' defense.

"He's not big, he's not whatever else, he's supposed to have impaired sight, but the guy's got the greatest sense and vision of anyone on the field. It's like a sixth sense."

What McMahon lacked was a sense of where he was off the field. Or maybe he knew exactly where he was, but didn't have the common sense to roll with the punches instead of throwing them. Whatever, records became the least celebrated of the things he broke at BYU.

"Jim has adventure written all over his face," Tuckett says.

$$\star \qquad \star \qquad \star$$

On a fall afternoon in Provo, there was a small sign on the door of the Brigham Young field house. "ATTN: FOOTBALL," began the notice, designed to remind the players of their obligations to the school's grooming code if they wanted to receive their monthly room-and-board stipend:

"Don't be surprised
"If your check is denied
"Because your hair needs a clip
"Or we can't see your lip
"Just come looking clean
"And you'll get all the green
"Pay day Friday."

The sign was accompanied by an illustration of a spike-haired outcast who bore a clear resemblance to comedian Martin Short and . . . Jim McMahon.

"Jim thrived on being different at BYU," Plater says.

The prevailing wisdom now is that he was always in hairy situations because BYU is BYU, with its prohibitions against alcohol, tobacco and caffeine, not that McMahon is McMahon, with his predilection for substances forbidden to Mormons. Thus, the logic goes, his differences with the school's Office of Standards were magnified.

"Jim was not a real major problem here," Edwards insists. "He's brutally honest, and some of the things he says and does disappoint me a little, but Jim is Jim."

McMahon has said leaving Brigham Young was like getting out of prison. He has said he would never go back there to finish the work for his degree. "It's not the easiest place to get an education, when they're playing mind games with you all the time," he says. Asked if the school would be ashamed or proud of him, he answered, "Probably a toss-up."

"Jim was detached from and indifferent to the mainstream of life at BYU, but not antagonistic to it. We have no problem with anything he says," insists Clayne Jensen, dean of BYU's College of Physical Education.

Chow, the receivers coach, disagrees: "They wish he would roll up and go away."

Although McMahon resented being the occasional object of the proselytizing that is part of the Mormon commitment, he had no trouble committing to relationships with Mormons, on or off the field. He became so close to one, Plater, that McMahon provided most of the down payment for his friend's house in a fashionable Los Angeles suburb. And he married another, Nancy Daines, whom he calls "the most positive influence in my life." So what if he showed up to meet Nancy's Mormon parents with a beer in his hand and a chew in his mouth?

"Her parents accepted me for what I was, not what everyone wanted me to be," McMahon says. "She never liked dating Mormon guys because they were boring. She grew up in California, and she knew that people drink beer and chew tobacco. Mormons outside of Utah are pretty normal; Provo is like a big bubble."

"He'd be a normal kind of guy in L.A.," says Pratley, a Mormon. "They didn't like him here because he wasn't (Dane) Iorg or (Dale) Murphy, and Jim sensed that, and it snowballed. The legends grew, and he did nothing to stop them."

He was guilty of drinking a beer on a golf course, of an occasional smart answer to the campus cops who ticketed his rattletrap Dodge Charger for minor violations, and of telling his coaches where they could stick the punting team they tried to send on the field with BYU behind by 20 points late in the 1980 Holiday Bowl. In the final 4:07, McMahon quarterbacked the Cougars to three touchdowns and a 46-45 victory in the game that, before Minnesota, established his reputation as the quintessential winner.

"Jim is a study in contrasts," Edwards says. "He's a real good family man, and then he paints this sort of thing."

When the Office of Standards decided McMahon's artwork looked more like spray-painted graffiti, it left Edwards to discipline his quarterback. Edwards accomplished that once by grabbing the quarterback by the facemask and pulling him to his knees. And yet the coach, too, kneels at the shrine of McMahon's ability.

"I'd sign a lifetime contract if I could keep a guy like him," Edwards says. "Jim is basically a good person."

Most of McMahon's indiscretions were, of course, negligible by any standards other than Brigham Young's. Those are, however, the standards which McMahon was purportedly going to obey when, at matriculation, he signed the agreement to honor the school's code of ethics and morals.

"That is a bad part of Jim," Pratley says. "He said that on his honor he had a commitment to live by that agreement, and he wasn't man enough to do it or mature enough to realize it."

"Jim didn't ever intend to honor it," says Eleanor Olson, a Roy High School teacher who counts herself among admirers of her former student. "His fingers were crossed the whole time."

It has been said that McMahon went to BYU because he confused it with BYO, which seems logical enough for a man who often lets "I drink, therefore I am" stand as 100-proof evidence of his existence.

McMahon admits he went to Brigham Young for one reason: to play football at a school where the passing game was emphasized and the quarterback's role was paramount. That is also why he stayed, despite impatience at having to play behind Wilson for most of three seasons, in one of which McMahon was redshirted. His father, Pratley and Edwards all claim some credit in talking McMahon out of transferring, but the quarterback probably listened only to his own angry voice.

"I didn't want to let them win, to let them make me leave," he says. "I just wanted to show them. Once I was on the field, they couldn't do anything to me. They would have to wait until after the game if they wanted to yell at me.

"After I redshirted, I said to Nancy, 'I'm going to break every one of those records the other guys (Wilson, Virgil Carter and Gifford Nielsen) set.' I got most of them."

Most of all, he got the education he wanted—or however little he needed—in the art of making the passing game work.

"Jim is a taker, an opportunist," Olson says. "He puts his needs above those of others, and his needs were to go to a school that would get him where he wanted to get. That was Brigham Young.

"Jim would never wear a sign that said, 'I am Third,' like the title of Gale Sayers' book. Jim's would say, 'I am First.' "

★   ★   ★

Both of Jim McMahon's parents encouraged him to think and act like No. 1. "If you don't feel you're the best, no one else will believe in you," Roberta McMahon says.

That might be one of the few points of agreement between McMahon and his family, especially his mother. She is a strict disciplinarian and a Mormon. His father, a Catholic, was closer to Jim until they had a bitter disagreement over the choice of Jerry Argovitz as his original agent. One of McMahon's friends advised against believing much of what his parents would say about him.

The McMahons, both 49, live in a modest two-story house on the other side of two sets of tracks in Roy, which is some 20 miles north of Salt Lake City. Jim Sr. is the vice president and general manager of a small packaging company for which one of his three sons drives a truck. The oldest son, Mike, is a salesman. Daughters Robin, Linda and Stacey are, respectively, a cosmetologist, a homemaker and a sales clerk.

Until this year, McMahon's fourth in the NFL, his parents had never been in the stands to see their son play for the Bears. This season, they said they were able to go to the game at Tampa Bay because a local airline offered promotional fares, the game at San Francisco by driving the 500 miles each way and the game at Dallas in a private jet owned by a Utah auto dealer.

The relationship between Roberta McMahon and her son became strained early, when she insisted on his not being able to play sports if he didn't play by her rules about grades and general conduct. She had him temporarily removed from teams in both junior high school and high school and, after an offense she preferred not to pinpoint, had her husband drop Jim from the Little League team he was coaching.

"If I couldn't play baseball, I was going to be an ass," McMahon says. "I was always fighting. Grade-wise, I didn't care. Eventually I turned myself around."

As a teen-ager in San Jose, he threw bats and helmets. As a teen-ager in Roy, when his basketball coach asked McMahon to stop lifting weights for football or turn in his uniform, McMahon immediately grabbed the uniform and handed it to the coach. The result, not surprisingly, was the coach relented because he wanted the talented McMahon on the team.

"Jim is the guy who can do it and get away with it," says Jacklin, who could only shake his head when McMahon stretched the meaning of a short pass to whatever distance he wanted.

As an adult, McMahon has thrown a table hockey game after Plater beat him. When golf beats him, as that game does almost everyone, he heaves the clubs. Or, if the spirit moves him, he brings a three-wood to its knees by bending it over his.

"When we first started playing golf together, the sound of the club was bigger than the sound of the ball, because he threw it," Pratley says. "When you play with McMahon, it sounds like helicopters: 'Whoop, whoop, whoop, whoop.' But I've never thought of him as a spoiled brat, just competitive as hell."

Ditka feels the same way about a quarterback with whom he has such a tenuous relationship that the coach's saying "shut up" were the only words they exchanged in weeks. "I expect that to change for the better," says Bears President Michael McCaskey, fully aware that getting one or the other to concede anything will be difficult.

"A lot of coaches try to make you into something you're not," McMahon says. "Mike saw Roger (Staubach) do things a certain way for a number of years, and I'm not like Roger. Coaches always tell you, 'If you don't do it like this in practice, you won't do it like that in a game,' and I don't believe that."

His confrontations with Ditka are a matter, to a degree, of two similar personalities coming to natural loggerheads, the same way McMahon has with his mother. "My temper comes from my mom," he admits.

"He looks like his mother and acts like his mother," says Jim McMahon Sr.

"I love him," she says.

"Does he love you?" she is asked.

"I don't know. I don't even know if he thinks of me as his mother anymore; I hope he does. I don't condone some of what he's doing, but I still love him.

"He can be mean and ornery and still be a halfway decent person. I'm mean and ornery, and I feel I'm a halfway decent person. Maybe he's rebelling; maybe he'll grow out of it soon. They keep saying, 'Hang in there, Roberta, he's going to grow up one of these days.' By the time he decides to grow up, I'll be six feet under."

★   ★   ★

Act your age, is how the expression goes. Act it, not be it, as if there is something of a put-on in being anything more than a child. At age 26, arguably one of the best men alive at his profession, Jim McMahon still can hear himself singing, "I don't want to grow up, I don't want to go to school."

McMahon says the only thing he wants to do after he retires is to own a golf course—a possible dream, given his five-year contract worth nearly $1 million a year—where the only rules would be his. "Yeah," says Plater, "and the first rule would be: 'Shoes and shirts, no service.'" McMahon wants to walk barefoot in the park, but with his luck, he'll step on a rusty nail.

"I want to go out and play where you can't be hassled by anybody," he says.

Not Mormons. Not mothers. Not coaches. Not by anyone who says Jim McMahon can't be Jim McMahon, whoever that is.

Lehigh's Sad Story Of Human Isolation

COLLEGE ATHLETICS

By *Dan Daly*

From the Washington Times
Copyright © 1986, by News World Communications Inc.

There were subtle signals early that Tuesday that something wasn't quite right with Lehigh University athletic director Dick Gibney.

It was Gibney's custom, for instance, to drop by football coach John Whitehead's office at the beginning of each day to discuss the department's state of affairs over a leisurely cup of coffee. "He'd put his coffee cup in here," Whitehead says, "and he'd walk down the hall and say good morning to everybody."

But on February 25, Gibney walked to and from the coffee room without the usual pleasantries. Later, he took his habitual late lunch and went downstairs in ancient Taylor Gym to work out. But instead of showering, he worked the rest of the day in his warmup suit. His secretary, Connie Harvey, couldn't remember him doing that before.

Associate athletic director Craig Anderson recalls Gibney coming out of his office to empty his trash basket about 2 p.m. but didn't see him after that. Gibney told Harvey he was going to be writing a paper and didn't want to be disturbed, then closed his door. At one point, Whitehead came by Harvey's desk and asked, "Geez, what's with your boss?"

"Working behind closed doors," said Harvey, equally in the dark.

At 4:45, Gibney briefly reappeared to tell Harvey to go home. "Funny he'd tell me to go home when it was time to go home," she says now. "He probably wanted to make sure I didn't stay late with him."

Soon, Gibney was the only person left in the department, a frequent occurrence during his 14 hard-driving months at Lehigh. Sometime around 6, he went into his bathroom, locked the door, and hanged himself with a leather jump rope tied around an overhead heating pipe in his shower, according to police. Campus police found him several hours later after Judy Gibney, worried that she hadn't heard from her husband, had called them.

Word that something had happened to Dick Gibney spread quickly through the close-knit Lehigh community. At first, wrestling coach Thad Turner said: "Campus police were very hesitant to give out any details, and my wife said to me, 'You don't think he's committed suicide?' And I said, 'Hey, listen, I'm not sure about many things, but that's one thing I'm sure of.' I just assumed he'd had a heart attack."

Only after Gibney's death did most people learn that he had been suffering from depression and had been taking medication since last April. Lehigh President Peter Likins knew. So did Marsha Duncan, the school's vice president for student affairs, who had hired Gibney. But no one in the athletic department knew.

"I wonder if, because of his athletic background, he was just able to shield it better than some other people," Anderson says. "Of course, it's something people don't want to talk about. That's one of the problems. People don't want people to know that they have a problem."

Less than a month earlier, Rick Carter, the highly successful football coach at Holy Cross College, also had committed suicide by hanging himself. He, too, was being treated for depression. He, too, was 42, raising the possibility that the two troubled men were in the throes of some kind of athletic change of life, farfetched as that may sound.

There was one other connection. In football, Holy Cross and Lehigh both belong to the Colonial League, a newly formed coalition of academic-minded schools that think competition, even on the Division I-AA level, has gotten out of hand. League teams won't be allowed to participate in the national playoffs.

This amounts to a de-emphasis of football at the six schools (Bucknell, Colgate, Davidson and Lafayette are the others). Holy Cross has decided it will discontinue football scholarships in 1989. After Carter took his life, Turner says, "I just went in (to Gibney's office) kiddingly one day and said, 'Geez, if wrestling loses its scholarships, I hope I don't do the same thing.' You know, just kidding with him.

"And then we got talking about that (Carter's suicide). What I remember him saying about it is, 'What did it accomplish?'"

The people who worked with Dick Gibney and grew to like and respect him have been tormented by that and many other questions the past few weeks because he was, above all, a man of accomplishment, a results guy. And in the short time he was at Lehigh, a school with 4,400 undergraduates known chiefly for its engineering program, he had moved a considerable distance the mountains that needed to be moved to modernize the old-fashioned athletic program.

Indeed, the day before he committed suicide, Whitehead says, Gibney told him he had good news: The administration appeared ready to let the athletic department raise funds on its own. It was a major victory, to say the least. Traditionally, Lehigh athletics have been totally dependent on the university for funding, which has kept the department in a permanently impoverished state.

"I wish he'd left a note," says Harvey. "I looked through all his papers after the police did. Who knows where he'd put it in that condition? But I didn't find anything. I'd like some day to know why he did it. I think I'll be asking myself for a long time."

Dick Gibney's suicide is a tragedy of the most American sort. His is the story of depression and its mysteries, the story of an ex-athlete who found it difficult to give less than his all in life. It's the story of the price of ambition, of the danger of human isolation. It's also the story of a serious-minded school's struggle with the contradiction of a big-time athletic program.

It's all this and probably a good deal more. No one at Lehigh claims to have any answers. "You could probably name 10 things (reasons), and you wouldn't be right or wrong on any of them," Anderson says.

Gibney himself apparently had no more of an insight into his condition.

In a meeting at the president's house last April, Likins recalls, Gibney said, "I can't understand what's going on inside my head. I have no reason to feel badly. Jesus, I've got a wonderful family (two boys, 15 and 10), I've got a wonderful job, I've got good friends, and yet I go through the floor with a depression that I just cannot control and cannot understand."

★   ★   ★

The relationship between Likins and Gibney was personal, not just professional. Both were former wrestlers. Likins was captain of the team at Stanford, Gibney a star at Springfield (Mass.) University. Both had sons who wrestled at Bethlehem Catholic High School. Often they would sit together in the stands during meets.

Gibney got his start in college athletics as Boston University's first wrestling coach in 1969. BU quickly became a regional power in the sport, losing just 15 matches in Gibney's seven seasons.

From there, he went to Syracuse and an eight-year stint as associate athletic director. His main job was running the Carrier Dome, the school's state-of-the-art athletic facility. In the two years before Gibney left to go to Lehigh, he interviewed for "three or four" athletic director jobs and was offered "one or two," according to Syracuse AD Jake Crouthamel, but turned them down.

"I think he was being selective," Crouthamel says.

When the Lehigh job opened in 1984, says Crouthamel, "I think there was probably some pressure (on Gibney) to take it. First of all, it was a good school with a good athletic program, and it was in the East. Second, his athletic background was wrestling, and that was

Lehigh's strongest program (the school perennially ranks among the nation's top 10 in the sport). I think he got some innocent pushing from people around here who thought it was the ideal job for him."

It was, and is, a period of transition for Lehigh athletics. An 18-month study of the department is nearing completion. Even before Gibney arrived, the administration had made the unprecedented decision to award athletic scholarships in wrestling on a provisional basis.

Lehigh had been one of the dozen colleges with major athletic programs that gave scholarships based only on need. Had the school not taken this step, Turner says, "there's no question in my mind" the nationally ranked wrestling program would have gone into decline.

Gibney was the man chosen to lead Lehigh athletics into a new era. But change came slowly at first and he grew frustrated, then depressed. There were too many sports (23) and not enough money. Some sports—even football, which produced a Division II national title as recently as 1977—were simply overscheduled, forced to play too many teams with too many more dollars to spend. Taylor Gym was "the pits," according to one athletic staffer.

Austerity wasn't completely foreign to Gibney. During his first year as Boston University's wrestling coach, the position was only part time, so he drove a school bus in the mornings and afternoons. But coming to Lehigh from a big-bucks athletic program like Syracuse's had to make it harder for him to do without.

"I remember him saying, 'We never had to say no to our coaches (at Syracuse),'" says Karen Adams, who heads the women's athletic program at Lehigh.

Gibney confided to friends shortly after coming to Lehigh that he wished he had taken other job offers. To complicate matters, his family had remained behind in Syracuse until the end of the school year. With no one to go home to, he worked—too hard, according to Anderson.

"Five months into the job, he really got physically sick," Anderson says. "He was visibly . . . he needed to take a blow, take a rest. We had a golf outing in May. I remember he came and spoke at the dinner that night, and he could hardly talk. He had like a strep throat. He had all these flu symptoms. He had lost weight. I thought it was just because he worked so hard.

"He didn't have somebody to say, 'Hey, slow down.' We were new to him, he was new to us, and he was doing his job and we were all doing our jobs. I think that was about the time he went to the doctor for some medication and maybe started to take it a little bit easier on the job. I would say by the middle of the summer, he was in good shape."

Says Whitehead: "I've been here 19 years, and I said, 'Dick, they're not going to change overnight. It's going to be a battle.' You have to be patient. I came here in 1967, came out of a very rabid high school football program. I mean, it was rabid. And some of the first days I was here, I often said to myself coming off the practice field or taking a shower, 'What the hell am I doing here? I was in a better situation (in high school).' But you learn to live with it."

Duncan says: "I do feel very confident that we did the best job we could in laying out—not only to Dick, but to all the (job) candidates —the extent to which we had some problems, and the depth and scope of those problems. For instance, I shared budgets with candidates, which is not something one always does.

"Dick was also one of the things that made him very good (as an athletic director)—he was compulsive. He was a perfectionist. He had never failed. And he wasn't failing here. But that kind of every-thing-has-to-move-forward-and-move-forward-quickly (philoso-phy) was one of the things that made him very attractive as a candidate initially."

★   ★   ★

By just about everyone's standards but his own, Gibney was making significant progress. He saw a need for an assistant business manager and got clearance to hire one right away. He got the reno-vation of Taylor Gym started about 20 years ahead of schedule. He made the administration aware of how underfunded his department was by obtaining the athletic budgets—invariably bigger—of the schools to which Lehigh likes to compare itself.

"Some of the big, big issues were behind us in terms of our ability to move forward," Duncan says, "and even some of the funding issues were behind us—not all, but we had started to make a dent."

Likins says: "Nobody had ever said, 'It's wrong for the basketball coach to have a big rip in his carpet.' Nobody ever *knew* the basket-ball coach had a big rip in his carpet, taped over, until these guys played Georgetown (in the first round of last year's NCAA Tourna-ment) and the reporters were all over the place."

Says Turner: "He (Gibney) lit fires under people. I just thought the guy did unbelievable things in just a short period of time. If that didn't satisfy him, the guy expected too much, I'd say.

"The pressures here are self-inflicted. I think as long as people are working at their jobs—and from a coaching point of view, as long as you're putting representative kids on the mat and trying to get out and recruit as best you can—I think that's what people expect. Everybody puts a certain amount of pressure on themselves regard-less of the job, I think. But it's very evident (now) that guy put a lot of pressure on himself.

"You know," Turner says, his voice growing softer, "this is the third time someone I've known has committed suicide. All three were wrestlers—and tremendously successful, too. One was a kid I wrestled with in high school, a Pennsylvania state champion. An-other was a kid I coached in high school. He was a New Jersey state champion.

"I've always thought wrestling was great training for life—it's a one-on-one sport, you learn to rely on yourself, all that—and I still feel that way. But it makes you wonder. There may be times when that kind of training works against you. And this may be one of them. If more people had known what Dick was going through, if he had been able to bring himself to tell us, maybe what happened could have been prevented."

Says Likins: "Much of it (the wrestling experience) is transferable, but with Dick, the transfer was complete. He didn't seem to distinguish in a balanced way between giving your all on the mat and giving your all in a job experience or in his son's wrestling. 'Giving your all' is a phrase that can carry too strong a meaning, and I suppose, in some sense, I've been haunted by that same kind of concern.

"You do learn in wrestling to suffer. You suffer because you lose prodigious amounts of weight to wrestle, and because you train so hard to wrestle. And then you also get beat, and you suffer through *that* experience. But you come back. The point is, you come back. The point is, you survive. And anybody who has really gone through the kind of mental and physical torture that high-level competition in wrestling involves ought to be a survivor above all else, ought to be a person who can just take it.

"I've always felt in my own experience that wrestling taught me not just how to win, but how to lose, how to come back, how to stay on the mat, so to speak, even when things go wrong. And Dick didn't stay on the mat. Dick didn't finish it. So in many ways I have to say that although his normal job functioning was very much in the spirit of a man brought up as a wrestler, his death was not."

The appointment of the 61-year-old Whitehead as Gibney's successor has caused some in the department to wonder reasonably whether Lehigh athletics might not return whence they came. But Whitehead, previously passed over for the job, assures that this won't happen. Likins is equally resolute.

"I don't think the course of Lehigh athletics will be altered at all," he says. "In the first place, Dick Gibney, like John Kennedy before him, set the tone, and fixed the path. And now it's just a question of who walks along the path. There may be a faltering because those of us left behind might not have the capacity that Dick had to get the job done so nicely, but we'll get the job done."

Traumatized Lehigh is slowly healing.

"I guess my biggest disappointment," Turner says, "is that I never told the guy I felt he was doing a great job."

Likins says: "I will never, ever in my life get past this. It's been a very painful personal experience."

That was evident from the eulogy Likins delivered at a memorial service held in the campus chapel.

"What went wrong?" he said in his conclusion. "I don't know. As I told you, Dick Gibney taught me enduring lessons in death, as well as in life. I learned from Dick in his flight from life how little I understand it, of the functions and malfunctions of the human brain. . . . I was forced to face the fundamental uncertainty of life, and I felt very small.

"I realize how foolish it is for me to ever imagine that I truly understand another human being or even myself. I learned a lesson in humility and discovered the power of the mystery of life. In relinquishing a bit more of the human illusion of understanding, I came close to my God. Perhaps I am not alone."

Jack Nicklaus Recaptures Mastery

GOLF

By *Mark Purdy*

From the San Jose Mercury News
Copyright © 1986, the San Jose Mercury News

The Beatles were back. They were singing just as well as ever. Mustang convertibles were rolling off the assembly line again. They were gassed up and ready to roll.

Jack Nicklaus was walking up the 18th fairway of Augusta National Golf Course. And he was winning the Masters. My God, he was winning the Masters.

There are some things so perfect, so right, that they make your heart explode. This was one of them. Sunday afternoon, the April sunshine filled up the Georgia sky with an adolescent glow, and Jack Nicklaus made every middle-aged man in America feel like a colt for a few hours.

★   ★   ★

All over the golf course, men were sucking in their beer guts and screaming. In living rooms all over the country, people were watching and willing him to win. Even the people who think golf is a stupid sport were paying attention. Nicklaus knew it. The noise told him.

It barked and rumbled across the gallery ropes every time he made a putt. It covered him like a soft blanket and almost made him cry. Nicklaus had not won a major championship in six years. He had not won any tournament since 1984. He knew this might be the last time he heard the noise.

"Several times, I started to get tears in my eyes and well up inside," Nicklaus would say later. "I had to remind myself that I still had golf to play. Earlier this week, I'd read a newspaper story that said golfers who are 46 years old don't win the Masters. And at the time, I kind of agreed."

★   ★   ★

He won it by a stroke. He won it by shooting a 30 on the last nine holes, which is as good as anyone has ever played them. He won it at age 46, four years older than any previous Masters winner. He won it down the home stretch against the best young players in the game today—Seve Ballesteros, Greg Norman, Tom Kite, Tom Watson. He beat them all.

He won it in the long shadows. By the time Nicklaus was playing the critical holes, it was late afternoon here and the sun was hanging low over the pine trees, casting a dusky light. Nicklaus has bad eyes now. He cannot see very far. The long shadows made it worse.

But there he was on the 15th fairway, behind by four shots, and deciding to go for broke. The 15th hole is the most dangerous one on the course. It is a par five. That means it should take three shots to reach the green. Nicklaus wanted to get there in two. He stood up the fairway, looking toward the flag, squinting at the creek in front of the green, a creek that was ready to swallow a bad second shot. Nicklaus turned to his son, Jack II, who was caddying for him.

"Do you think if I got a three here, it would help?" Nicklaus asked his son.

Jack II smiled and handed his father a 4-iron.

His father hit the shot only one 46-year-old man in the world could hit. It flew 202 yards, kissed the green and began rolling toward the flag as if they were old chums. It stopped 12 feet away.

★   ★   ★

"Where'd it go?" Nicklaus asked his son.

He never heard the answer. The noise again. When he made the putt to give him an eagle three, the noise grew louder. Then he birdied the 16th hole. And the 17th. He was no longer behind by four shots. He was ahead by one. When he walked up to the 18th green, his shadow spread nearly all the way across it.

"I couldn't hear a thing," Nicklaus said. "The noise just kept building. All I knew is I wanted to keep making birdies. It may be as fine a round of golf as I've ever played."

He parred the 18th hole, waved to the crowd, hugged his son and went off to a nearby cabin to watch the younger men try to match his score. One by one, they came to the 18th green and failed. Norman had the last chance, and when he missed his par putt, Jack II ran across the cabin and practically knocked down his father to embrace him.

★   ★   ★

Barbara Nicklaus, Jack's wife, said they had never talked about whether his career was finished, or whether he would ever win another major championship.

"I thought he could win another major if he would *think* he could win another major," Barbara said. "You know what I mean?"

Jack said yes, the mental part was important. Until Sunday, he'd kept missing putts. A putt is a tender stroke. It requires no physical strength. A putt is mental. Last week, a friend had put a newspaper story on the refrigerator at the house Nicklaus rented here, anchored the story there with a magnet. Nicklaus kept thinking about that story all week. NICKLAUS DONE. NICKLAUS THROUGH. NICKLAUS WASHED-UP.

He also thought of his mother. She was here. Helen Nicklaus is 78, and she had not attended the Masters since the first time Jack played in it, as an amateur in 1959. After that, Jack's father always made the trip with his golfing buddies from Columbus, as a sort of annual stag field trip. Charlie Nicklaus saw his son win three Masters before passing away in 1970. Helen Nicklaus had seen her son win none.

★   ★   ★

Jack Nicklaus thought of all these things, and he made the putts. He won the Masters for the sixth time. The trophy presentation on the putting green outside the clubhouse drew the biggest crowd ever. First, the golfing officials from around the world were introduced, the men from England and Japan. Then a trophy was given to the tournament's low amateur, Sam Randolph, who was not even born the first time Nicklaus won here, back in 1963. Randolph took the microphone and congratulated Nicklaus for playing an "awesome" back nine.

Then it was Nicklaus' turn.

"For a guy who's won only $4,000 this year, this isn't a bad win," he said. "I want to thank all you people from the bottom of my heart. You're terrific."

At that, the golfing men from around the world came to their feet and gave him a standing ovation. Bernhard Langer, the defending champion, placed the traditional green jacket around Nicklaus' shoulders. He buttoned it, pulled on the lapels, smoothed the sleeves. The sun was sitting on the horizon, and Jack Nicklaus' shadow was stretching from here to forever. The noise never stopped.

Follow the Bouncing Ball

by Billy Weeks of the Chattanooga Times. Bo Jackson goes one way and the ball goes the other after the Memphis Chicks right fielder had missed connections on a diving catch during a game against the Chattanooga Lookouts. Copyright © 1986, Billy Weeks, the Chattanooga Times.

Double Trouble

by Sam Forencich of the Palo Alto Times Tribune. The perfectly timed click of the camera caught Oakland A's infielder Mike Gallego in flight as he makes the relay to first over San Francisco runner Dan Gladden during an exhibition baseball game. Copyright © 1986, Sam Forencich.

The Black Pioneers

PRO BASKETBALL

By *Richard Hoffer*

From the Los Angeles Times
Copyright © 1986, Los Angeles Times

The integration of professional basketball has come, like all other integration, at a frightful expense. But in the National Basketball Association, where it seems most complete, the men who paid the most are largely forgotten and badly compensated, the game's considerable debt to them apparently written off.

Consider that of the three men to break the color line in 1950, one has passed so unheralded that his death may yet be unreported in some parts. Another, his whereabouts unknown even to the team for which he once played and coached, counsels quietly in a big-city school district. A third, perhaps the best of them, drives a cab.

Yet their legacy is profound. Today, easily three-quarters of the players in the NBA are black. The players are now paid vast sums, and in accordance with their skills, not the color of their skin. Black men coach and attain front-office jobs. Equality, in many of the important aspects, has finally been achieved.

"And you know what I am, after all that?" asks Earl Lloyd, one of the men responsible for that equality. "I'm the answer to a trivia question: Who was the first black to actually play in the NBA? Through a scheduling quirk, I beat Chuck Cooper by a day, even though he was the first drafted and signed. You can win money on that one." He laughs.

★　　　★　　　★

It may be difficult now, having experienced a civil rights movement and seen the comparatively rapid reform in race relations, to imagine what it was like in 1950, when the black man first tried to play in the NBA. By then, it is true, Jackie Robinson had broken through to the major leagues in baseball, establishing an inevitability of integration in other sports. Still, that inevitability was small comfort to a black man who walked into a gym of 10,000 white fans, escorted uncomfortably by white teammates. The word "nigger" somehow resounded oh so distinctly above the crowd noise.

Lloyd, who along with Chuck Cooper and Nat (Sweetwater) Clifton, was the first to brave the unknown, admits to all the little injustices, all turned into cliches over the years. "It was all the things you hear," he says. "You couldn't stay at certain hotels, eat at certain restaurants. You took your chances on the streets in some towns. Remember, these were the '50s. When we played towns like Paducah, Ky., or Fort Wayne—well, I wasn't there by choice."

Lloyd has vanished from sight as far as the NBA or even his old team, the Detroit Pistons, are concerned. He now works in a youth program that prepares students for employment in Detroit. He seems to have distanced himself from the days when he had to cower in his hotel room and take room service alone. But he remembers.

"Most of it was just isolated instances," he says. "And it's hard to be bitter about something that happened all the time. We more or less took it in stride. One year, my second year when I was with the Syracuse Nationals, before we opened in Baltimore, we played an exhibition in South Carolina. I was left behind. I can look back now and say you shouldn't schedule a game where one of your players can't play. I can say the players should have stood up for me. But it was different then and I could hardly be bitter. I didn't appreciate it, I will say that. But I wasn't bitter then, and I'm not now."

The black pioneers, to a man, startle by their lack of bitterness. Sweetwater Clifton, who was drafted by the New York Knicks that same historic year, almost apologizes on the fans' and owners' behalf. "It was different," says Clifton, who drives a cab in Chicago after a 10-year career in the NBA. "I had been playing with the Globetrotters, to white crowds, but when you walked in with an all-white team, well, it was different."

Clifton, when pressed, can recall a few race-related incidents. No, he didn't always stay with the team, but he didn't make anything of that. "I knew all the hotels in all the cities from my days with the Globetrotters," he says. "Some cities I had no problem staying with the team. All over New York, Boston—I had no problem. Other towns, I just moved on over to another hotel. I had more fun that way.

"It was no problem, really. At that time I had no time to be bothered. I had a place to stay and most times friends were looking for me. Life was going too fast to think about racism."

There was, however, one semi-legendary incident involving Clifton. Once in an exhibition game with the Celtics, Clifton threw a dazzling pass by Bob Harrison. Clifton had been a Globetrotter, remember. "He said, 'No nigger do that to me,' " recalls Clifton with a chuckle. "It was a one-lick fight. I was lucky enough to knock him out."

That KO, among the three blacks in the league, was a satisfying amusement for years. Lloyd tells the story differently but with the same glee. "Way I heard it," he says, "Sweets just turned and clenched those two meathooks of his and you could smell burning rubber for miles. Sweets was 6-7, about 230 pounds. Never mind being broad-minded, just think some small intelligence. Why call Sweets anything. It could be detrimental to your health."

Chuck Cooper, in an account he provided Art Rust's "Illustrated History of the Black Athlete" before he died two years ago, claims a fight for himself, though not a one-punch knockout. "I had only one fight in the NBA that was clearly over race," he recalled in the book. "That one fight was against the Tri-Cities Blackhawks. After fighting for a loose ball, a player said, 'You black bastard.' Not looking for a fight, I gave him a chance to back down by asking him not to say that again. He looked me dead in the eye and said it again. So I took my open hand and shoved it as hard as I could into his face."

A brawl broke out between the Celtics and Blackhawks, bitter rivals anyway, but Cooper was later acquitted of any wrongdoing when the commissioner heard the whole story.

But racism mostly worked in silent and less visible ways. It was more than hearing "nigger" or being refused service. Cooper, in his account for Art Rust, said: "There were things I had to adapt to throughout my career that I wouldn't have had to if I were white. I was expected to play good, sound intensified defense and really get under the board for the heavy dirty work. Yet I never received the frills or extra pay of white players.

"I remember Sweetwater Clifton, the first black on the Knicks, was told to play less of his game."

Yes, there was something to that, Clifton says. "I realized that, being the first black, I couldn't do anything people'd notice. So I had to play their type of game—straight, nothing fancy. No backhand passes. It kept me from doing things people might enjoy. My job was to play the toughest guy and get rebounds and not do too much throwing.

"The fans that saw me play before with the Globetrotters wondered why I didn't do more. My teammates used to say, don't play Globetrotter style. So I didn't do certain things, didn't play my game. They missed out. I missed out."

Clifton doesn't make too much of this either. "I had been in the Army, you know, and I was a disciplined, quiet kind of guy," he explains. "I was used to following orders. I suppose it was why I was chosen to play in the NBA because there certainly were blacks better than me. Marques Haynes—how could he not be in the NBA?"

Looking back it is possible to say these pioneers went along, got along. But there is no way to know the grinding effect of racism, which is what prepared them for the NBA. Cooper, who played basketball at Duquesne, after all saw a college game flat-out canceled at the last minute when Tennessee learned of his presence. Tennessee refused to come out onto the floor if he was allowed to play. Duquesne did not back down.

Mostly, though, life was a process of backing down, accepting

one inequality after another to achieve even a little equality somewhere down the line. It is against this background that the smallest
gestures loom heroic.

"Once in St. Louis, I walked across the street to join my teammates at a coffee shop," Lloyd recalls. "Their food was practically on
the table when I was told I wouldn't be served. They got up and left.

"Something else that impressed me. Hotel in Fort Wayne said I
could stay there but I couldn't eat in the hotel restaurant. Now what
can I do? Am I going to go out looking for a restaurant that will serve
me? Not likely if the hotel that's keeping me won't serve me. You
understand? Room service was all I could have.

"My coach at the time, Bones McKinney, who was described by
folks other than me as redneck, came to my room and ate with me
that night. Doesn't sound like much, but in 1950. . . ."

And then there was the matter of pay. Clifton learned about that
inequality first-hand in his dealings with the Globetrotters of all
teams. "We played an all-star game my last year (1949) against a
team Bob Cousy was on. After the game, Cousy, who got to be a
pretty good friend, asked what Abe Saperstein paid us. He showed
me his check for $3,000. I was ashamed to show him mine. It was for
$500."

Of course, by then, Clifton had somewhere else to go.

★   ★   ★

"It was probably amazing that the color line was broken as soon
as it was," says Richard Lapchick, who directs the Center for the
Study of Sports in Society at Northeastern University and who observed the integration first-hand as the son of the man who signed
Clifton. "The world still had not changed that much by 1950. The
blacks had come back from the war and found a country where an
anti-lynching bill still couldn't get through Congress."

Still, Lapchick says, there was no doubt that the NBA would soon
be integrated. In fact, there was a meeting in 1948 to consider the
addition to the NBA of the Rens, an all-black barnstorming team
which was arguably the best team during the '30s. "My father (Joe
Lapchick), who had played against the Rens, convinced the league
to give them a hearing," Lapchick says. "It seemed a good possibility
because they were bringing teams in that represented large black
populations. He brought in Bobby Douglas, the founder of the Rens,
and he made a presentation. The owners got up and said they didn't
need the Rens and that was that."

The problem, Lapchick says, is that, "they just weren't sure what
would happen. It wasn't like in baseball. The dominance of the Negro
leagues in baseball was much greater than it was in basketball,
which really just had two teams, the Harlem Globetrotters and the
Rens."

Another problem, incredibly, was one of those black teams, the
Globetrotters, who would definitely not benefit by integration. In the
early NBA days, the Globetrotters would bring their act to the NBA

franchise and build the gate with a doubleheader. It was not money the NBA teams could afford to lose, which they certainly would if the NBA was integrated. In fact, when the Celtics did finally draft a black player, the Globetrotters struck Boston from its list of destinations, at some cost to the Celtics.

But by 1950 some owners and coaches began to recognize, however slowly, what might be called the competitive imperative. That is best summed up by Walter Brown, the Celtic founder. When he announced that his team had selected Charles Cooper in the second round, the closed door meeting in Chicago fell mute. "Walter," said another owner, "don't you know he's a colored boy?"

Brown's famous rejoinder: "I don't care if he's striped, plaid or polka dot, so long as he can play."

The Knicks followed by buying Clifton's contract from the Globetrotters and the Washington Capitols followed by drafting Lloyd out of West Virginia State.

For such an important breakthrough, it was still many years before the number of blacks in the league grew. "In 1954, there were four black guys in the league," Lloyd says. "That went to maybe seven in 1957."

Adds Bill Russell, who joined the league in 1956: "I'll just tell you this, the first championship the Celtics won in 1957, I was the only black player on either team to play for it."

Even when teams began drafting black players in numbers, it was still years until they would play them in numbers. It was Russell who famously identified the NBA quota system. "The general rule," he once said, "is you're allowed to play two blacks at home, three on the road and five when you're behind."

UCLA Coach Walt Hazzard, who played for several NBA teams in the '60s, says the number of blacks per team was pretty much held to three. "It was unstated," he says. "Nobody had more than three until the emergence of the American Basketball Association. Then the owners were forced to go after talent, not color."

Lloyd says the eventual equality in the NBA was really assured when major colleges began letting blacks into their programs. "How could you deny blacks to the NBA when major universities are taking black kids? Who's going to draft and leave Kareem Abdul-Jabbar sitting there? Nobody's crazy. When you get Bill Russell, you can justify playing blacks in the NBA."

But in the meantime, NBA owners were wary of antagonizing the white fans, who, they assumed, wanted to see as many white players as possible. "It was the old adage that you needed a white star to attract fans," Lloyd says.

But this, too, was eventually disproved. "I really believe this," says Lloyd. "They'll come to see you if you're winning, and you could be putting gorillas on the floor. Losing? Then you might have a problem."

The Boston Celtics, largely under the guidance of Red Auerbach, was the team to disprove this adage, not so much by drafting Cooper, but by playing as many as four blacks at a time in the '50s. "What Red did basically was get the best people for the job, period," Russell says. "He might have ended up with an all-white team, or an all-black team. Gorillas would be especially good, because he wouldn't have to pay them but bananas. Is the team any good? That's what it's all about for Red."

One wonders why the Celtics stood out in this respect for so many years. To which Russell says, "One wonders why we won all those (11-of-13) championships."

Russell, though he came late to the NBA, was a pioneer in his own way. He was the first black superstar in the league and he correctly gauged that, as a superstar of any color, he had some leverage. "In 1961, in an exhibition in Lexington, the black players could not get served at a restaurant," he remembers. "The black players left, didn't play that night. Best thing could have happened."

Why? "Well, let's just say that without us, it was a different game. We never ran into that again."

Another pioneer, in another way, was Wilt Chamberlain. "Keep in mind that there are some weird ways to express racism," Russell says. "The blacks never got a fair hand until Wilt came along. I'm talking about being underpaid, never getting endorsements and weird things like not getting cars. The white players often were given cars, for advertising reasons. The black players got discounts. But Wilt, I have to give him credit. He was the first to have leverage and the first to exercise it. Whether he was threatening to box professionally or play tight end for the Kansas City Chiefs—he was getting his money, I guarantee that."

Russell, who was the first black coach—for Auerbach of course—still does not see integration in the NBA as complete. Front offices are largely white, for one thing, and there are more marginal white players than marginal black players.

Lapchick, who has researched the subject, confirms that. "The league is 75 percent black, yet front offices are just 5.6 percent black." And, he says, the lingering suspicion that marginal white players are retained in favor of marginal black players has some statistical basis. "The scoring average for black athletes was about 2 percent higher than for whites," he says, indicating that a black player still has to be better to be equal.

But, as Russell says, "If we didn't have that to change, we wouldn't have anything to do."

★   ★   ★

It almost seems that when the NBA was integrated there was a kind of grandfather clause for the first blacks: they could always be discriminated against, regardless of reform.

Cooper told Art Rust, "Another thing I'm somewhat resentful about is that at the time, I would have liked to get into coaching. I felt I knew the game and how to handle young men. But there were no opportunities for black coaches then. I got one offer from a school in Piney Woods, Miss., but they were still killing black people down there then. So I declined."

Lloyd, who did coach briefly with the Pistons, found a similar problem. He was invited to interview for a head coaching job at Wisconsin and was asked such questions as what kind of "balance" he'd have on his team. He didn't get that job.

And Clifton? It is interesting to look at a roster of a team he played on. "It's a very tough situation for Nat," Lapchick says. "He has to know that all his teammates, all the guys that started with him, have been wildly successful. Vince Boryla is vice president with the Denver Nuggets, Ernie Vandeweghe is a doctor, Carl Braun a stockbroker, Dick McGuire's still with the Knicks. Nat never got those opportunities, which is one of the enduring aspects of racism in sports."

But the pioneers reflect no bitterness and claim little achievement, which would prove how special they are. Chuck Cooper presumably rests in peace, never having taken, or gotten, credit for what he had done. Earl Lloyd, the answer to a trivia question, secures employment for underprivileged kids who have never held jobs. "I sleep good at night," he says.

In Chicago, a man asks a black cab driver, a man in his 40s, if he knows a fellow cab driver, a man named Sweetwater Clifton. The cab driver remembers, if so many others don't. "Yes," he says slowly. "But he's *Mr.* Clifton to me."

The Silence

BASEBALL

By *Glen Duffy*

From the Philadelphia Magazine
Copyright © 1986, Philadelphia Magazine

Clearwater, Fla., is not a place to look for resurrection. It is a place where working men retire to sit in the sun, develop breasts and complain about how the world is being ruined by the younger generations. It is a place to enjoy the modest privileges of seniority as you allow seniority to get the best of you. It is not a place for a 41-year-old man who could not comfortably pull on his own shirt last year to prove that he can still throw a baseball for a living.

But Steve Carlton—acknowledged to be the greatest lefthander of his day—is attempting that now, trying to show that after more than 20 years of throwing a ball with serious intent, with a major shoulder injury because of it, he still belongs in the game.

Nearby, about a dozen sportswriters watch the spring training workout. They give it as much attention as they deem it deserves—which is not much. In truth, the central act of the game is just one part of the scenery today on what has come to be known as Whale Beach, the bleachers where sportswriters gather to view spring baseball, work on their tans and wonder which players will turn horseshit this year.

They are all here, all but the self-proclaimed best of them. And now, among other things, they are wondering where the hell Conlin is.

"How can he miss this game? What if Carlton's arm falls off?"

"What if he dies right on the mound?"

"What if he gives an interview?"

There is comic pause, and then general agreement that they should not get carried away.

This year is the 10th anniversary of what is widely regarded as the longest-running media silence in baseball history. Coincidentally, Steve Carlton's comeback has become the best story in camp. Too bad. Lefty's still not talking.

For all but the oldest writers, the Silence is something they've inherited. The Silence has become as much a part of the job as ruining your shoes in the tobacco juice players spit on the floor, and waiting outside the clubhouse door until you hear someone say, "OK, let those negative bastards in," and having some 20-year-old with a brain the size of a rosin bag try to string three syllables together while you write it down as if Dr. Teller were giving you the secret of the H-bomb.

All part of the living.

The Silence has been around so long that most writers have no idea what they might be missing. Or, for that matter, exactly how it began. But most of them blame Conlin, if only because it feels so good.

Bill Conlin is the sort of man who doesn't allow anyone to have a higher opinion of him than he has of himself. There are those who would call him the best baseball writer in America. No one is more vocal in expressing that opinion than Conlin himself. He has been covering the Phillies for the *Daily News* these past 21 years—predating the team's ownership, the stadium and many of the current rules.

Conlin knows the sport and the team—really *knows*—and he never lets the others forget it. The others are forced to listen to him repeat his own most clever lines and proclaim his expertise in matters ranging from meteorology to American history. No one would deny his talent. His reports are consistently more entertaining than theirs, and often more entertaining than the game itself. He has the late deadline, the high sources, the talent. It comes so easy for him, and it galls the others. He didn't even show up at half of the spring training games.

Worst of all, he seems to think of himself as being above the game and the many indignities of their profession. Despite the competition among the best writers, there is a sense that they are in this together. The younger ones talk about needing sex on long road trips. The older ones worry about dying alone in some hotel room. They spend their working lives pursuing the truth of a trivial institution. They understand their common predicaments—not the least of which is their standing with the players, who regard them as the ones who dampen victories and post-mortem defeats. The sportswriters remain prisoners of the players' actions—and their words. Their words. Those could be the worst times, the times when the job of getting intelligent quotes from a ball player resembles a miner's sorry struggle with a bed of bad rock.

Conlin considers himself more writer than reporter. He presumes to understand the spin of things—from the break of a good slider to the way weather patterns slip across the globe. There are those who resent him for this, for this and the widely held belief that he caused The Greatest Lefthander of His Day to fall silent for what may be the rest of eternity.

While the sportswriters sun themselves and consider all these things, down on the field Carlton has left the game and the dugout, smiling, quite clearly, to himself. The writers enter into the third phase of Conlin imitations now—a vocal affectation that suggests a gorilla with a gin hangover.

"This had to be the greatest spring training performance I've never seen," says one.

"I saw the game," says another. "I had a satellite dish set up next to the courts and I watched as I played doubles."

Shortly thereafter, in the midst of the fifth inning, the Best Baseball Writer in America makes his entrance in tennis shorts, a T-shirt advertising a restaurant, and dock shoes that look as if they've been dredged from the bottom of the Gulf of Mexico. He perches his massive bulk at the top of the Whale Beach bleachers, sending shock waves through the lower levels.

A pause.

"So what's your read on Carlton's performance?" he asks no one and everyone, "Professional?"

"Why don't we go ask him?" one replies.

"Shouldn't we wait till he showers?" another comments.

In truth, they'd rather Carlton didn't break his silence now. It would just mean more work. But in the unlikely event that he did talk, they share one satisfying thought: It would be the one story Conlin couldn't get no matter how hard he tried.

★   ★   ★

Being the best baseball writer in America isn't as easy as most readers believe. The Best Baseball Writer in America is a critic, not some hack. Does a theater critic go backstage to interview the actors? Does a restaurant critic interview the maitre d'? Conlin is quite capable of understanding a game without the benefit of the players' often meager powers of articulation. If it were up to him, he'd rarely print what they have to offer.

Conlin has been at it since the days when most writers covering the Phillies were extensions of the team's PR machinery. He was one of the first to print the whole truth about players. In what would later become a widely accepted approach to the profession, Conlin saw what happened in a player's life off the field—in the clubhouse and beyond—as being within his bounds. This did not make him popular. But he had the courage to print it, and then walk into that clubhouse the next day and the next and the next. Unlike many writers who are rendered toothless as they grow close to those they cover, familiarity only serves to inform Conlin where best to place his bite.

He has been at it long enough to have gone from the brash young guy on the beat to the brash old guy on the beat. If he had any inclination of walking away from it, it would be due to the repeated insult of having to deal with some low-intelligence bully who knows that you know he can break your neck like a twig. Or the born-again babble from some limited individual who expects you to be a conduit for his muddled evangelical ramblings. Sometimes it takes all of your considerable ability just to translate what some of these players say into your tape recorder. Sometimes you play it back and wonder what part of Ethiopia they are from.

Which is one of the things the Best Baseball Writer in America used to like about the Greatest Lefthander of His Day.

Look, Carlton was no genius. But his brain was more than you'd expect to find hiding under a peaked cap. And for a time they were as close as is healthy for a writer and a player to be. They were neighbors in Florida. Conlin's daughter baby-sat Carlton's kids. They would talk. Carlton would go on about Eastern philosophy and its applications to the national pastime—Zen and the art of the breaking ball. And Conlin, as was only appropriate for a man of his station, would evaluate where Lefty was right and where he was wrong.

Things were fine as long as Carlton was winning. Then, in 1973— the year after his 27-10 season for the last-place team—Carlton lost 20 games. And Conlin started looking for reasons.

If Conlin had stated his opinion directly, he would have written that Carlton failed because he had spent the off-season getting blasted on the banquet circuit. But the Best Baseball Writer in America has his own way of stating things.

"Blame it on the 1972-73 banquet circuit. . . . Blame it on dry charter flights, not getting on top of the fastball, tipping pitches, tippling between starts and it still comes down to the same stark bottom line," he was still writing in 1975. "It is difficult to avoid confronting the unspoken judgment on Carlton: That he is a shot pitcher."

This was stated repeatedly in so many words under Conlin's byline, even as the Greatest Lefthander of His Day began shopping for a new baby sitter.

For a long period, Carlton continued speaking to all writers but Conlin. The Best Baseball Writer in America would simply go write his story, knowing it would be no less great minus one ball player's meager input.

Then they started speaking again, on and off. An occasional game comment, a friendly hello. The long season in intimate quarters had a way of softening grudges.

But in 1976, the final break was made. There were labor problems, and the players' grievances included uncomfortable travel arrangements. Conlin informed his readers exactly how tough the players had it after one particular flight delay. Carlton had shown great leadership in pooling money for a Bloody Mary binge that left the Philadelphia Phillies merrily bumping into walls.

Shortly thereafter, the Best Baseball Writer in America was holding court by the pool in his condo complex, enlightening everyone within earshot with his theories regarding baseball and most of the universe as he defined it. The Greatest Lefthander of His Day happened to live in the same complex, and happened to be sitting nearby with some friends, including his own personal catcher, Tim McCarver. So Conlin went up to this group and gave out a friendly, collegial, "Yo, Tim." And Carlton, his voice quivering with anger, turned to Conlin and said, "Don't you *ever . . .*" leaving the rest unsaid to this day.

The two men spoke one last time three years ago, in the Phillies clubhouse. Conlin was conducting an interview near Carlton's locker when he felt this electric presence behind him, this pulsating cloud of yin and yang. And this is what he heard: "Would you get that fucking *cigarette* out of here?"

Well.

Conlin turned off his tape recorder. He rose majestically from his chair. He crushed the cigarette in his hand. And the Best Baseball Writer in America walked out of the clubhouse without giving the pure and mighty Zen master the satisfaction of turning around to look at him.

And if it ever comes down to it—in the event that the Greatest Lefthander of His Day ever comes after the Best Baseball Writer in America with the intent of making one last, emphatic "no comment" —Conlin imagines himself taking one good shot at the pitcher's groin. And then hoping that Carlton would hurt him badly enough in turn to result in a civil judgment that would send reverberations through the major leagues. Not in the tennis arm, of course. Anywhere else would be fine.

The Best Baseball Writer in America would not willingly speak to the Greatest Lefthander of His Day even if he begged for a chance to give an interview. Conlin would have to be ordered to do so, and even then he'd do it with great reluctance. He has made a very nice living for himself over these past 10 years without Carlton's help. So fuck him. And if the rest of those writers don't like the situation, fuck them, too.

After all this time, Conlin knows every nuance of every one of Carlton's pitches. And he can describe them far better than Carlton ever could. What could be gained by talking to him? Why bother? To talk to a guy who's read maybe four books in his whole life—on the religions of the Far East, for chrissake—none of which he has any chance of understanding? Books that contain words he's unfamiliar with and ideas that are beyond him? Some Dade Junior College dropout? Are you kidding?

★   ★   ★

Bill Giles first came to prominence in the Phillies organization as the man who twice tried to deliver the opening day game ball via a human kite. Both attempts crashed, but Giles' fortunes continued to rise, and in 1982 the one-time promotion man was named to run the team.

Giles, who put as much faith in packaging as he did in content, mandated that the players cooperate with the media. He even wanted them to be polite. Before long, everyone in a Phillies uniform was media-slick.

Everyone except the Greatest Lefthander of His Day. Giles

ended up convinced by Carlton's argument that talking to the media would harm his performance on the field. It would be a distraction. He might not win as many games.

And when Carlton asked Giles if the Silence was hurting his image or helping it, the new owner had to agree that, yes, it seemed to add to "the mystique." And so Carlton—and only Carlton—was given a special dispensation from interviews.

It was always Carlton's nature to regard groups of writers—particularly writers he didn't know—the way an antelope regards a pack of wild dogs. Since childhood, he had fallen mute when called upon to speak publicly. Still, when he felt like it, Carlton was capable of expressing himself on a level uncommon for a ball player. He was thoughtful and, on occasion, quite forthcoming. In 1972, as he went about the business of having the best season any pitcher would have that decade, winning the first of four Cy Young awards and becoming perhaps the first Philadelphia athlete to complete an entire season without being booed, Carlton came forth quite frequently. His theories on the importance of concentration—philosophies of baseball that went beyond when to shift the infield in—became a curiosity throughout the game. They were also quoted in a different light the following year—one of Carlton's worst.

The truth of the matter, Carlton's friends would say, was that while he may well have enjoyed the various beverages available on the banquet circuit, finding Steve Carlton with a drink in his hand was no more unusual in 1973 than it had been in his record-setting season of 1972. The real problem in '73 was both physical and mental —a case of pneumonia that spring and the distraction of writers and fans and guys on the street asking for his attention throughout the season. It was then that Carlton stopped giving so freely of his thoughts and his interviews, and started asking his closest friends if he should give at all. He began staring spookily into vacant corners during interviews. He began saying things like, "I have to re-establish my thoughts."

His personal withdrawal did not extend to his teammates. He continued to be generous with a joke or a word of encouragement or a crate of fresh fruit for the team. He was well-liked, though not exactly a regular guy. There was always some barrier—the difference between a man who has a half-million dollar collection of rare vintage wines and men who wonder why buy the stuff if you're not going to drink it.

He just liked having it. Liked looking at it, they guessed. It was like that Zen thing of his. Weird.

Which is also how the writers felt at first, uneasy, before the Silence fell heavily and real resentment brewed. He broke his silence for only two mass interviews—after his 200th win in 1978 and again that year after a playoff victory. The latter scene featured a national media horde firing urgent questions into the air as the big lefthander suffered the sort of verbal paralysis common to the cast of grade-school plays. It even made Conlin feel sorry for him.

Since then, Carlton has been approached by reporters for everything from hunting stories to business stories. The last full interview he gave to a newspaper was in 1979, when he opened up to a local writer solely on the subject of wine. When some of the comments appeared the following day without attribution in a New York paper, Carlton declared there would be no more statements on any subject to any writer anywhere.

As the mystique grew, so did the curiosity. Everyone was interested—from McCarver, his catcher-turned-broadcaster who did three Carlton interviews before being included in the media blackout, to Barbara Walters, whose interest was aroused after the Phillies' 1980 world championship. He spoke to the author of a book on the team, but only after much cajoling. After his 300th victory—acknowledged to be an automatic ticket into the Hall of Fame for any pitcher—Carlton came close to granting a television interview, but decided the interest surrounding his historic words would overshadow his historic victory.

These days, he's asked to speak only occasionally. If it's a friend approaching him with a request that is half joke and half hope, Carlton may promise to sit down and talk "after my 400th." If it's anyone but a friend, he will walk away, eyes fixed on some faraway thing beyond the clubhouse wall. He simply pretends the person isn't part of the dimension in which he currently chooses to reside. Over the years, he has mastered this to the point where sometimes he can even block out Conlin—whose daily presence in the clubhouse sits with Carlton like stale Ripple. A baseball clubhouse is a small place for two men who require so much personal space. The only difference is that Conlin's space is filled with the sound of his own knowledgeable voice, while Carlton's is filled with quiet. Ten years and counting.

While Carlton's clubhouse spot is usually buffered from the media by empty lockers and hand-picked neighbors, arrangements on the road are not so considerate of his retiring nature. Once in Chicago, for instance, Carlton was placed next to a teammate who was speaking to a pack of writers at great length regarding a great game. The Greatest Lefthander of His Day threw a folding chair into his own locker, throwing a damper on the mood. The teammate decided it was time to shower, and the writers decided it was time to allow Lefty access to his locker.

After another game, in the same clubhouse, a group of Chicago writers decided that this would be the day they got the interview that others had been after for years. Their strategy was simple—wait the sucker out. Carlton sat in the trainers' room as the clubhouse cleared and the writers continued to blockade his locker. The standoff continued at uncomfortable length before Carlton finally emerged, elbowed his way to his civilian clothing and returned to the trainers' room to dress without so much as a colorful obscenity for the writers' notebooks. The last serious incident occurred several years ago, involving Thomas Boswell of the *Washington Post*—who is also considered by many to be the best baseball writer in America. Carlton has trouble with these guys. On this particular evening, Boswell took it upon himself to chronicle the contents of Lefty's locker for his readers, trying to gain insight into the long-silent man. Carlton walked up behind him, full of great rage and several words. "You can't do that," Carlton said in a whine that might have been humorous if the man weren't so large. "You have no right to *do* that."

That's about as ugly as it's gotten and probably will get, barring the unlikely event that Lefty finds someone camped out on his doorstep with a tape recorder. Under the circumstances, throughout his career, the only thing nasty about the man has been his slider. Carlton will speak off the record to small groups of media types. As for the rest, he is known to offer the occasional hello to certain writers with whom he can trust such a comment. (Never Conlin.) He has even been known to utter full sentences. There was, for instance, the time in Miami last year when Carlton leaned over in the dugout after a game and said to a writer, "Would you please pass me that towel?" And there was the day when a sportswriter approached Carlton and explained that his tape recorder was off and his notepad was in his pocket and couldn't they end this silly game?

"Sorry," Carlton replied in words that have found their place in history. "Policy is policy."

In the last 10 years, that is as close as they've gotten to having Carlton speak out on his personal philosophy.

Policy is policy.

It has not been easy. A decade of silence in the close quarters of a long season might have caused a lesser man to give in. But not the Sphinx of the Schuylkill. Not even when a group of writers was shown to the only available table at a Clearwater restaurant only to find themselves seated next to Carlton, who finished his meal entombed in silence. Not even on those occasions when Carlton might step into an elevator without checking it first for media terrorists only to find one lurking in the corner, leaving the Greatest Lefthander of His Day staring dead through the floor.

For Lefty, life in the big leagues is one big elevator. Close and too crowded. Too many strangers brushing up against you while you're looking for your floor. It's the nature of the season and the nature of the men. And it is the nature of the sportswriters to declare with some satisfaction that these days, Lefty's elevator now is quite clearly on the way down.

★   ★   ★

The Greatest Lefthander of His Day throws in the bullpen as the coaches watch and pray that his shoulder obeys. Again and again, Carlton repeats the precise motions he has depended on for all his adult life. He rocks back on his left leg, raises the right to a critical juncture of leverage and balance, then exhales and uncoils, producing a respectable pop of leather for a damaged middle-aged man.

Nearby, the Best Baseball Writer in America and a dozen other guys with notepads gather around in a casual way, watching Lefty throw and discussing whether he's horseshit. There is some disagreement. Many of them would like The Greatest Lefthander of His Day to have turned horseshit, but their eyes tell them different.

One writer, who just a week earlier said Carlton "looked 30," now says he has "The body of a 25-year-old." The number goes down after every outing, as it becomes likely that Carlton will defy the predictions and the wishes of many sportswriters and stay in the game for at least another year of the Silence.

"He's a special case. I wouldn't say anything's beyond him," one says.

"He's a strange man. Very determined."

The sportswriters stand there and give what they can to the game. Most are in the kind of physical condition that comes from a diet of free buffets heavy on starches, a lifetime of the sedentary urgency of deadlines and the occasional airport dash. Theirs is not the well-cultivated Buddha belly of wealth, but the paunchy disrepair of old luggage. They will endure, most of them well beyond the playing days of the ball players around them. Enduring has good points and bad points. The best part of it might be that you have the last say.

Sportswriters call a young player who is polite to his elders a "nice kid"—as in, "You hate to see that happen to a nice kid." An older player can be a "good guy"—someone who knows what the writers want, and gives it to them. He's quotable, and he never spits on their shoes. Later, if he's lucky, a ball player who has seen his better days can become a "good man." You almost have to become horseshit before you can be a good man. It helps if you're dead.

Of course, we all will be horseshit someday. The difference with ball players is that it happens in front of 40,000 fans and a couple million readers. Everyone knows you're horseshit, and the only thing that can redeem you is if you also have been a good guy.

Carlton? Maybe he'll hang on for another year. Maybe more. But he will be horseshit someday—someday soon is the general opinion—and then he'll wish he had been a good guy when he had the chance.

★   ★   ★

Another pop of leather. Again, again.

Carlton is alone inside the act. When he pitches, he doesn't acknowledge the hitter—it's just him and the ball and the target. It's all in his hands. Just as he refuses to allow writers to disrupt his concentration with their negative thoughts regarding what he can and cannot do. He works as hard as any man in baseball, and this spring he might be working harder than ever before, just to stay in the game.

Conlin breaks from the group. "Are we allowed to say he's throwing a screwball?" he asks a coach. "Last year he didn't like us to use that word, you know. He apparently felt we were implying that he was hanging on. Of course, I heard this fourthhand. I guess we have to use special words with him. We wouldn't want to *offend* him."

As some other writers approach players for interviews, Conlin chats with a veteran about the possible purchase of a condominium in his development, and whether he would prefer his with a ceiling fan or a wet bar.

Nearby, Carlton steps off the mound and begins a brief exercise with Gus Hoefling, a man who is part fitness coach and part personal guru. Carlton stretches himself into several improbable shapes, just a small part of the daily Samurai workout that has helped him stay in the game long after certain critics declared him horseshit. Then Hoefling takes over, applying a hold to Carlton's upper body that produces a sound similar to that of a cook getting serious with a chicken.

Conlin acknowledges all of this only after it stirs his wit.

"I'm calling Hoefling 'The Exercist' this year," Conlin announces. "I'm spelling it e-x-*e*-r-c-i-s-t. Isn't that a great name for him?"

Everybody hears this, and then, as Hoefling exerts pressure on Carlton's spine, everybody hears the Greatest Lefthander of His Day grunt. It is the last comment he will be making this afternoon.

Cracking Up

TRACK AND FIELD

By *Judy Mills*

From Women's Sports & Fitness
Copyright © 1986, Judy Mills

To hear some tell it, Kathy Ormsby was perfect. She had never gotten a grade below an A in school. She always wore a smile. She was so outstanding in every way that her hometown named a day in her honor. Then she threw herself off a bridge.

Her former high school principal refused to believe her act was a suicide attempt. "I don't think she was Kathy Ormsby," he told the Associated Press. "Not the Kathy Ormsby we know. . . ."

But did he know the *real* Kathy Ormsby? Did anyone?

The event itself is cloaked in mystery. Ormsby, one of North Carolina State University's best runners, had set the women's intercollegiate 10,000-meter record earlier in the year. Then last June, while competing in the NCAA Outdoor Track and Field Championships, she suddenly broke away from the pack, ran outside the Indiana University stadium and jumped off a 50-foot bridge two blocks away. Her body's impact on the flood plain below left her paralyzed from the waist down.

Why did she do it? That's a puzzle only Ormsby herself can work out and, since her memory of the events is still unclear, it may be a long time before she's able to put all the pieces together—if, in fact, she ever does.

But Ormsby is not the first athlete to jump—either literally or figuratively. Mary Wazeter, another promising runner, leaped from a Pennsylvania Railroad bridge in 1982 and was paralyzed from the chest down. Last spring, top triathlete Joy Hansen was hospitalized with an emotional breakdown. And several other women athletes, including Olympic figure skater Rosalynn Sumners and endurance runner Judy Milkie, have mysteriously dropped out from their sports and gone into seclusion at what seemed the height of their careers.

What pushes these athletes over the edge? Is it simply the

pressure to succeed or something more complex? And are female athletes more vulnerable than their male counterparts?

★   ★   ★

According to her father, Kathy Ormsby had always been an overachiever who put tremendous pressure on herself. She was a perfectionist, a "pusher," as one of her teammates put it. Whenever she didn't come in first, she felt she was letting herself and everybody else down.

This mind-set is not unusual. Indeed, the drive to be No. 1 is often what makes a true champion different from an also-ran. But with some athletes, the obsession with winning becomes so strong that life's other pleasures lose their appeal and "playing the game" becomes no more than an inconvenience on the way to victory.

"When you are an athlete," says Rosalynn Sumners, "you live for those highs. You train. You go through the drudgery. You peak and feel wonderful. Then you come crashing down."

Sumners admits that she's addicted to winning, a high that drugs could never duplicate. "I don't want a fake high," she says. "I want the real thing." Now, at 22, as she searches for a new direction, she confessed, "It's still hard to believe I can get a high that isn't skating-related."

Like Ormsby, Sumners was a victim of her own success. A promising young skater from a small town in Washington, she rocketed to international fame in 1983 when she won the world championships in Helsinki. Overnight, reporters started showing up at Sumner's door, and she became the overwhelming favorite to win the gold medal at Sarajevo.

But things didn't quite work out as planned. Instead of taking the gold medal, she had to settle for the silver—which, in her mind, was tantamount to failure. She was so embarrassed by her loss and the media's coverage of it that she fell into a post-Olympic depression that has plagued her ever since.

She joined Disney on Ice and began touring the world as one of the stars of the show. But the pressure to excel made her even more depressed and, at times, she found herself bursting into tears for no apparent reason. She also had trouble keeping her weight down and slid into a bulimic cycle of binging and purging with laxatives. Finally, last summer, she opted for a hiatus from her professional commitments, lest she end up like Ormsby.

"That's why I quit, because I didn't want to get to that point," she explains. "And believe me, it's crossed my mind. I don't think I would ever have the nerve to carry through with it, but I didn't want to have to do something drastic before people would stop and say, 'Oh, well, she *was* burnt out. She *did* need a break.'"

Not all athletes, however, have the presence of mind to stop before something terrible happens. In Joy Hansen's case, her collapse occurred so quickly that it caught everyone by surprise, including her closest friends.

"Joy was the kind who had to do everything perfectly—she had to be above and beyond the best, in all aspects of life," says Charlie Graves, her manager. Last spring, she had just won the opener of the U.S. Triathlon Series. She was No. 1—at least for the moment—but she realized, because of an injury, that she would not be able to sustain that position for long. "She knew she was going to lose and not be perfect," Graves recalls. "And that played terrific havoc with her mind."

What gets athletes like this into trouble, says sports psychologist David Coppel, is their inability to maintain a sense of inner balance, to realize that they amount to more than their scores or a roomful of trophies. Athletes who focus on the outcome of their sport rather than on the process of playing it, he adds, can get caught on a "real roller-coaster where self-image is tied to performance." As a result, they will have more problems with anxiety than other competitors.

Like any other form of addiction, victories are short-lived, as the athlete soon must look to the next conquest. Psychologist Thomas Tutko compares it to drinking saltwater—each sip quenches thirst momentarily, but eventually causes even greater thirst. "Winning can never satisfy the thirst completely. So, it's not just to win; it's to win again. It's not just to win again; it's to have a dynasty. That is how you define neurotic behavior."

Tutko believes that "competition and the obsession with winning are driving everyone crazy," and that Ormsby's story is not an isolated case but a manifestation of a problem that is getting worse. "It's all right in the business world, where you can have 15 computer companies that can all be successful," he says. "But in sports there's usually only one winner and a large number of losers."

For many athletes, especially women, this means living in a constant state of apprehension. When they win, the pleasure is illusory, and when they lose, they become crippled with guilt.

"We hear that a lot at the finish line," says Cathy Plant, spokeswoman for the U.S. Triathlon Series. " 'What are my sponsors going to say?' they ask. 'They invested so much time and money in me.' Women tend to internalize a lot of people's expectations."

"We athletes have lived so long under the fear of disappointing our family, our coaches, the public, that we get used to the dread," adds Sumners. "When we start feeling OK about ourselves and kind of happy, it freaks us right out. I am scared of being happy. I am scared of not having that worry, that fear of what people will think."

Judy Milkie won the 100-mile Western States Endurance Run in 1984, but an accumulation of personal problems and a stress fracture drove her away from running and into seclusion. "Withdrawing was my way of dealing with things," she says. "Everyone has her own way of coping. Some people overeat; some use drugs; some use alcohol." Her whole self-concept had hinged on running, and she spent two years learning to develop other sides of her identity. This year, at 36, she returned to the Western States and made it only as far as the

17-mile mark. It was a disappointing experience, she said, but not so much for herself as for "a special friend I didn't want to hurt."

Coppel calls this the issue of "entitlement"—Mom, Dad, coach, and Aunt Jessie are all entitled to a win because they've invested so much time, money, effort, and love in the athlete. They may even demand it. Winning, then, becomes a payoff. "That's what it feels like," he says. The danger is that an athlete's motivation will switch from "intrinsic" to "extrinsic"—that she will stop doing well for herself and let performance become an obligation.

This risk is especially great with athletes who attain success in high-visibility sports. "The public doesn't know the stress you are under," says Sumners. "All of a sudden you get all this stuff thrown at you—the fame, the money. You're thrown into this public image, into upholding 'the dreams of the American people,' and the press is there with all these expectations, and you're 19 or 20 and all you want to do is go to the prom."

In Sumners's case, she felt as if she were competing for herself until she won the world championships. Then she started competing for the nation. "By the time I was ready to get on the ice at the Olympics," she admits, "I didn't even want to be there."

Even though she is no longer competing, Sumners still feels an obligation to her public. She rarely goes out—even for a quick trip to the grocery store—unless she is with somebody else or ready to make a celebrity appearance. And she feels bad if she isn't giving a reporter a good story. In fact, she says suicide is out of the question because she's afraid of bad press.

Sumners talks about the "public" athlete versus the "real" athlete—what Coppel refers to as the "distancing" that makes the person no longer feel part of the persona. "I would love to talk to Mary Lou Retton," Sumners says. "Everyone's in love with her, but I want to know what's going on *inside* her."

Many athletes besides the superstars have experienced these feelings, but few talk about them because they don't want to appear unable to cope. The role model for the successful athlete, both male and female, is stoic, cool-headed, and macho. So, to voice one's insecurities is a sacrilege, and quitting is absolutely off the scale of possibilities. Some athletes have shown that they would rather kill themselves—or at least try—than give up.

"It's possible these are individuals who would face an amazing amount of disapproval and disappointment if they quit," observes Coppel. "They might feel intense guilt or shame. That can result in their taking drastic measures to remove themselves from the situation—perhaps forever. They may see no other way out." One can't help but notice that both Ormsby and Mary Wazeter disabled themselves in such a way that they can never run again.

Tutko laments the fact that women athletes are "doing the same dumb things men do" by putting winning above everything else. While men tend to vent their frustrations in more violent, flamboyant ways, women tend to suffer in silence. But the cause and effect are essentially the same.

Triathlete Gayelene Clews, a friend of Hansen's, believes women suffer more because of their passion to please. "Women are brought up to be selfless," she says. "A man is brought up just the opposite—to do what's best for himself first."

Coppel sees balance as the key to mentally healthy athletes. "People believe if you let up your intensity—say, taking an hour off to play instead of training—that some other athlete is not going to take that hour off and will have an edge on you," he says. However, it is the balance achieved through doing and enjoying things outside one's sport that puts performance in proper perspective.

Some of the warning signs Coppel has observed are:

• Drastic mood swings accompanied by a lack of a sense of self-worth.

• An outward appearance of perfection and obvious efforts to keep it up.

• Loss of joy in training.

• Indications of other psychological problems such as a weight fixation, sleeping problems, lack of concentration, or eating disorders.

Eating disorders are of special concern in sports such as skating, gymnastics, and aerobic dancing where maintaining a certain weight is vital to success. "They can create some of the same feelings of loss, identity confusion, and disapproval that a poor performance can," says Coppel. "The athlete thinks, 'Gee, I wasn't able to stick to my diet. I wasn't able to win.' "

To regain inner balance, Coppel recommends making mental skills as important a part of training as physical skills. "I'm advocating this as enrichment rather than psychological repair," he says. "We'd like to make our athletes supermen and superwomen who don't need any of this psychological stuff, yet there is clear evidence that it works."

The Ormsby incident has prompted Henley Gibble, president of the Road Runners Club of America and member of the Women's Long Distance Running Committee, to ask those organizations to set up a pool of advisers or some similar forum to help athletes make their way through the "labyrinth of pressures."

Hansen's breakdown has had a similar impact on the triathlon community. "She made a lot of people sit back and take it a little easier on themselves," notes Clews. "She helped others realize that the only thing you owe anybody is to be true to yourself. When it comes right down to it, that's all that matters. If you're feeling tired, if you're struggling and not on top of things—stop."

Ultimately, athletes will have to find the resources within themselves to keep their sport from taking control of their lives. A good example is marathon swimmer Julie Ridge, 30, who recently made the *Guinness Book of World Records* by swimming a lap around

Manhattan every day for five days. She had planned to swim a sixth lap, but weather prevented it. "What was neat is that the world didn't end," she says. "The weather beat me. I did my best.

"Sometimes we look at a race as being the whole world," she continues. "That's distorted. Think about Kathy Ormsby. How many people know who won that race she ran out of? How many care?"

Taylor: A Troubled Giant

PRO FOOTBALL

By *Bill Brubaker*

From the Washington Post
Copyright © 1986, the Washington Post

If Lawrence Taylor isn't the finest all-round athlete in the National Football League, he is certainly one of the wealthiest. He lives with his wife and two children in affluent Upper Saddle River, N.J., in a $400,000 house with a $36,000 Mercedes and $35,000 BMW in the driveway. The house is a dandy: five bedrooms, 3½ baths on an acre of wonderfully landscaped property. There is a Doberman pinscher to guard the grounds, a maid to clean the floors and a live-in former teammate to look after the kids.

Who could ask for anything more?

There is more: Taylor is the highest paid defensive player in NFL history. He will earn $750,000, or $46,875 per game, playing outside linebacker for the New York Giants this season. Next season, his salary will increase to $850,000, then to $900,000, $1 million and $1.1 million. If that isn't enough, Taylor also has the use of a 25-year, $1 million loan. Interest free.

Who could ask for anything more?

There is more: Taylor's investment portfolio includes interests in Arabian horses, Holstein cattle, a sports representation agency, a house in Virginia, a hotel in New Jersey, and a horse farm and apartment complex in southern California. At one point last year, he had between $400,000 and $500,000 in a New Jersey bank account. Ready cash. As for walking money, Taylor has needed only to snap his fingers: In 1982, for example, he earned $37,500 for wearing a brand of shoes, $20,000 for endorsing a chewing tobacco, and $7,500 for signing autographs at a bar mitzvah.

Who could ask for anything more?

★   ★   ★

Today, Lawrence Julius Taylor is asking for something more. Help.

On March 20, in a statement released through the Giants, Taylor surprised some of his closest friends by disclosing that in recent months he has been seeking "professional assistance" to combat a "difficult and ongoing battle" with "substance abuse."

The announcement did not surprise Giants and NFL club officials, who had suspected for more than a year that Taylor was abusing alcohol and cocaine. For more than a year, Giants Coach Bill Parcells also had expressed concerns about Taylor's off-the-field habits and associates, including a friendship with a New Jersey bar manager who has a criminal record.

In his statement, Taylor did not reveal the exact nature or cause of his problems and, in a recent phone conversation with a *Washington Post* reporter, he declined to discuss any aspect of his life, including his football career.

But from interviews with Taylor's friends and associates—and from testimony by Taylor in a little-known court case—a picture emerges of a small-town athlete who has been overwhelmed by the enormity of his big-city success.

"Lawrence Taylor lives in the fast lane—the *serious* fast lane," a longtime friend of Taylor's recently observed. "If we lived the way Lawrence does, maybe we'd have the same problems he's having now, who's to say? But before you judge Lawrence Taylor, you have to look at the road that he has traveled."

★   ★   ★

He grew up in a four-room frame house in Williamsburg, Va., the second-oldest of Clarence and Iris Taylor's three sons. His father was a shipyard worker who could afford only to provide for his family's basic needs. "I couldn't spend money on candy and stuff," Taylor once said. "I didn't have it." At times, Taylor stole to get what he needed. "Sometimes I had to," he admitted.

He didn't play high school football until he was a 5-foot-10, 180-pound junior. "At first, the other kids were just head and shoulders above him, and I looked for him to pack it in any day," recalled Melvin Jones, a coach at Williamsburg's Lafayette High. "But he hung in there, and by the middle of his senior year he was playing like he was possessed."

Although he had grown to 6 feet, 210 pounds, Taylor was never a darling of college recruiters. "Being a late bloomer, even Norfolk State didn't talk to the kid," Jones said. "But one day a North Carolina coach came by the school, just looking around. When he saw Lawrence on film, he offered him a scholarship, even though his grades were right on the borderline."

In Chapel Hill, Taylor struggled to attain an identity. "Having only played two years of high school ball, I'm not sure he had the respect of the guys at first," a former Tar Heels coach recalled. "So Lawrence felt that he had to prove himself—and to act out the image he thought a football player should portray."

"The image was mean and nasty," said North Carolina assistant coach Bobby Cale, a former teammate of Taylor's. "As a freshman playing on the special teams, he'd jump a good six or seven feet in the air to block a punt, then land on the back of his neck. He was *reckless,* just reckless."

Off the field, Taylor figured the same image would fit nicely. "Lawrence always talked about gaining respect," said Steve Streater, Taylor's roommate for three years, "and we'd always juke him about how he wasn't getting respect at this bar downtown. So one night Lawrence walked into this bar and busted up everything—chairs, glasses, everything. That's what he thought it took to gain respect." (The bar owner at the time recalled that Taylor threw a chair against a wall, but added that Taylor was generally well behaved.)

By his junior year, Taylor had won respect: In 11 games, he terrorized opponents with 80 unassisted tackles, five quarterback sacks and seven fumble recoveries. His teammates nicknamed him Godzilla. "He even had a bodyguard," Streater said, laughing. "If we were going to the club where there were a lot of people, Paul Davis (a teammate, who now lives with Taylor and his family) would open up the way for him, saying, 'Let Lawrence through.' "

Once he was through, Taylor was determined to have a good time. Often with alcohol.

"Lawrence could put away a case on a night," Cale recalled. "I mean, 24 cans of beer. And still have a lot of spunk left. I've seen him do it . . . . And if we ran out of beer, we'd start chugging wine. Sometimes we'd be up almost 24 hours doing that."

"I thought he could have a drinking problem," said former North Carolina linebackers coach Mel Foels. "At the Bluebonnet Bowl in Houston his senior year, he showed up for practice early one morning with a hangover. Hell, I could *smell* it on him, so I just got on his butt and ran him more and more. Finally, he threw up."

Understandably, Taylor, who majored in Industrial Relations, wasn't setting any classroom attendance records.

"We used to joke Lawrence about how the only time he'd come on campus was when it snowed—so he could have a snowball fight," Streater said. "But Lawrence didn't need to go to class. All the women gave him all the notes he needed. So he'd just read a little bit here and there, pass the tests, then go uptown and have a good time."

"He's a very intelligent individual, but he was really there to have a good time," said Foels, who is now coaching at Tennessee. "He was also a con man. He could talk his way into and out of a lot of things with the professors. He'd say, 'I had this problem, I had that problem.' Most of the time, when I had to get hold of him, I called the pool hall."

Foels said he never worried about Taylor's academic progress. "He would always say, 'Don't worry about it, coach. I'll get my 2.0. The professor doesn't take roll,' " Foels recalled. "He was one kid about whom we just said, 'Hey, we're not going to worry about it. He'll do it. He'll get it. He'll be eligible.' "

Taylor remained eligible, although he did not earn a diploma.

"Lawrence told me he didn't need a degree," Foels said. "He said, 'Coach, I'll make more money playing football.' " And who could argue? As a senior, with opponents running the ball away from him, he had 55 unassisted tackles, 16 sacks and three fumble recoveries. Now a 6-foot-3, 235-pounder, he was a consensus All-America, a certain first-round draft pick and the target of agents.

Taylor said in a 1981 interview that he was wooed by "women, drugs, money, everything." He added: "That turns me off. I used to try a little of this and a little of that until I got real sick. With better judgment I learned to stay away from it."

On April 28, 1981, the Giants made Taylor the second overall pick in the draft. Two days later, he asked to be excused from the club's minicamp when Streater, who had just signed as a free agent with the Washington Redskins, was paralyzed from the waist down in a car wreck. Taylor rushed to his roommate's bedside. "People like that cannot be forgotten," said Streater, now the North Carolina coordinator of Students Against Drunk Driving.

Taylor signed a six-year, $1.35 million contract that included a $250,000 bonus. Out of the bonus, he said he paid a $100,000 fee to his agent, Mike Trope, gave a total of $10,000 to members of his family, bought a three-bedroom house for his parents, and began sending $700 each month to his mother for "being my mother."

At the Giants' training camp, teammates called him "Superman" and offered to replace his locker room stall with a phone booth. Faster than a speeding quarterback, more powerful than your average offensive lineman, Taylor quickly became the toast of the Metropolis. He was named All-Pro that season, the following season and every season thereafter.

Taylor couldn't ask for anything more—except, perhaps, peace of mind.

★   ★   ★

On March 29, 1982, his former girlfriend, Kathy Louise Davis, filed suit against him in the Orange County (N.C.) District Court, seeking support payments for a child he had fathered in Chapel Hill.

While the case was being litigated, Taylor married another college sweetheart, Linda Cooley, bought a Mercedes, built a dream house, and set out to make the most of his fame and fortune.

He passed some of his time at The Bench, a boisterous go-go bar in Carlstadt, N.J., in the shadows of Giants Stadium. Somehow, Taylor felt at ease at the bar, where women take turns gyrating on a platform bathed in red and amber lights.

"This is where everybody (on the Giants' team) went," recalled Brian Kelley, a former Giants linebacker. "It was the first stop. After games and after practice. You stop and you have a few beers. You go to any team, and as soon as practice is over I guarantee you that 10 or 12 players will go to a certain place and drink."

Taylor established a close friendship with the bar's manager, Vinnie Ravo. "Lawrence and I have gone out, taken vacations together, and socialized together," Ravo said. "His family has been to my house for Christmas. I've been out to dinner with him many times. We're very close."

But their friendship apparently disturbed Parcells because Ravo has a criminal record that includes felony convictions in New Jersey for larceny and receiving stolen property. The latter conviction came after police found a stolen, fully loaded, 9mm automatic handgun under a floorboard in Ravo's attic.

"(Giants coaches) know The Bench has all the possibility of becoming a bad joint, a type of joint where a drug guy would hang out," Giants defensive end Leonard Marshall said, adding that Parcells has told players, "Don't make yourself too visible in this place." Marshall described The Bench as a "strip joint where a lot of guys go to have fun and laugh and get as drunk as possible." Parcells declined to answer any questions concerning Ravo. Ravo's lawyer, Miles Feinstein of Clifton, N.J., said: "Vinnie has nothing to do with drugs. If Taylor had any problems, Vinnie was not responsible."

New Jersey law enforcement officials interviewed by the *Post* also had concerns about professional athletes hanging out at The Bench. One reason is that Frank Scaraggi, who has been identified by law enforcement authorities as a major sports betting figure and an associate of Genovese crime family soldier John DiGilio, has been a customer at the bar. Feinstein said his client knows Scaraggi. "Vinnie doesn't throw out people and say, 'Hey, are you a member of organized crime?'" Feinstein said. There is no indication that Taylor has associated with Scaraggi.

Ravo said he is not associated with any illegal activities. "I think Parcells is a fat (hyphenated epithet)," he said. "I wish you could put that in the paper. I don't really give a damn because I'll spit in his face." As for Taylor: "L.T. is a friend of mine, so what's the big deal? My bar isn't the only bar that L.T. has gone into. He must've been into 500 bars."

While Ravo was awaiting sentencing on the receiving-stolen-property charge, Taylor was being questioned about his assets by lawyers representing his former girlfriend. In a deposition taken on July 21, 1983, Taylor said of the financial interest he has in his agent's company: "(It's) like a savings account. It's my money. They keep it there. I get some interest on it . . . around 15 percent maybe." Of his horse ranch, he said: "I guess it is (a) horse farm, a breeding farm. Not a breeding farm, but just a place where they graze and stuff." Asked for the name of the ranch, he said, "I don't pay attention to that."

As he sat in a lawyer's office in Chapel Hill that afternoon, Taylor seemed uncertain about his future as a professional athlete. "I might not play at all (this season)," he said. "I might be tired of football."

That summer, Taylor refused to report to training camp until his contract was renegotiated. He relented only after the Giants promised to discuss his contract at season's end.

In the midst of a dreadful season (the Giants would finish 3-12-1) Taylor received a message to call Jim Gould, an adviser to New Jersey Generals Owner Donald Trump. "There's the possibility of a million dollars in your pocket within a week," Gould told Taylor, "but you've got to be in my office in an hour. Do you think you can get free?"

An hour later, Taylor, dressed in an elegant dark silk suit, was in · midtown Manhattan, having lunch with Gould in the marble atrium of Trump Tower.

"Lawrence looked sharp," Gould recalled, "but the suit jacket was a bit tight on him, and one of his buttons kept coming off. I kept watching him fiddle with this button, and I got the impression that this wasn't something that he wore all the time. So I think he was hungry and ready to go with the deal."

Taylor hired a Washington, D.C., lawyer, Richard A. Bennett Jr., to negotiate a contract that would pay him $3.25 million over four years, starting in 1988, when the option year of his Giants contract expired. The deal also provided him with an on-the-spot $1 million interest-free loan and a lifetime $100,000 annuity that would begin in 1998.

Taylor celebrated his new fortune by flying to the Bahamas with Ravo. "We just went out there to fool around," said Ravo, who was still waiting to be sentenced.

On returning, Taylor learned that the Giants had countered with a six-year $6.55 million package that also included a $1 million interest-free loan. This deal, negotiated by Trope, was contingent upon Taylor getting a release from the Generals. Trump obliged, but only after Taylor returned the $1 million loan with $10,000 interest and agreed to make a $750,000 settlement over several years.

With Ravo's sentencing date approaching, Taylor wrote a letter on Giants' stationery to Passaic County Superior Court Judge William J. Marchese. The letter read in part:

". . . I have had the sincere pleasure of knowing Vinnie for the past (3) years. I am aware of his family life and his relationships. Based on that knowledge, I must tell you that he is a sincere and devoted man who is a hard worker and cares very much for his family life at home. . . .

"Vinnie has always been there when I needed him for personal advice or just someone to talk to. I trust him with my life because he has always been to me an honest, sincere, and kind person . . . I think it would be a tradgedy (sic) to have this man go to jail . . . Please consider this before you sentence him and I know that you will do what is right."

The judge sentenced Ravo to three years in prison. (He would serve 10 months at the Leesburg, N.J., state penitentiary.)

By the 1984 season, Taylor's fast-track lifestyle had been a topic of conversation among NFL club officials. "We were hearing that he had a terrible drinking problem and a cocaine problem," one club executive said. "Some of his teammates said they were scared to death to be with him in a car." Taylor was again selected All-Pro, even though he made only 3½ sacks in the last 12 games.

On February 20, 1985, an Orange County (N.C.) District Court judge ordered Taylor to pay Davis $900 a month in child support, $11,000 for back payments, and to purchase a house for his child, Whitney Taylor Davis, that costs between $70,000 and $90,000. Taylor also was ordered to pay $43,000 of Davis' legal costs, the child's medical bills and private-school tuition, and to provide a $250,000 life insurance policy. (Taylor has appealed the order to pay the legal costs.)

Taylor refused to talk to the media when he reported to last season's training camp. When he finally granted an interview, he said he had spent the off-season traveling and playing golf. "Golf is just like drugs," he said. "Once you start it, you can't stop it."

As the season progressed, writers covering the team noticed a marked change in Taylor's personality. One day, he was spotted dozing on a couch in the Giants' clubhouse. Another day, he was seen weaving his Mercedes around the steel drums that section off the players' parking lot. His onfield performances were equally erratic. In one three-game stretch he made a total of only eight tackles. But in a game against the Redskins, his two-sack, 11-tackle effort helped the Giants to a 17-3 victory. "I prepared well for this game, got some sleep and didn't go to the bars as much as usual," Taylor explained. Some writers wondered whether Taylor was serious when he said that. Sadly, he was.

★   ★   ★

When Lawrence Taylor admitted last month that he was undergoing treatment for "substance abuse," some of his closest friends were surprised. Others weren't.

"Lawrence is mysterious in that something like this could happen," said Dylan Pritchett of Williamsburg. "There must be something he's trying to get in his life that he's not getting."

"To me, Lawrence is a 27-year-old built into a 19-year-old who's got a lot of money," Steve Streater said. "Lawrence has got a good head on him, he knows what he's doing, but there are just so many things that come across his desk every day, he doesn't know where to turn."

In New Jersey last week, Giants General Manager George Young said he was closely monitoring Taylor's progress. Yes, said Young, he fully expects to see the linebacker at next month's minicamp.

"Lawrence has got a setback right now," Young said, "and he'll get as much support as we can give him. But he has to help himself. And right now, that's what he's doing. He's helping himself. You couldn't ask for anything more."

Now, Touch Your Toes

by Louis DeLuca of the Dallas Times Herald. Gymnastics is not a sport for the faint of body, as this picture clearly demonstrates. Olympic hopeful Kristie Phillips is the subject for this photo as she concentrates on her balance beam routine during competition in the United States Olympic Festival in Houston. Copyright © 1986, Louis DeLuca, Dallas Times Herald.

Passing Fancy

by J.B. Forbes of the St. Louis Post-Dispatch. It could be mistaken for a Globetrotter-type pass, but Webster Groves High School player Martin Coleman is really in the awkward position of having just lost his balance during a game against rival Ladue. Copyright © 1986, St. Louis Post-Dispatch.

The Knee

GENERAL

By *David Levine*

From Sport Magazine
Copyright © 1986, Sport Magazine

"Man, will you look at that!" says Frank Hare excitedly. "They're *crushin'* that thing!"

Frank, a large young man from Kentucky and a rookie lineman for the Houston Oilers, is looking through an observation window into an operating room at the Hughston Sports Medicine Hospital in Columbus, Ga. The "they" Frank refers to are Dr. James Andrews and his surgical team; "that thing" is the left knee of his friend and former teammate Tony Mills, a freshman on Kentucky's football team.

Tony, normally a large young man himself, now resembles a large felled tree, being spread-eagled and thoroughly unconscious on the operating table. His knee, propped up and wrapped in a brownish, sterile stocking, looks like a plump Christmas turkey. And Dr. Andrews is, well, *crushin'* that thing; an arthroscope enters one side of the knee, a surgical tool enters the other and Andrews is twisting and maneuvering each instrument with an unsettling abandon. Unsettling to Frank, anyway, since he's scheduled for similar surgery tomorrow. "Damn, he's diggin' in there!" Frank mutters. "I ain't gonna sleep tonight."

Up on the wall in the observation room, two Sony TV monitors are broadcasting the surgical action. One camera is mounted in the OR and focuses on Tony's knee. The other is in the arthroscope itself. Like Jacques Cousteau, it plunges deeply into the watery and mysterious world of the knee.

"See this," Andrews says, his voice crackling over the intercom as he pokes at what looks like a little-neck clam viewed from the side. "This is what a meniscus should look like." He moves over to a clam that appears to have been cut with a scissors. "This tear here is what catches in his knee, it's what bothers him. And this here," he continues, pointing to a frayed mass swaying in the currents, "this thing floppin' around is his anterior cruciate ligament. It should be a good, strong rope. But it's not. It's all torn and rolled up."

Andrews proceeds to clip and shave at the torn meniscus; pieces flake off like bits of smoked fish and get sucked out of the joint. Soon, the tear is gone. That done, Andrews removes the scope and, taking up his scalpel, slices Tony's knee open faster than your uncle carves into that holiday turkey. Rather than repair the torn ligament, Andrews moves another ligament on the side of the knee over and down, to give the knee the stability it lost. The whole process includes some power drilling into bone, from which a cloud of smoke arises and surrounds the knee, and chipping at the bone with a chisel, roughing up the surface to help the graft attach. "Man, I don't need to see that," Frank mumbles.

What Frank is seeing is a startlingly common result of physical activity—knee repair. The knee, as any casual sports fan, weekend athlete or physical laborer knows, is perhaps the most vulnerable, injury-prone part of the human body.

You see bad knees in little girls who have fallen off bikes, in old men who have stepped awkwardly off curbs. Popes were known to have bad knees from kneeling so often; your grandmother got house-maid's knee from scrubbing floors. Doctors recognize Jumper's Knee, Swimmer's Knee, Cross-Country Knee. Dancers are regular victims. One researcher has studied "Knee Joint Changes Among Welders in Ship Building."

Being so vulnerable, the knee is often hurt. And often severely. Think of the metaphors: an athlete's knee is blown out, destroyed, torn up, totaled. Crushed, as Frank Hare might say. Play-by-play announcers whisper prayerfully, "Let's hope it's not a knee."

The knee has its own lore, its own mythology. From the Latin *genu*, as in genuflect, the bended knee is a symbol of vulnerability. It is a place of supplication, of submission ("on your knees, slave"), of humility, of marriage proposals.

Sure, the knee has had shining moments of greatness. The history of art was changed when the classical Greeks, stuck with the then-rigid style of figure representation in which the human body was more or less columnar, took one knee and bent it, which shifted the body's weight, which turned the hips and shoulders and which invented physical movement in sculpture. (Picture Michelangelo's "David" with stiff knees.)

The knee can be a sex symbol, as in Eric Rohmer's film "Claire's Knee." To Claire's admirer, "the knee is an obscure, refined taste," says film critic David Denby. "He's not hooked on something as obvious as her breasts."

But the knee means, mostly, pain. In 1890, the last major battle of the war with the Indians occurred at Wounded Knee, a resonantly named area in South Dakota that has come to symbolize the entire history of the Indian Wars.

And above all, there is the knee in sports. Joe Namath. Bobby

Orr. Gale Sayers. Mickey Mantle. More recently, Kellen Winslow, Bernard King, William Andrews. For all their touchdowns and goals and home runs, they will always be known as well for their shattered knees.

And now you can add Frank Hare to the list. As his friend Tony Mills is wheeled out of the OR, Frank sighs.

"Man, they're gonna crush *me* tomorrow."

★   ★   ★

The embryonic knee forms between the sixth and 12th weeks of gestation. Dr. William Southmayd describes this process in his book "Sports Health" as a solid mass of gristle that develops "as if a sculptor were working inside the joint." The gristle disappears, leaving the cavity that will become the knee.

That the knee is a special part of the body is not lost even to those who have to patch it up. "The knee has it's own language," says Dr. Andrews, "meaning that it's different than other joints. There are really only two parts of the orthopedic anatomy that have their own language. One is the hand, because it's so intricate. The knee is just the same. Some people become knee specialists just to spend all their time trying to figure it out, working on it almost as a hobby."

The knee joint, the largest joint you own, is the conjunction of the two largest bones in the body, the femur (thigh bone) and tibia (shin bone). A third bone, the patella (knee cap) floats in front. Unfortunately, none of these bones fit together terribly well. The hip and the shoulder are ball-and-socket joints, the ankle is a hingelike mortise joint; they and all your other joints have well-defined places where the bones meet and fit together, like pieces in a jigsaw puzzle. Not so the knee, which is essentially two flat, slippery surfaces held together by soft tissues like ligament, cartilage, tendon and muscle. Instead of a mortar and pestle, or a door hinge, the knee is more like two big sticks held together, end to end, by rubber bands.

The knee is classified as a hinge joint, but, as "Gray's Anatomy" points out, "It's really of a much more complicated character." The knee does more than flex and extend. It rotates, it slides, it glides—in almost every direction. Its center of rotation changes as it moves; the tibia, femur and patella are constantly separating and pulling together, putting remarkable stress on those soft tissues trying to keep everything in order. Under normal conditions, like walking, climbing stairs and light running, the knee handles those stresses well. But sports aren't normal.

"Certain joints have a predilection for injury because they're constructed in such a way that if they are exposed to the slightest bit of extra force, they get hurt," explains Dr. James Nicholas, founding director of New York's Lenox Hill Institute of Sports Medicine and Athletic Trauma, and fixer of Joe Namath's knees.

Four ligaments do the main job of keeping the bones in line. Inside the knee, between the femur and tibia, are the two cruciates, so named because they cross (cruciate, from the Latin *crux*, which also led to *cruciare,* to torture, as in excruciate, as in what it feels like to tear a cruciate). The anterior (front-to-back) cruciate and its partner, the posterior (back-to-front) cruciate, keep the femur from sliding too far back and forth on the tibia, and also restrict rotation.

The two collateral ligaments, on the medial (inside) and lateral (outside) sides of the knee, keep the joint from buckling inward and outward. Ligaments are generally tough stuff, described by Gray as "pliant and flexible, so as to allow perfect freedom of movement, but strong and inextensible, so as not to yield readily under the most severely applied force." Writing in 1858, though, Henry Gray couldn't have foreseen the most severely applied forces of crackback blocks.

The end of the femur forms two elliptical notches, called condyles. The top of the tibia is essentially flat, with a small central spine to fit between the condyles. The femur sits on the tibia like a rider straddling a horse. But the fit isn't tight, so the knee has evolved a sort of saddle—the meniscuses. Padding the area between the femur and tibia are two semicircular, crescent-shaped pieces of cartilage that help stabilize the two bones and absorb the shocks when they crash together. Gray found these types of cartilage "in those joints which are most exposed to violent concussion and subject to frequent movement." Too many violent concussions will do them in; when an athlete is said to have torn cartilage, most often he has in fact torn a meniscus.

What really holds the whole joint together are the muscles. The quadriceps, the hamstrings and others are powerful pieces of work and do the job the ligaments and tendons can only begin to do. In fact, the muscles work in tandem with and are often triggered by their aides-de-knee. The knee is full of nerve fibers, and along with holding the knee together, the ligaments and tendons act as sensors. When things begin to get too tough to handle, they signal the muscles for help, reporting the forces on the knee and firing the muscles to respond. That's why your doctor taps your knee for reflex responses —the unusual force on the kneecap fires the muscle, causing you to kick.

But those nerves do more than tell your muscles how to act. "They also tell you when you're hurt," says Dr. Kurt Jacobson of the Hughston Hospital. "And they're pretty good at reporting. In fact, they're severe." Indeed, a blown-out knee is among the most painful injuries sufferable. "You see a lot of big guys, 300 pounds, who crush people for a living," says Jacobson, "and they're in tears."

★   ★   ★

"Stick your finger in there," Dr. Nicholas says as he pulls a rubber model knee from his desk drawer. The model is bent like a catcher's knee in a crouch. The finger slides easily between the rubber femur and rubber tibia. "See how loose it is when it's bent. It's only held together by the ligaments in the back there. If you stand perfectly straight . . ." he straightens the model, and the finger is crunched like a walnut, ". . . it's stable. It doesn't need ligaments to hold it together. It doesn't wobble. When it's bent . . ." he bends the model, for which the finger is grateful, ". . . it wobbles all over the place.

"The body is a chain of systems linked together," Nicholas continues (though the finger is having trouble concentrating). "When you throw a football or swing a golf club, the weight shifts, it transfers from the ground, up the leg, through the knee, hip and spine and into the arms. Now, the hip is intrinsically stable. The foot has many bones to dissipate the force. But the knee doesn't have that. The knee is the fulcrum of two big lever arms that transfer the loads, placing those loads on the ligaments and cartilage. And since they're inherently unstable, you see many more knee injuries."

You certainly do. Nearly every study you find, regardless of age, sex, sport or activity, finds the knee at the top of the list. Some of the more startling numbers include these:

• Between 1961 and 1970, 70 percent of all football players had knee surgery by the age of 26, including half of all running backs and virtually every quarterback.

• The NCAA's "Injury Surveillance System" studied seven sports as diverse as football, gymnastics, volleyball and lacrosse, and concluded "the knee is the most commonly injured body part across all seven sports."

• Big skiing centers like the Aspen Clinic see "about six acute anterior cruciate tears per day," says Dr. Andrews. Nationwide, he figures about 50,000 anterior cruciates are torn each year skiing.

• In 1984, 38 percent of all players on the NFL's injured reserve list were there because of knee injuries; 1984, in fact, was the worst year in recent memory for football knees, as the likes of Billy Sims, William Andrews, Kellen Winslow, Billy Johnson and Curt Warner all, to use the heart-stopping metaphor so appropriate for knees, went down.

One could go on and on. The greatest number of injuries by far are seen in high school athletics; the numbers actually decrease as you move up in ability toward the pros. Dr. Jack Hughston, the knee specialist whose name graces the hospital where we left Frank and Tony, estimates that "more than twice the number of sports injuries occur in nonorganized sports, compared to organized athletics." And that, of course, doesn't begin to count coal miners, train brakemen, loggers or those poor ship welders.

★   ★   ★

"It sounded like a miniature firecracker went off." That's how Derek Smith of the L.A. Clippers described his knee injury last November.

The knee can be injured in any number of ways. "A lot of injuries are associated with specific tasks in sports," says Dr. James Garrick, director of the Center for Sports Medicine at St. Francis Memorial Hospital in San Francisco. "There's tennis elbow, pitcher's shoulder.

Ninety percent of ankle injuries are sprained ligaments. Shoulder and hip problems are generally specific to one or two things. Many things can go wrong with the knee."

In both Frank's and Tony's cases, the injuries came not from a specific hit or tackle, but from general overuse—football knee, if you will. Indeed, thanks to rules changes pushed for by doctors and trainers in many sports, "most injuries we see now are not from hits, but from noncontact trauma," says Andrews. "You get a guy 6-6, 250, runs the 40 in 4.7, he doesn't have to get hit to tear up his knee."

"If someone who weighs 180 pounds runs wide open, plants his leg and stops to cut, about 2,000 pounds of force goes across the knee," says Jacobson. "To stop like that in a split second, turn and accelerate in another direction is more than enough to generate an injury." It's these *de*celeration forces, occurring so quickly and powerfully, that can shred a ligament. "Often, it's not how fast you're going," Jacobson says, "it's how fast you stop."

With knees, any of the ligaments and cartilages can be injured. "You can get smoldering overuse injuries or acute trauma," says Garrick. Ligaments can be sprained, simply stretched a tiny bit too far, or they can tear. Kellen Winslow's ligament was shredded in what is called a mop-end tear, because that's what it looked like. The menisci can be sliced and diced as well, and since most of the meniscus has no blood supply, it doesn't heal. Ligaments do heal, but not that well. No matter how the knee is fixed, it's a long, slow recovery.

And knees never come completely back. They always remind you of it, too; the knee might be the noisiest joint in the body. Derek Smith's knee exploded. Even a healthy knee often pops, cracks, clicks and snaps like a bowl of Rice Krispies. A bum knee, as one writer put it, feels and sounds "like peanuts, shells and all, being ground in a mortar."

★   ★   ★

The best way to understand anything is to go to one of that thing's trade shows. At the annual Sports Medicine Congress and Exposition, held last summer in Indianapolis, the knee was the star.

That shouldn't come as a surprise; with all those bad knees out there, the knee business is booming. It's so good, in fact, that a business magazine, *Forbes*, recently reported that 600,000 arthroscopies, 68,000 ligament repairs, 30,000 osteotomies and 75,000 total-knee replacements were performed in 1984, making the knee probably the largest segment of the orthopedic market. When you consider that the vast majority of knee injuries are treated nonsurgically (and knowing as you do the cost of medical care these days), the knee business is a multi*billion*-dollar industry.

The convention's opening session, "Injuries to the Knee—Past, Present and Future," drew such experts as Drs. Nicholas and Hughston as panelists. But the true sense of the knee's importance was out on the exhibition floor, where Serious Business meets High Camp, and the free gift is raised to an art form.

It doesn't take long before one's free Medtronic "Pain Management is our Bag!" bag is filled with free brochures, pamphlets, technical manuals, a DONZIS IS SPORTS MEDICINE baseball cap, a Camp Orthotic Supports and Appliances comb, a Genucom notepad and Knee Analysis System Test List, as well as pens, buttons, posters and T-shirts from such groups as the American Trauma Society (sponsoring Trauma Week, followed by the Trauma Banquet) and the Academy for Sports Dentistry. Nautilus and Cybex were there, as was Pregnagym. Someone at the Gatorade booth mentioned Gatorade and scotch, a highball whose time may have finally come.

But the most prominent category was easily the knee. Salesmen were strapped to beds with their knees in traction. Salesmen were rolling up their pants legs and strapping on their braces. Salesmen were limping stiff-legged through the aisles, fitted with all manner of pads and braces and supports. It is not athletes who come to mind; it is the zombies in *Night of the Living Dead*.

One of the more popular booths was manned by Lenox Hill Brace, Inc., owing partly to the large picture of their poster boy, Dan Marino, whose braced knee drew far less attention than did his curly hair and blue eyes, at least among the female conventioneers.

Actually, the Lenox Hill brace hardly needs Marino to draw attention. The brace, originally designed for Joe Namath, is the top dog in bracedom, holding a 75 percent market share since 1970. There were many pretenders to the knee-brace throne at the show, some frightening high-tech models seemingly capable of immobilizing a small aircraft, others looking like felt-and-gauze cutouts offered by mom-and-pop orthotics shops. None, though, possesses Lenox Hill's place in history. Last August Joe Namath entered pro football's Hall of Fame. So did his knee brace.

★   ★   ★

Your mother is knock-kneed. So is your father, but, being a man, not as much. So are you, for that matter. In fact, everyone you know is knock-kneed. It's one of humankind's most striking adaptive features. It helps us walk upright.

The most famous anthropological knee, as famous to anthropologists as Namath's knees are to sports fans, is the Hadar knee, a 3-million-year-old joint named after the region in Ethiopia from which it was unearthed. It belonged to a creature named Lucy, more scientifically known as *Australopithecus afarensis*. Lucy was knock-kneed too; hers is the first knee to show the human characteristics that allow upright walking.

This knock-kneedness is called the valgus shift, and it gets the knee under your center of gravity. If your leg hung straight down from the hip, you'd have to sway from side to side while walking to support yourself on one leg, like chimpanzees, our nearest relatives, do. That being a terrible waste of energy, man evolved the valgus shift—natural knock-knees.

You can stand for a long time without tiring because of another uniquely human development called the screw-home mechanism. When the knee is fully extended, it sort of screws itself tightly into a locked position. The finger remembers that if you stuck it inside the joint while extended, it would be crunched like a walnut. That keeps the knee locked and stable during standing and allows the muscles to relax. (And also allows for a practical joke as old as humanity—tapping a knee from behind while a person stands will cause him to fall, because his muscles are relaxed.)

"The human knee was probably the first of the joints to restructure," says Dr. Jack Stern, a professor of anatomical sciences at the State University of New York at Stony Brook. "As soon as you get up on two legs you develop the valgus knee. Some fossils with human-like knees have shoulders like chimpanzees. The hip is somewhere in between."

But while the knee was made for walking and standing, it wasn't made for much else. It had finished evolving while man was still a scavenger. It could handle chasing down food when the species became so inclined, and for several million years it worked fine. It was only when man started chasing down quarterbacks that the knee collapsed.

"The human knee is the best around for what it was designed to do," adds Dr. Owen Lovejoy, a professor of anthropology at Kent State. "But we're not adapted to bearing cleats and running on AstroTurf. We do things early man never did. *Australopithecus* never ran around end."

★   ★   ★

There is no evidence that Lucy played on a girls softball team; her knee was sound. But as long as there have been sports, there have been sports injuries. And that means knee injuries. A papyrus dated back to around 2500 B.C. describes how the ancient Egyptians treated various knee sprains, fractures and dislocations, many of which probably came from whatever version of football they were playing at the time. Hieroglyphics from Egypt depict some of the citizenry with canes and crutches, all suffering from knee and leg troubles still seen today.

The first known jock doc was probably a fifth-century-B.C. Greek named Herodicus. Actually, he was more a trainer than a physician. A sickly man, Herodicus found that exercise helped his poor health and he passed on his training techniques to athletes and non-athletes alike.

His reputation spread and he drew many visitors, including Hippocrates. As physician to the Olympic athletes, Hippocrates is called the father of sports medicine, yet in his writings he gives curiously little attention to the knee. He spends more time discussing hemorrhoids than knee sprains. Still, he was perceptive enough to call the knee "compact, regular and elegant in construction."

Galen of Pergamon, a Roman physician who cared for the gladiators in the second century, compiled a large amount of research and writing in sports medicine, but he was a rather crotchety sort, disdainful of sportsmen and their trade. "Athletes live a life quite contrary to the precepts of hygiene," he wrote, "and I regard their mode of living as far more favorable to illness than to health. They lose their eyes and their teeth, and their limbs are strained."

But like the knee itself, the evolution of its care and treatment peaked early. From the Middle Ages up to our own lifetime, orthopedics made little progress.

"In the first three decades of this century, knee surgery centered on providing stability at the expense of motion," Nicholas says. Surgical repair was limited, ligament repair unheard of. Bad knees were generally put in casts and allowed to heal however they might.

But in the 1940s, an orthopedist named Don O'Donoghue, widely regarded as the father of orthopedic sports medicine in this country, showed that bum knees could be repaired surgically.

Since then, advancement in the understanding and treatment of the knee has been phenomenal. In many ways, treatment outpaced understanding, to unhappy results. For a long while, a torn meniscus was simply and totally removed. Little was known about just what the menisci did, and doctors, for all the good they do, have a history of chopping things out before they're fully understood. More recently, however, much of the advancement in knee care has been in the simple understanding of anatomy. "We didn't realize the sacrifice made when you remove all the cartilage," admits Nicholas.

Then came the arthroscope. Actually, the scope has been around longer than football has. In the early 1800s candlelight was reflected into a tube placed in the body. By the 1880s incandescent light bulbs had been attached, and lenses were added to provide better viewing angles, but it wasn't until the birth of fiber optics in the late 1950s that arthroscopes were made small and light enough to really maneuver with a joint.

The Japanese—surprise! surprise!—were the first to use a scope regularly, but they employed it mainly for diagnosis. Arthroscopy didn't really take hold as a surgical procedure in this country until the late '60s. New York Knicks star Willis Reed, in 1968, was one of the first athletes to undergo arthroscopy.

The scope has vastly increased the knowledge of the working knee and allowed the preservation of many of its structures. "What the arthroscope saves is more important than what it can extract," says Dr. Hughston.

Hughston's hospital, where Frank and Tony came to fix their knees, represents the future of the knee. Soon, much of the knee's repair will be done arthroscopically. Torn ligaments will be replaced with artificial structures, arthritic bones will be resurfaced, and the debilitating and costly repairs done by open surgery will be reduced. The damaged knee will be restored, giving it back what James Nicholas calls "the troika of motion, power and stability."

★   ★   ★

For all its problems, your knee is really quite remarkable. Considering its often conflicting requirements of stability and flexibility, in motion and at rest, while starting and stopping, the knee is a marvel of design.

The fact is, many animal species have knees that, while showing specialization, are very similar to yours. "The knee joint may be more similar crossing animal boundaries than any other joint," says Dr. Garrick. Much of the early research on repairing cruciate ligaments was done on dogs. "We work with a veterinary medicine school with cruciate-ligament problems in bulls," says Hughston. "When they're mounting and breeding and another bull hits 'em it tears their ligaments. If you've got a million-dollar bull, it's just like a million-dollar football player."

So you should be happy with what you have. It could be worse. You could have birds' legs, where the knee is tucked up near the body and the ankle is at the center. That would have grave consequences in sports, but even more so in the furniture business. Try to imagine what a chair would look like if your knees bent the other way.

Bird Gift-Wrapped Celtics' Title

PRO BASKETBALL

By *Paul Attner*

From The Sporting News
Copyright © 1986, The Sporting News

Larry Bird's flair for the dramatic has never been better. Just when it seemed the National Basketball Association championship series would become Wrestlemania III, Bird all but gift-wrapped a 16th title for the Boston Celtics by playing so well that a highlight film of his performance in Game 6 deserves a spot in the Hall of Fame.

Bird was never better on a day when the NBA needed all the *basketball* help it could garner. An awful fight in Game 5 initiated by Houston's Ralph Sampson had cast an ugly shadow over what had been a quality series. Suddenly, the focus no longer was on Bird's playmaking or Akeem Olajuwon's quickness around the basket. Instead, everyone wondered if Marvin Hagler would be putting on a Celtics uniform.

But Bird brought skill and quality back to the series. "My team came to play, not to fight," he declared after the Celtics had reclaimed their NBA supremacy with a 114-97 victory over the Rockets June 8 before a joyful Boston Garden crowd. Indeed, it was "his" team, fueled by his intensity and driven by his desire to repay the Rockets for all of Sampson's sins in Game 5.

The Celtics were an angry bunch in the hours leading up to the concluding game. Not only had the hotheaded 7-foot-4 Sampson stunned them by picking on 6-foot-2 Jerry Sichting to start the fight ("my girlfriend could beat him up," Bird said of Sichting), what happened after the altercation hurt them even more. Sampson was ejected, but the Rockets didn't miss half of their Twin Towers. They played inspired basketball, running over the Celtics, 111-96, and sending the series back to Boston with the Celtics leading, 3-2.

"You can't believe how down we were," said Boston reserve center Bill Walton. The Celtics, who had pulled out Game 4 on Bird's three-point field goal and Walton's rebound basket in the final 2½ minutes, fully expected to win the next contest and conclude the series in Houston. Now they had to return home, wondering if overconfidence was letting the series slip away.

What's more, the Sampson controversy had taken the spotlight away from the Celtics, who already were being compared to the greatest teams in NBA history. Instead, the NBA and the Celtics now were being quizzed about security precautions in Boston Garden, and the Boston Globe was writing about past "villainous" NBA big men and the fights they had started. Accompanying that story was a drawing of Sampson, holding a blackjack.

The NBA decided not to suspend Sampson, but he was fined heavily after the series ended. The Celtics, their enormous pride wounded, didn't want him on the sideline. They had a debt to pay and the more they thought about Game 5 and the way Houston beat them on the boards (56-37) and outfought them for loose balls, the more upset they became.

At practice the day before Game 6, Coach K.C. Jones had to send everyone home early after it got so rough on the court he feared someone would get hurt. "I've never seen anything like it since I've been here," said Jones. And how irritable were his players in the locker room before the game? "Some guy walked through and they wanted to know how he got in," said Jones. "And it was the trainer."

No one was more prepared than Bird, who admittedly had thought "the hell with it" when the Rockets kept pouring it on in Game 5. Bird had been superb all season, winning his third consecutive Most Valuable Player award, and he was determined not to blow everything by having a lackluster final round. But he had been inconsistent during the first five contests, playing well enough for most players but not always up to his harsh standards. He finally decided he had been "too pumped up" for the series, which was causing him to force things to happen instead of letting everything come naturally.

For Game 6, he wanted things as natural as possible. The Celtics helped out by making some changes. Dennis Johnson and Robert Parish suggested they take on new defensive assignments. Johnson would move from Lewis Lloyd to Robert Reid, who had 17 assists in Game 5, and Parish would switch from Sampson to Olajuwon, who was devastating in the same contest (32 points, 14 rebounds). Jones, who usually is quick to agree to player requests, gave his approval.

With Johnson hounding his every step, Reid became passive. "I went flat," he said. "Blame the loss on me." He finished with 12 points—he had only four when the game was still in doubt—and six assists. Olajuwon had a team-high 19 points and 13 rebounds, but missed eight of his 14 field-goal attempts and couldn't keep up with Parish's headlong dashes down the court that helped ignite Boston's dormant running game.

More importantly, the Celtics decided they had been ignoring Bird too much on offense. Bird had said as much after Game 5, when he took only 13 shots and went long stretches without touching the ball. Bird is a realist; he has proven over the years that when he is allowed to control the offense, the Celtics normally win. Give me the ball in Game 6, he said, and we'll likely win.

"The stage was set and the time was right," he said. "I didn't want to go away disappointed."

So his teammates complied. When the game was still undecided, which wasn't much beyond halftime, Bird initiated things on almost every Celtic half-court offensive foray. "You see those five fingerprints on the back of Larry's jersey?" said Jones. "That's because he carried us all the way and I grabbed hold at the hotel."

With Bird orchestrating, the Celtics played sweet music all afternoon, methodically dissecting the younger Rockets and all but putting the ugliness of Sampson's Game 5 outburst out of mind.

"Kick our tails and see what happens," yelled forward Kevin McHale in the locker room afterward as champagne was poured on anyone who moved. The Rockets certainly learned a lesson: If you beat the Celtics, don't gloat about it, especially if the next game is in the Garden—and especially if Bird knows about it.

If there was any doubt about Bird's unique greatness, Game 6 answered any and all questions. Someone told Walton that Bird's 29 points weren't all that exceptional, considering he averaged 26 points during the season. Walton laughed and said, "With all the pressure out there and with everything he does, 29 points is exceptional."

But it was more than the points. The Celtics needed help on the boards after being outrebounded, 102-77, the previous two games, including a pitiful 48-21 at the offensive end. Bird decided he should concentrate on rebounding and wound up with 11 for the game, including eight at halftime, one less than McHale.

But it was more than rebounds. The Celtics had been standing around too much in Houston, depending on individual skills, not their characteristic unselfish passing, to generate points. Bird changed that in Game 6 with his 12 assists. The Celtics would give the ball to him, isolated against Rodney McCray to the right of the basket, and Bird would improvise a give-and-go play or wait until the last minute before tossing a pinpoint pass through a mass of defenders to an open Celtic on the other side.

But it was more than assists. "When we play defense, no one can beat us," Bird had said earlier in the series. For this game, the Celtics came out alive and active on defense. The Rockets had an incredible seven turnovers in the first six minutes as they fell behind, 20-9. Bird had three steals in that span, including two from Olajuwon, who was not allowed to wheel and deal near the basket without three Celtics hanging on his every move.

But it was more than steals. It was Bird's very *presence*. Bird played the game's first 46 minutes. After three periods, he said he was as tired as he's ever been. That's because he pushed himself relentlessly, setting an example for his teammates. If he could keep running, why couldn't they? And the more they all ran, the closer that 16th title came.

"I've never been so pumped up," he said. "I thought I was in Game 2, but this takes the cake." So did some of his plays. In the first quarter alone, he had seven points, three steals, four assists and four rebounds. But that was just setting the stage. He kept diving on the floor after loose balls and knocking away errant passes and leading fast breaks up the court, never letting up the pressure on the Rockets.

And when he could see Houston was on the verge of crumbling, he applied the final blows. A give-and-go pass to Parish that was just impossible to make . . . a three-point basket to put the Celtics up by 20 . . . a dazzling pass to Walton early in the fourth quarter . . . and, finally, a second three-point goal that had the Garden in an uproar. Time was running out on the 24-second clock when Bird tried a spin move. It didn't work, so he decided to push the ball out to the three-point circle and fire away. "I hoped I had enough strength," he said.

He did. The ball swished in, putting Boston ahead, 87-61. The fans were still cheering when Walton took a Bird feed for another layup, Houston called a timeout and the crowd kept yelling even when play was stopped. "I was hoping (the three-pointer) would be the backbreaker," said Bird. It was.

"We still haven't seen the best of Larry Bird," declared Walton, "because we aren't good enough yet to push him as hard as he can be pushed."

It was Bird's second triple-double of the series, and he missed a third by only one rebound in Game 4. Until Game 6, choosing a most valuable player was difficult. But he made it simple.

His performance atoned for what he considered to be an embarrassing effort in last year's final round against the Los Angeles Lakers. Bird's shooting arm was ailing then and he could never dominate a game as he did this one. So he practiced hard during the summer, vowing that the Celtics would win their third title since he joined the franchise in 1979.

Whenever Bird struggled in the series, the Rockets were competitive. But the NBA's youngest team couldn't handle the intense pressure generated in the heat of the Garden. They shot a dismal 28 percent in the second and third periods, scoring 15 points in the second and 23 in the third, while losing the boards to their older rivals. No matter where Coach Bill Fitch turned, he couldn't find anyone to neutralize Boston's onslaught.

Sampson especially had a dreadful time. He claimed that reaction to his fight did not affect him, but he was a timid, passive player in Game 6, just as he had been outlandishly aggressive in Game 5. McHale, who scored 29 points, consistently wheeled around him for baskets. Sampson didn't counter with his first points until two minutes were left in the half, after he had missed six shots.

To give Olajuwon more room inside, Fitch moved Sampson to the high post to start the game. That took away the hooks and dunks which he had used to hurt Boston earlier in the series. Sampson went 4 for 12 from the field and scored just eight points.

"I played bad," said Sampson, who was greeted by numerous signs—such as the one that read: "Ralph, I'm 5-foot-2. You'd probably hit me, too"—and booed each time he touched the ball. "If I had played well, we would have won. But I've had some good days, some bad days and some tough days. This was a bad day. I feel frustrated but it's a learning experience. I look forward to being on top for a long, long time."

After falling behind in the opening minutes, the Rockets could make just one run at Boston. Olajuwon made three straight steals late in the second period and scored after each turnover, drawing the Rockets to within 22-21. But the Celtics went on a 13-2 streak, McHale and Bird scoring all the points, to open up a 44-30 lead. Only horrid foul shooting (11 for 21) and turnovers (10) prevented the Celtics from being in front by more than 55-38 at the half. It was never close in the last half, when Boston led by as many as 30.

"I think they were embarrassed by what happened to them in Houston," said Rockets forward Jim Petersen. "When they are mad, it's tough to beat them in the Garden." Thankfully, the Rockets didn't vent their frustration with any more fights. Referees Jake O'Donnell and Darell Garretson never let the game get out of hand.

Even playing against Olajuwon and Sampson, the Twin Towers who vanquished the defending champion Lakers in the Western Conference final, the Celtics thought they could win the series in four straight. And they probably should have. After winning the first two in Boston, they blew an eight-point lead in the final four minutes and lost Game 3 in Houston. Then they overcame the Rockets' superior rebounding and hustle to pull out Game 4 when Walton laid in a rebound with 1½ minutes left.

"We want to end it here," McHale said before Game 5. But Reid said he didn't want the Celtics "opening champagne in this building." The Celtics had the bubbly ready, but it was never uncorked in Houston. The Rockets thoroughly whipped them in Game 5, getting superior efforts from Reid, Olajuwon and Petersen, who stepped in for Sampson and grabbed 12 rebounds.

Boston played as if its tradition and reputation would be enough to win. They weren't. Neither was the loss of Sampson, who became the center of controversy with 9:40 left in the second quarter.

He and Sichting bumped at the foul line and Sampson's elbow smacked the Celtics guard on the head. When Sampson went to the low post, Sichting and Walton sandwiched him, and shoving and more elbowing followed. Sampson, who claimed Sichting hit him, suddenly stepped away and swung at his foe, then punched again. Johnson hurried over and got smacked for his troubles before Walton tackled Sampson.

By now, both benches had cleared and Johnson had been hit by Olajuwon. Sampson broke free and tried to get at Sichting again before finally stomping off to the Rockets' bench, kicking a basketball as he went. The Houston Summit crowd was incensed by the ejection and Sampson wasn't too pleased, either. In the corridor outside the Rockets' locker room, he told CBS television it was a "bull - - - -" call. Later, he said he swung to protect himself, but he apologized to everyone but Sichting, saying he would not be fighting again. Then he returned to the floor to be saluted at a postgame fan rally, a gesture the Celtics couldn't believe.

Sichting, who was acquired this season from the Indiana Pacers, giving the Celtics a much-needed outside shooting reserve guard, cast himself as innocent in the whole affair, although he admitted he told Sampson, "I'll get you for that" after being banged by the first elbow. "My little boy hits harder than that," Sichting said of Sampson's punches. Johnson got the worst of the ordeal. He had a cut near his left eye, which was bloodshot.

The Twin Towers are gaining quite a fighting reputation. That was the fifth time Sampson had been ejected this season—the second time for fighting. Olajuwon already had been kicked out twice in the playoffs for brawling, including a scuffle with the Lakers' Mitch Kupchak in the final game of that series. The Celtics' Danny Ainge didn't help matters by referring to the Rockets as "freaks," a remark that was overheard by a Houston reporter.

Still, the Rockets, who now feel they should rule the Western Conference for years to come, were proud of what they were accomplishing in the finals. "The Celtics went fishing and landed a barracuda," said Reid.

In Game 6, the Celtics landed much bigger game. More than a 16th title, they staked a claim for their place in history.

Milwaukee Bucks Coach Don Nelson, a former Celtics star, already had proclaimed them the best NBA team ever. By sweeping the Houston series, they would have finished with the best-ever winning percentage, including playoffs, in NBA history. Instead, they had to settle for being among the top five. Still, their numbers were impressive: a 67-15 regular-season record, which had been bettered by only three other teams; a record 41 straight victories at home (50-1 at the Garden this season); and a 15-3 playoff mark, including a 4-0 blanking of the Bucks.

"I don't think it's right to compare eras," said Fitch, "but in this era, they certainly have been the strongest. A measure of how good they are will be how good my team turns out to be. If we get very, very good, then this win over us will look even more impressive."

Once the Celtics won the title, Jones, who played with Bill Russell on some of the best Boston clubs, said the team was the greatest he had seen. Until then, he had maintained it was the most talented Celtics club, not necessarily the best. Club President Red Auerbach, the architect of all the Celtics' championship teams, hasn't been able to answer one question: Would this team be able to beat the finest Russell clubs?

Certainly, these Celtics were a delight to watch. They were the essence of teamwork, featuring two outstanding passers (Bird and Walton), a bona fide big-game player (Johnson) and a top-notch scoring forward (McHale). They had great size and shooting touch and, when motivated, they played wonderful team defense, one reason they never lost more than two games in a row all season. It wasn't an exceptionally quick team, but it was smart and confident. And Bird usually more than compensated for any weaknesses. Jones helped by preparing his players well in practice, then letting them have great leeway in games.

"He was a lot more laid back in the playoffs this year," Bird said of Jones. "It was the right approach for this team."

The addition of Walton, who last played for the Los Angeles Clippers, improved Boston immensely from the team that lost to the Lakers in last year's final round. He gave the Celtics added strength in the frontcourt and brought with him a zest for playing that became infectious.

When Bird heard Walton had signed with the Celtics, he told Auerbach, "That's our championship." Now Bird says, "As long as Walton stays healthy, we can win a lot more (titles)."

But for now, Walton will settle for this one. Nine years ago, before foot injuries all but ended his career, he had been the center on Portland's championship team. He had called the Celtics in the off-season, hoping he could talk his way onto a contender before his career ended. His persistence worked and, after the Game 6 victory, he hugged Bird and thanked him.

"He should thank me," said Bird, tongue firmly in cheek. "I carried him the whole season." Walton wasn't alone. He had the rest of the franchise along for company.

If Athletes Abuse Drugs, It's Their Problem

GENERAL

By *Scott Ostler*

From the Los Angeles Times
Copyright © 1986, Los Angeles Times

The Dodgers were boarding their private jet at a New York airport several years ago. The players and others in the traveling party were ushered around the metal detector, where a long line of people waited for the standard scanning for bombs and weapons.

One lady in the line was indignant.

"How come *they* don't have to go through the metal detector?" she demanded of an airport security cop.

"Lady, the Dodgers have their own airplane," the security cop explained. "If they want to blow it up, that's their business."

That's the way I'm starting to look at drugs and athletes.

We should be educating and informing these athletes about what drugs do. We should do our best to cut off the supply. Throw in lots of peer pressure, counseling, testing if there's probable cause, second chances, rehabilitation, incentives, any help we can give.

Then, after all that, if they still want to blow themselves up, that's their business.

There's only so far we could and should go to baby-sit these people. Should we test them every month? Every day? Follow them around in the off-season with surprise visits from roving urine-test-mobiles?

Pete Rozelle has announced a plan to randomly test every NFL player at least twice during the season. The players' union is protesting, and the union will probably prevail. Without union agreement, Rozelle's new plan is probably unworkable.

That's just as well, because I don't believe random testing of every pro athlete is the right or effective way to go.

But what about Lenny Bias and Don Rogers? What about the kids who are influenced by their pro athlete heroes?

Drug testing wouldn't have saved Bias and Rogers. Both had been tested, in season, and found clean, but each tragically overdosed in the off-season. Which only shows that drug testing, while an effective momentary deterrent, doesn't knock out a person's inclination to partake of drugs, doesn't protect him from evil outside influences.

As for the impressionable youth of America, looking up to pro athletes, I'd tell them to keep looking. This is real life. The athletes you admire are not perfect. Some of them take drugs, even some real nice guys and gals. By taking drugs, some of them ruin their careers and their lives, and a few of them even die young of overdose. And all of them were sure they could handle drugs. Most started drugs as a lark, innocent fun.

But keep looking kids. Some of your heroes, while not perfect, choose *not* to take drugs. Look at them, too. Check 'em out. Whatever problems they have, they don't wind up in gutters or rehab houses or morgues. Some of them even seem to enjoy life for more than 10-minute stretches of time.

Take your choice, kids. Do you want to grow up to be a Walter Payton, or a Don Rogers? Do you want to grow up to be a Magic Johnson, or a Micheal Ray Richardson?

We'll help you all we can. But we can't follow you around all your life, testing and spying, even if you're a famous athlete. Somewhere along the line, maybe a lot of places along the line, you're going to have to take responsibility for yourself.

I object to Rozelle's random blanket testing of everyone, not simply because it infringes on the players' rights, although it does. The NFL Players Association will file a grievance. Had the union been around when the team owners voted to make helmets mandatory, the union would have filed a grievance.

I object to Rozelle's plan because it's cosmetic. Testing, as the tragedies of Bias and Rogers showed us, is only a momentary deterrent at best. Even baseball commissioner Peter Ueberroth, who comes off as a hard-core, pro-test guy, sees random testing as only a short-term measure, not the key to an anti-drug program.

Maybe the intentions of the various league commissioners are pure, but their rushing to implement strong anti-drug programs, especially the testing parts of the programs, smacks of marketing strategy, smart PR. Why don't they crack down on steroid abuse, a dangerous and widespread practice? Because steroid abuse doesn't discourage the paying customer.

Why can't the commissioners of all the pro sports leagues, and all the reps of the various pro players' unions, get together and come up with a monster drug attack plan? Because they are in competition, even to see what league can have the fewest arrests and scandals and advertise itself as the cleanest.

I asked Ueberroth why, if he's so sure his anti-drug program will be effective, he doesn't phone Rozelle and NBA commissioner David Stern and offer to share his plan.

"I did," Ueberroth said. He indicated that Stern and Rozelle were not interested in meeting with him.

I like Ueberroth's zeal in attacking the problem at the junior high school level, where the real drug action is, and at the government level, trying to control the supply. Let's drug-test kids in junior high, in high school, even college, where they are young and impressionable and naive and need protection. By the time they are pros they should be making their own decisions.

As for Rozelle's random testing, better he should put the league's time and energy into the education, information and assistance of the players. Give them a chance to be clean by personal choice.

And those unfortunate few who resist all efforts of sincere guidance, who in one way or another blow themselves up, well, that's tragic, but that's their business.

The Most Majestic Rivalry Ever

TENNIS

By *Barry Lorge*

From Tennis Magazine
Copyright © 1986, Golf Digest/Tennis, Inc.

Flashback to 1973, an indoor arena in Akron, Ohio, and the first meeting between Chris Evert Lloyd and Martina Navratilova.

"She was 16 then, I was 18 and I beat her 7-6, 6-3," Lloyd recalls. "It was a shock that the first set went to a tiebreaker because I had never heard of her before. She had this big lefty serve and she was about 25 pounds overweight and she was moaning and crying on the court but, boy, did she have talent! Good wrists, a lot of power, even at 16. It was kind of scary.

"It was the first round, I was seeded No. 1 and nobody knew anything about her. She had the shots, the weapons, if she ever got into shape. I didn't know if she had it mentally. She was a wreck emotionally—so young to be playing in America. She didn't have any direction or discipline in her life. Everybody was saying after that week: 'Gosh, if this girl ever gets organized and has some discipline, she's going to be tough.' And that has turned out to be true."

Lloyd already had been to the semifinals of the U.S. Open twice and Wimbledon once. She had won a handful of pro tournaments. She was known as "the Ice Maiden"—regal, imperturbable, a paragon of backcourt consistency. Navratilova was a pudgy, tempestuous Czechoslovak playing her first pro tournament overseas, discovering fast food and the fast life—an immense but as yet unconsolidated talent.

Little did they know that day in Akron that their match would be the first episode in the greatest rivalry tennis has known ... that they would play more than five dozen times during the next 13 years, 13 times in Grand Slam finals ... that they would drive each other to higher levels of play than either protagonist would have achieved without the other as antagonist ... that they would prolong each other's careers and force one another to change their approaches to the game and their bodies in an ongoing, uncompromising quest for supremacy.

Now a flashback to 1985 that illustrates the intensity and majesty of the rivalry—the test of personal pride and professional prejudice that is always near the surface when these two champions confront each other across a net.

Paris, June 8, the French Open final at Stade Roland Garros. After nearly three hours of exceptional shotmaking and twists and turns as unpredictable as the swirling breeze, Lloyd is at match point. Navratilova has beaten her in 15 of their previous 16 matches, dating back to late 1982, but Lloyd is on the threshold of claiming at least one of the four traditional major championships for the 12th consecutive year.

Their sneakers are covered with clay the shade of salmon. Both are drained. It has been a torturous match. Lloyd's pale yellow skirt flutters in the wind as she crouches to receive serve. Navratilova wipes the perspiration from her glasses.

Navratilova serves and wants to attack—her natural inclination, although this day she has fiddled too much with drop shots and baseline rallies. Lloyd goes for the laser-beam backhand down the line, the consummate counterpuncher's best weapon. Navratilova's window of vulnerability is small; she and her coach believe that a superb net-rushing game will trump a splendid baseline game every time. But Lloyd's passing shot shatters it. She wins her sixth French title, dethroning Navratilova 6-3, 6-7, 7-5.

Navratilova heaves a primal sigh (it sounds like a vacuum cleaner exhaling) and strides around the net to hug Lloyd. They are like two prizefighters after a glorious bout. Exhilaration, disappointment, satisfaction, frustration, exhaustion and a mutual admiration that perhaps only they can truly appreciate is embodied in that embrace. "It's too bad someone had to win," said Navratilova. "It was one of those matches that should go on forever."

She was speaking of their 65th encounter, but the same sentiment could apply to their extraordinary 13-year rivalry. They are the superpowers of the women's game and, for years, everybody else has been Third World.

"The only reason that Chrissie has stayed in the game is to be No. 1 again," said Don Candy, coach of Pam Shriver, Navratilova's doubles partner. "That wasn't just a win in Paris, that was a victory in her life. That was a triumph from her toenails to her hair. She didn't just beat another player; the lady of ice was back on the throne."

The great rivalries are contested on several levels—on the court and in the hearts and minds of the combatants. They are fascinating psychological battles as well as chess games of strokes and strategies. The tactical thrusts and counterthrusts are reflections of the personalities of the duelists. The most intriguing rivals have contrasting temperaments and styles, and their matches become tangible clashes of will as well as skill.

So it is with Navratilova and Lloyd. Fire vs. Ice. Volcano vs. Glacier. Irresistible force vs. Immovable object. The most forceful and acrobatic serve-and-volleyer in women's tennis vs. the most dogged competitor.

"Martina is the best athlete I've seen in tennis, and probably the best ever," says Lloyd. "I think if you combine strength and quickness and agility, she is the best athlete, without a doubt. Mentally, I would have to say I've seen a few better ones."

Historically, baseline players have developed earlier than netrushers, whose attacking style takes longer to jell. Lloyd, entrenched atop the women's rankings, dominated the first five years of the rivalry, winning her first five matches against Navratilova, 14 of the first 16, and 20 of the first 24 from 1973 through 1977.

Those were turbulent years for Navratilova. Her temper often overcame her talent. One questionable call could dissolve her into tantrums or tears. She defected from Czechoslovakia during the 1975 U.S. Open. She was unsettled and still undisciplined.

But by 1978, she was getting a grip on herself and her career. In the final at Eastbourne, a grass-court tune-up for Wimbledon, she defeated Lloyd 6-4, 4-6, 9-7 in a magnificent match. She won again a fortnight later to take her first Wimbledon title 2-6, 6-4, 7-5. Navratilova considers that the biggest match in their rivalry. "I was down 4-3 in the final set and came back to win," she says. "That was the first time I beat her in a Grand Slam final. She had won it twice already. That was special."

But Lloyd won their last three meetings of 1978, and six of the next 15—including a 6-0, 6-0 thrashing on clay at Amelia Island, Fla., in early 1981. That one stunned Navratilova, who had gotten her life and training regimen in order but had begun a new stage of dedication. Supervised by a series of coaches, confidantes and trainers, she geared her diet, conditioning and practice to becoming the best athlete she could be. She consulted a nutritionist and used a computer. She lifted weights and played full-court basketball and drilled for hours, building up her body as no woman tennis player ever had before.

She next met Lloyd in the semifinals of the 1981 U.S. Open and beat her 7-5, 4-6, 6-4. Through the end of 1984, when Lloyd decided she had to go to the gym and get fitter, Navratilova won 18 of 20 matches and finally forged ahead in the head-to-head rivalry, 31-30.

They had drawn deep reserves of resourcefulness and determination from each other. "I had to do something to beat her because she had so much the better record during the first years," says Navratilova. "I knew I had to do something to make my game better, and I did, and then she had to do something to make her game better, and she did. So we sort of fed off each other over the years and improved each other's games, which is great." That may be the ultimate measure of their rivalry: Neither could stand to be No. 2, and both were willing to sweat gallons to gain the upper hand.

"I think that I probably changed her first and then she changed me second," says Lloyd. "I'll never forget that 6-0, 6-0 win at Amelia Island, and I think after that she just really started to get in shape. Mentally she committed herself more, and she became this bionic athlete. Then I saw what she had done to her body, and that inspired me. I figured if you can't beat 'em, join 'em.

"I'm definitely a better athlete and a better tennis player now than when I was dominating six years ago, in that period when I was ranked No. 1 for five years. I was kind of just cruising along, trying to keep up my game but not to improve. I could beat everybody, so I never felt any desire or pressure to change anything or add new shots. I look at pictures of myself now and see that I was 15 pounds heavier, and I see films where the tennis was played at a much slower pace, and I realize that Martina has really drawn things out of me that probably wouldn't have come out otherwise."

Lloyd had rivalries with Billie Jean King and Evonne Goolagong, who also has prided memorable contrasts of style and personality, and with Tracy Austin, who was her clone. But in the game's record books and lore, she will always be linked first and foremost with Navratilova. They define each other's ambitions, limits and place in history—legendary rivals like Muhammad Ali and Joe Frazier in boxing, Bill Russell and Wilt Chamberlain in basketball, Nashua and Swaps in horse racing, Jack Nicklaus and Tom Watson in golf.

"I don't mean this to sound conceited, but I could play to 90 percent of my potential and still win most of my matches against the other players," says Lloyd. "With Martina and me, whoever wins has to play 100 percent."

Lloyd admits that she probably would have become bored with tennis and retired by now if it weren't for Navratilova's looming presence—always there, like Everest. But Navratilova was not always a tower of strength on the court. A gifted athlete, yes, but she had to pull herself up by the laces of her sneakers and overcome the emotional fragility that characterized her early years on the tour.

Contrary to popular image, Lloyd is more the cold realist of the two. Navratilova is more sensitive and probably more vulnerable—the romantic dreamer with a wild imagination. When she beat Lloyd in the 1984 Wimbledon final (her 12th straight victory, which tied the rivalry at 30-30), she almost seemed sad to be dominating the player who had once set the standard to which she aspired.

"Thirty-all, can you imagine?" she said softly, as if drifting back through a book that had taught her much about herself. "There have been some rivals, but nobody has ever played as many finals. God, I wish we could quit right now and never play each other again. I wish that we could end up even, believe it or not, because it's just not right for one of us to say we are better."

They grew up in different environments, in Czechoslovakia and south Florida. Navratilova strained against the constraints of a confining political system, and she was as impetuous as she played. Lloyd was raised in a strict, close-knit Catholic family, and she was as meticulous as her upbringing.

They were close friends and doubles partners early on, before Navratilova matured and became a threat to Lloyd's position. They drifted apart when she was no longer a pretender but a legitimate contender for the throne. They remained bound by a profound professional respect and by proximity on the board of directors of the Women's Tennis Association (WTA), but separated by a fierce desire to stand atop a pedestal only one player can occupy.

"It has always been easier for me to be really close friends with players who aren't around me in the rankings," says Lloyd. "I think that's true with everybody. I don't think I'm any different from the other top players in that. I really don't know what happened with our relationship. We were always friends. We got to be real close when we played doubles. But Martina wanted to play doubles every tournament, and I never did that, so that split up our doubles. When the doubles broke up, we weren't best of friends anymore. We were still friendly, but she had her group of friends and I had mine.

"Now we don't really hang out together. I feel we have a very good professional relationship. We work well together. Away from the courts, we're fine. We enjoy each other's company and sense of humor. We have a good time. We can relate to each other. Once or twice a year, we get together and have a long, deep talk about how things are going in our lives. But she basically hangs out with her circle and I hang out with mine. We don't socialize all that much."

With the greatest of rivalries come some professional jealousies that cause tension. That was evident in 1985 when Navratilova and Lloyd jockeyed for the top spot in the biweekly WTA computer rankings. Going into the Australian Open at the end of the year, the last major battlefield of the season, Navratilova was rankled by comments that Lloyd had regained parity, especially when Lloyd made them.

★   ★   ★

"There might be some friction," says Lloyd. "Tennis is such big business now, it gets so much publicity, and players never go to tournaments by themselves. They've got the entourages around them, and everybody's talking. There are rankings and points involved, and it magnifies everything.

"We both have a lot of pride, probably more than any of the other players. We take pride in what we've done, and that makes it hard at times. We try to be honest with each other and not believe everything we read about what the other supposedly said. But we've both achieved a lot, and somebody is always favoring one of us, and it gets difficult. . . . We've needled each other at times because we both want to be No. 1 so badly. We both want it and both deserve it, and there's such a big difference between No. 1 and No. 2."

There have been other enduring, enthralling tugs of war in the game's history, but nobody has ever played more frequently with so much on the line—major titles, million-dollar bonuses, stardom in the video age—than Navratilova and Lloyd. Head to head, they have produced reservoirs of blood, sweat and tears, volumes of suspense and drama.

"Every time I play a match against Martina," Lloyd says, "I want it to be new and fresh. I don't want to think in historical terms because I don't want it to seem stale. But we have gone through so many different phases, physically and mentally, that I suppose when it's over, I'll look back and reflect and say, 'Yeah, it's probably the most interesting rivalry ever.' "

Navratilova sometimes flashes back to that first meeting in Akron 13 years ago. "I remember losing the tiebreaker 5-4 and being upset because I could have won a set against Chris," she says. "That would have been something else. But I also recall that I figured she'd probably remember me after that match. I thought to myself that I had made a mark, you know."

The impression has grown into legend. "It's hard to imagine two people lasting this long at the same time and winning so much," Navratilova says. "So it may very well be the greatest rivalry in tennis history."

Feller Still Pitches Coast to Coast

BASEBALL

By *Malcolm Moran*

From The New York Times
Copyright © 1986, The New York Times Company
Reprinted by Permission

The light towers almost always offer the first clue that Bob Feller is near his destination. Sometimes they are silhouetted against a sunset, and sometimes they are the brightest lights for miles around, but almost always they tell him that he can put away that dogeared road atlas because he is close to the ball park.

Tonight, the ball park is the Bomber Bowl, the home of the Tri-Cities Triplets of the Northwest League. Tonight is Bob Feller/United Way/Pasco-Richland Chambers of Commerce Challenge Night. Just after the softball game between the Pasco and Richland chambers of commerce, Bob Feller, No. 19, takes the mound in his double-knit Cleveland Indians uniform to make his pitches one more time. These days, he encourages everyone to hit them.

His pitches are an important part of his livelihood. "I'm a promoter," he says. "People say, 'Well, you're out promoting Bob Feller.' Well, who else would I be promoting?"

For several years, Feller has been an ambassador for the Indians, working with pitchers during spring training and making his own schedule of appearances the rest of the year. He crisscrosses the country, enduring a punishing pace in a one-man business that allows him to see old teammates, Navy buddies or friends from previous stops on the road.

"I could be in the insurance business, or I could be in the hotel business," says Feller. "I could probably do a lot of other things. Be on the circuit like all these defeated politicians. I'm doing what I want to do. If I want to go out and work on my tractor, plow the ground, put in some alfalfa or beans or fiddle around at home, I'll do that. I can afford to do it."

After his exhibitions, Feller sits behind card tables and reminisces with old fans who remember the outcomes of games played decades ago, or a moment when he pitched to Rogers Hornsby, or a confrontation with Mickey Mantle. Feller speaks with people who know his name from listening to baseball games on the radio in the 1930s, or watching television in the 1950s, or from the movie that showed his fastball outrace a speeding motorcycle. He pays attention, remembers specific games from decades ago and challenges opinions. He signs autographs for children far too young to understand the irony of asking Bob Feller to write his name on a bat. His double-knit uniform reveals sags that did not exist when Feller wore the flannel of another era, but his strong forearms still bulge with muscles, and some of his pitches still hiss.

Feller drives—sometimes alone, sometimes with his wife, Anne— long enough for eyes to sting, feet to burn and backs to ache, at least until the next fast-food stop. But his appearances and his speeches allow him to share an outlook shaped by a father who took two 2-by-4s and chicken wire and built a backstop in Van Meter, Iowa; by the anguish of the Depression; by the national bond that grew from a war, and by the shattering speed of a fastball that helped Feller win 266 games and become the most spectacular pitcher of his time, perhaps of any time.

He feels strongly that the fabric of America cannot be found in the major cities, for all their power and excitement, and that baseball, in its purest form, is not the game that is played at Yankee Stadium or Dodger Stadium, or even worse, at all those cement bowls with their artificial fields. He feels the fabric is out there amid all those small light towers.

"I always say to a lot of these kids when I speak, 'Nobody plans to be unsuccessful, but if you don't plan ahead, you *will* be unsuccessful,' " he says one day, behind the wheel on the way to another ball park in another town. "And touch all the bases. Don't cheat, don't cut across the infield. If you haven't touched all the bases, go back and touch 'em now, before it's too late. Before somebody throws you out."

After warming up, Feller calls to the first batter, "OK, hit this one out of here."

A superintendent of schools takes the first pitch. "Good eye, Doc," the pitcher says.

"Hit him," a young voice yells from behind home plate.

Another man hits a line drive to right-center field and tells the pitcher, "Thanks a lot." A younger man, with broad shoulders and thick thighs, with spiked shoes on his feet and a batting glove on each hand, does not do nearly as well. A Little Leaguer steps in, and Feller steps forward to the edge of the mound. His gentle overhand tosses occasionally become weak, but triumphant, ground balls.

Soon, the infield is being dragged for another game, and Feller walks toward the locker room in the adjacent high school football stadium. Just before he reaches the door, a recording of the national anthem is played. Feller turns around, faces the flagpole in center field and places his cap over his heart.

Today's trip began in Salem, Ore., at 5 a.m. It will end at 2 p.m. tomorrow, E.S.T., after flights from Portland to Pasco to Seattle to Kansas City to Chicago to Battle Creek. When Bob and Anne Feller leave Pasco to catch a connection in Seattle for an overnight flight, bolts of lightning are shooting everywhere. When they arrive in Battle Creek, three of their bags do not.

★   ★   ★

At a luncheon celebrating the Stan Musial World Series and the 50th anniversary of the American Amateur Baseball Congress, Feller knows how to start his speech. "I started off the day by having a double order of Product 19," Feller says, and in a city were cereal is made, his line gets big laughs. "They named that cereal after me. My number is 19."

He remembers names and faces and places. He recalls the first championship in 1935, when, at the age of 16, he lost, 1-0, to a team from Battle Creek. "I seldom ever won a game when I got shut out," Feller says. "And neither will Dwight Gooden."

He brings the reminder that the old days and the achievements of those times should not be forgotten.

"They're in the book," he said. "And they'll always be there." Feller brings up his record and how it was affected by his nearly four seasons in the Navy during World War II. "The lucky ones that came back—and I was one of them—we have no regrets. I'm very proud of my military record," he says. Upstairs, in a briefcase in his room, a set of numbers prepared by a statistician in Seattle projects Feller's statistics if his career had been uninterrupted. Victories increase from 266 to 357, strikeouts from 2,581 to 3,516, shutouts from 46 to 65, complete games from 279 to 378. At the top of the page, in red felt-tip pen, the title reads: WHAT IF NO WARS.

The teen-agers in the ballroom are hearing about a very different time.

"When I was 9 years old, in 1928," Feller says. "Babe Ruth and Lou Gehrig came to Des Moines. They had been playing these games around the United States with their own uniforms, and picking up semipro players. The Larrupin' Lous and the Bustin' Babes.

"They made all the Middle West. It was advertised in the paper that they were going to sell baseballs for $5 apiece. Autographed, by both Lou Gehrig and Babe Ruth. I wanted one. My dad was taking me to the game. This is October 28, 1928. A couple of years before, I started driving that Caterpillar through those corn fields and wheat fields of Iowa.

"I had to get $5. I figured, well, I'll get this old Dodge truck out and put a hose over the exhaust, and go out and smoke the gophers out of the gopher mounds in the alfalfa field. The county treasurer gave you 10 cents bounty for every pair of claws you brought in.

"So I got one of the neighborhood kids that played catch with me all the time, who I went to school with. I gave him a big potato sack or gunnysack, and I say, 'You get over there, Paul, and I'm going to stick this hose in there, and I'll pull down the choke and open up the accelerator wide open and it's going to be very smoky, and those little gophers are going to come out of there like bullets.

"I caught 50 of 'em, and I went to the county treasurer's office. My dad drove me up there in the old Rickenbacker car we had. And I got five bucks. Went down and got Babe Ruth's and Lou Gehrig's autograph on a baseball. And I still have it at home. The first gopher ball I ever had."

★   ★   ★

After a dinner in Kalamazoo, Bob and Anne Feller are on the way home for a one-night stay, and the rain and the windshield wipers are smearing the oncoming headlights, when suddenly there is an unscheduled stop. Nearly everywhere he goes, Feller is asked about the speed of his pitches, measured long before the radar guns that scouts and coaches use today. He tells them about the promotion at Griffith Stadium in Washington, when one of his fastballs was measured at 107.9 miles per hour. He hears the question at every stop: How fast were you clocked?

Tonight there is no question.

He has been clocked at 74.

By the Ohio State Highway Patrol.

In a 44 mph zone.

He pulls over, and a flashlight shines into the driver's side. An officer stands in the rain, asks for the license and registration, explains how the offender can post a bond with a credit card and then asks an odd question: "What's your occupation?"

"I work for the Cleveland ball club."

The officer leans his face closer to the open window.

"That's who I thought you was."

The officer goes back to his car, and returns with a request. "I'm a Tiger fan," he says, "but Sergeant Stroble has been a Cleveland fan for years, and he asked me if you could sign an autograph."

At this moment, Feller is signing the credit card form to post bond. He examines the slip, grim-faced. "I don't think so," he says.

The officer backs away from the window. "I understand," he says. "He just wanted me to ask."

"I'm only kidding," Feller says. Using the same clipboard he leaned on to pay the penalty, he writes, "To Ron Stroble. . . ."

Miles later, at 2:10 a.m., they stop at a convenience store for milk and orange juice. Five minutes later they are home. Eleven hours after that, they will be gone again.

★   ★   ★

In the basement of Bob and Anne Feller's home in a Cleveland suburb, there is evidence that when Feller told his gopher ball story yesterday, he had omitted one item of historic significance. For in a wooden cabinet in the basement, there rests the ball signed by Ruth and Gehrig, dated October 28, 1928. But what Feller did not mention was that just before his 10th birthday, in his best but wobbly script, he had added his own name long before any admirer would ask: Robert W A Feller. Bob Feller's first gopher ball may also have been his first autographed one.

In his office hangs the official scorer's report, with some of the ink smudged, from his no-hit victory at Comiskey Park in Chicago on opening day, April 16, 1940. There are old covers of *Time* and *Newsweek* showing Feller in his prime. Throughout most of the house, however, there are not nearly as many baseballs as there are bears. They have big bears and the tiniest of bears.

His wife has a round, friendly face, and an easy laugh, and enough energy and imagination to have planned the design of this new house.

Anne dusted off her new husband's old posters and knick knacks that had been left forgotten in closets. She took them to a do-it-yourself frame store and created displays for the most colorful and memorable items. She is responsible for much of the warmth of this house.

When Anne travels with her husband, she washes his baseball uniform for the exhibitions, often hanging it to dry in the back seat of the car. At each stop, she sends a postcard to her mother in California, and rates ball-park hot dogs, and seeks whatever cultural attractions each town offers.

Occasionally, the laundry business can get complicated. Once, trapped in a hotel in Butte, Mont., without facilities, they asked if the clubhouse man could wash their laundry at the ball park.

The clubhouse man said yes but did not mention he had been having problems with the dryer. Late in the game that day, Anne noticed her nightgown hanging over the left-field fence.

When Feller arrives at Sal Maglie Stadium, a converted football field in Niagara Falls, he walks through a raw mist. Places are beginning to look alike; an intersection on the way to the ball park reminded him of another in Salem, Ore.

There is no game tonight, no appearance, and no appearance fee unless he can return on Sunday. At least the rain has created time for a real meal. Instead of more ball-park hot dogs, the Fellers dine overlooking the Falls.

★   ★   ★

On their way to Pittsfield, Mass., rather than speed along another interstate, they traveled east along Ridge Road, taking turns behind the wheel, looking for antique stores and piles of junk.

"You're going too fast," the husband said from the passenger seat. "I want to see something."

And every so often they would stop, and he would get out and wade into piles of rusted metal. Once, a horse emerged from a barn to see what was going on. Birds fled. Cows followed and inspected the visitor. The Fellers would pull the car over if there was the most remote possibility that Bob would find some valuable, hidden piece of equipment. He says he would love to go through here with a convoy of flat-bed trucks "and buy every pile of junk the trucks could carry."

"But what would you do with it?" Anne says, a sense of urgency growing in her voice.

At last, a place without a fast-food strip. They see old stone churches and morning glories and sleighs and turkey farms and family-run fruit stands.

A few miles west of Rochester reality returns: a complex of six movie theaters, a shopping plaza, electronic time and temperature signs, the 20th century.

At Wahconah Park, the small wooden home of the Pittsfield Cubs, one fan wonders loudly: "Where's Bob Fellah?"

When he emerges, there is applause, extended, respectful applause. And the public address announcer finally says, "Ladies and gentlemen, in case you don't already know. . . ."

He pitches to a stud in a Yankee hat, with spiked shoes and pine tar and eyes that say I'm taking this guy deep. He pitches to a reporter, the team orthopedist, the team organist and a banker.

And then comes a first in the career of Rapid Robert William Andrew Feller.

He pitches to a mouse.

A 6-foot-6-inch mouse.

A light brown mouse, with pink feet.

Mr. Whiskers is a promotional mascot. Mr. Whiskers gestures toward the center-field fence, calling his shot, then hits a ground ball, and takes a bow.

"It's part of the deal," Feller says. "It's supposed to be funny. Sometimes it is. Sometimes it isn't."

He finishes signing autographs and as the organist plays "Auld Lang Syne" on the last night of the season, Feller receives his fee from the office. "I'm making a few bucks along the way," he says. "Which is what you do in America."

★   ★   ★

On Main Street in Cooperstown, N.Y., a young man hands out small mimeographed pages with the news that Bob Feller is in town.

Just inside the door of a souvenir shop not far from the Baseball Hall of Fame, a man softly says to a woman: "Remember when you asked me about Gooden? This is the man whose record he broke. He was the greatest."

On August 25, at the age of 20 years, 9 months and 9 days, Dwight Gooden of the Mets had become the youngest pitcher to win 20 games in a season in the 20th century. Until then, Feller had been the youngest at 20 years, 10 months and 5 days in 1939. Reporters were calling, and lately, as fans everywhere would ask for an autograph, they would also ask his opinion of Gooden. At one stop, Feller pointed out that he had struck out 17 batters in one game at the age of 17, and 16 at the age of 18. "He'll never do it," Feller said. "He'll never complete 36 games in a season. They don't pitch him enough. He gets four days' rest between starts. I only got three."

The listener looked horrified.

Feller smiled. "He's a heck of a good pitcher," he said. "I'm only kidding you, son. Don't get excited."

Beneath the surface, there appear some strong feelings. This afternoon, down the street from the Hall where Feller's likeness appears on a small plaque and where Gooden's may appear one day, Feller tells a Mets fan: "He's got a great arm. But what should they do, put him in the Hall of Fame tomorrow? Are you kidding?"

He says an accurate evaluation must wait until Gooden has pitched five years. Feller praised the strong role Gooden's father had taken in guiding his son, but ridiculed the care the modern pitcher receives—the counting of pitches, the concern of the number of innings, the careful scheduling of enough rest. Gooden will rarely have to pitch with just three days of rest. He will not have to serve on a battleship or lead a players' association, and he will never have to go barnstorming to capitalize on his popularity.

Feller does not know how long he can continue making all his promotional pitches. After the last autograph here, he and Anne will leave for that makeup game in Niagara Falls, and go on to an afternoon game tomorrow in Erie, Pa. "And then," Anne says in the warm sunshine outside the store, near Doubleday Field, "We're going to go"—she takes a deep breath—"home."

And then?

Her husband turned 67 before the start of another season. He would like to go for two more years, at a less demanding pace. He would like to visit, or revisit, places without seeing ball parks: Alaska, England, Gettysburg, Yosemite, Nantucket. He would also like to be able to usher in church on Sunday and spend more time working in the yard.

As she waits in a filling station on the way back to Niagara Falls, Anne Feller is willing to confide her husband's dream. After more than 50 years of playing, traveling and barnstorming, after all those airline meals and drive-through hamburgers and roadside peaches, this is the dream: Take a year off, get in a car and drive all over the United States, checking out old barns.

"I think it's called breaking and entering," she says.

He says he will slow down by the age of 70.

"He told me the same thing when he was 65," Anne says.

He can't ignore the fact. It's in the book. And they have many pages to go.

Proposition 48 Teaches Athletes a Hard Lesson

COLLEGE ATHLETICS

By *Dave Krieger*

From the Rocky Mountain News
Copyright © 1986, Denver Publishing Co.

If Mike Vaughn had been born a year earlier, he would be finishing his first year at the University of Colorado or some other major university this spring.

Instead, because of something called Proposition 48, the Aurora prep football star is left to choose between a junior college and a community college in Arizona.

"I knew some rules were coming out," says the Rangeview High School senior, "but I didn't know what they applied to."

"The administrators, the coaches, the kids all felt it was never going to happen," says Dick MacPherson, head football coach at Syracuse University. "It has to hurt first. This is the year of the hurt."

Coast to coast, the Mike Vaughn story is being played out in the first high school class to be affected by Proposition 48.

Sitting in the quiet home at the end of an Aurora cul-de-sac that he shares with his mother, Vaughn refers to his discovery of Proposition 48 during the winter of his junior year softly and a little sadly.

"It was," he says, "kinda too late for me."

It was too late for many of his classmates, too.

"They're finding out the hard way," says Gerry Faust, the former Notre Dame football coach who moved to the University of Akron this year.

"High schools were not well-informed," agrees LaVell Edwards, head football coach at Brigham Young University. "For some reason, the word didn't get out."

It's getting out now. The National Collegiate Athletic Association will no longer allow an incoming freshman at a Division I school to participate in intercollegiate athletics unless he or she meets minimum academic standards.

To be eligible, a student must maintain a C average in a core curriculum during high school—2.0 or better in a 4.0 system—and achieve a minimum score on a college entrance examination—15 on the ACT, 700 on the SAT.

Mike Vaughn has the C average, but his ACT score fell three points short of the new standard. As a result, four Division I schools that recruited him to play football ended up backing off.

"We thought he was a terrific football player and a good running back," says Leon Fuller, head football coach at Colorado State University. "We didn't feel like we could get him in academically."

Idaho State, a Division 1-AA program that checked into Vaughn, withdrew as well.

"We had him rated fairly close to the other running backs we were considering," says Idaho State football coach Jim Koetter. "He would have been in the group that we were considering to recruit and to visit."

Idaho State did not visit, though. "That was just based on academics more than anything else," says Koetter. "We just didn't have a real good feel that he would be a good academic risk."

The University of Kansas, too, contacted Vaughn and then retreated, although KU Coach Bob Valesente says, "I don't recall that case at all."

But for Vaughn, the key school was the University of Colorado. CU wanted him and he wanted CU. That's what he thought, anyway.

"They did a recruiting job," says Vaughn. "They told me they needed me, they could use me. Then, at the last minute, they told me they couldn't take me."

Would Mike Vaughn be a CU running back today if he'd emerged from high school one year earlier?

"Conceivably," says Colorado head coach Bill McCartney.

How close did CU come to signing him anyway?

"Very close," says McCartney. "We evaluated him as a guy who had enough ability to play in this conference (the Big Eight). Then it became a concern whether or not he could do the work. In that particular case, we had a surplus of running backs we were recruiting, so it became a position thing."

Across the country, the story is the same: Major college coaches say they are no longer even considering many high school athletes with poor academic credentials.

"Of the players that we would normally be talking to, scholarship players, I would say it decreased the talent pool by about a third," says Nebraska football coach Tom Osborne.

"We didn't even contact the people that were questionable," says Louisiana State basketball coach Dale Brown.

"A lot of kids we backed off on," adds Faust. "When they don't have the grades, you just don't take 'em."

"We did on two or three kids," says BYU's Edwards. "We've recruited a lot of Polynesian kids over the years, and they've had difficulty taking the ACT or the SAT tests. They have not had difficulty so much in graduating."

Establishing academic standards for college athletes became a crusade in the late 1970s and early '80s following a series of horror stories about functional illiterates who used up their athletic eligibility and found themselves dumped into the world without an education by the institutions that used them.

The NCAA responded to the gathering sentiment by approving Proposition 48 in 1983. It's now known as NCAA Bylaw 5-1 (j). When it was approved back in '83, the NCAA delayed the effective date until this year to help schools prepare for it.

Even so, when the principle became a rule with specific requirements, some coaches started getting off the bandwagon.

The most controversial aspect of Proposition 48 is its reliance on the standardized test scores—and the racial implications of those scores. White students have historicaly fared much better on these tests than non-whites, many educators and coaches say.

"I've heard the phrase that the ACT is a white test," says Dean Stecklein, Mike Vaughn's football coach at Rangeview.

★   ★   ★

"I have no problems with the grade-point average," says Dr. Walter Reed, athletic director at Jackson State University, a predominantly black school in Jackson, Miss. "If there's anything we should have done, it's upgrade the grade-point average. But I do have a problem with the test scores. Most of your testing agencies have already indicated that the test scores are not good predictors of academic success."

"There's a lot of minority students that have trouble with those standardized tests," adds Jim Brandenburg, the University of Wyoming basketball coach who took his team to the finals of the National Invitation Tournament this year.

"I think we really need to come up with a different type of a test that might be a little more fair to all concerned," says Brandenburg. "I'd say if you really take a look at these types of standardized tests, there is definitely some built-in bias. I think if we went to a type of a test that really didn't test information as much as the ability to learn, we'd be better off."

Indeed, a study conducted by the NCAA itself provided the most damning evidence of the tests' discriminatory effect. Examining students who entered college in 1982, the NCAA found that 51% of the black men scored below 700 on the SAT, and 60% scored below 13 on the ACT.

The NCAA found that more than four times as many blacks would be ineligible for Division I athletics under Proposition 48 as whites.

"There's no question about that," says Oklahoma football coach Barry Switzer. "Those statistics are valid. You can look at any review of that and it's just different for them."

Even the logistics of the testing—particularly the conflicts between national testing dates and athletic commitments—have left some players' eligibility in question.

"We found out some young people did not take the test early," says Ohio State football coach Earle Bruce. "We have about three or four of our recruiting class who are still taking the test to try to make it."

★   ★   ★

Still, two attempts to eliminate the impact of test scores on eligibility were defeated at the NCAA convention in New Orleans earlier this year. Reformers insisted the need for standards arose in the first place because high schools were graduating functionally illiterate athletes. To rely solely on high school grades, therefore, would gut the reform effort, they said.

One minor modification was approved. It established a temporary sliding scale of test scores and grade-point averages. A higher grade-point average would compensate for a slightly lower test score, and vice versa. But the impact appears to have been minimal. The leeway in the test scores is just 40 points on the SAT and 2 on the ACT.

Caught in the middle of this experiment with social values are members of the class of '86 like Mike Vaughn.

Those familiar with Vaughn's transcript say a decline in academic performance coincided with his parents' divorce when he was in the fifth grade. He began to apply himself in 11th grade, but by then a great deal of educational water had rushed under the bridge.

"You can't make up for a 5-year period in there where he was turned off, particularly in the English area," says Stecklein.

The fact remains, however, that Mike Vaughn would have liked more time to prepare for the new requirements.

"What brought my GPA down was my freshman and sophomore years," he says. "I just wanted to fool around and do what everybody else was doing. Coaches would tell me I had to hit the books, but they'd never tell me why."

Says Stecklein: "Telling them their senior year isn't good enough. You've got to tell them their freshman year because that's where they goof up their GPA."

Vaughn may attend Arizona Western Junior College in Yuma or Mesa Community College in Mesa. It's possible he could move on to a Division I school after earning a junior college degree. In fact, one CU assistant coach recommended that route. But Vaughn is not sure he ever wants to attend the major colleges that courted and then dropped him.

Late last week, he was leaning toward spending his entire college career at Mesa. His dreams of big-time athletics at a big-time university are gone.

"When it first hit me, it was a big letdown," he says. "All I talked about, all I thought about was CU. My mom has a part in it. I like to see her happy. Sam Perkins is a second-cousin and she goes crazy whenever she sees him on TV. She says one day she'd like to see me on TV."

It's not likely now. By the time the recruiters and coaches got around to telling Mike Vaughn what he had to do to play college football under the new rules, his dream was already a casualty of his past.

A Shady Shot

by Adrian F. Keating Jr. of the Manchester Journal Inquirer. When 89-year-old Agnes Green of East Hartford, Conn., plays golf, she plays by the rules. Green, who plays at least three times a week all year long, does not let weather or other natural barriers keep her from her appointed rounds. Copyright © 1986, Journal Publishing Co. Inc. of Manchester, Conn.

Crunch!

by John Walker of the Fresno Bee. Long Beach State catcher Sue Trubovitz grimaces as she takes the impact of Fresno State baserunner Karin Ritcher during a women's softball game. Ritcher scored as the ball popped out of Trubovitz's glove. Copyright © 1986, John Walker.

Verdict Raises No Cheers In NFL Camps

PRO FOOTBALL

By *Ken Denlinger*

From the Washington Post
Copyright © 1986, the Washington Post

The United States Football League got exactly what it deserved in its lawsuit against the NFL: pennies in damages and millions in ridicule. Probably, the perky new guys on the sporting block were doomed the day a flamboyant hustler strutted into their lives and said: "Hi, I'm Donald Trump." Still, a just verdict produced far more losers than winners.

Think about who actually prevailed. Was it the NFL? Nope. Commissioner Pete Rozelle won. Jack Kent Cooke won. So did the other 27 owners. The rest of the NFL lost. Nearly everybody except the commissioner and maybe five dozen others in the NFL are poorer because the USFL failed.

The USFL almost certainly is history. This means that every Redskin and 1,500 or so other players in the NFL have lost what little bargaining leverage they had with ownership. No longer can a vital player use the possibility of jumping to a rival league to coax a decent raise. Nowhere in any training camp were high-fives spotted when the jury's 31-hour deliberation ended Tuesday.

General managers in the NFL said they were elated, because no competition makes their jobs easier. No longer must the San Diego Chargers scrounge because several of their top draft choices opt for USFL teams. Bobby Beathard seems even more astute, having drafted Kelvin Bryant three years ago in hopes that the USFL would go out of business about the time John Riggins walked into retirement.

The addition of Bryant and more than a dozen other very good USFL players also will cheer coaches such as Joe Gibbs. Temporarily. When Beathard, Gibbs and others in management look beyond their own lives, they will be sad for a hundred or so colleagues suddenly out of work.

A former Redskin, Ted Marchibroda, is one of them. He presumes that the head-coaching job with the best team in the USFL, the Baltimore Stars, would have been his had the award damages not been a matter of about $500 million less that the league demanded.

The Stars were waiting "until the litigation was over" to officially sign him, Marchibroda said from his Falls Church home yesterday, and he was set "to go to war." Almost surely, his troops have been wiped away before he could even lead them in one practice.

Marchibroda had been let go as the offensive coordinator of the Philadelphia Eagles with one year left on his contract. How many others also will have no job options once their work no longer pleases the NFL?

The pity is that the USFL could have worked if its founders had been strong enough to stick with the original game plan and resist speculators such as Trump. As a one-buck league, a diversion in the spring, the USFL could have been steady work for players and executives either on the way up or the way down from the NFL.

Also, competition is necessary so the establishment does not become unbearably powerful and arrogant. New leagues are bold and imaginative; if an idea, such as using television replays, happens to work, the stodgy league steals it.

Early on, the USFL showed a remarkable lack of foresight. Expansion was announced before the first games were played. Some owners hired bright people to promote their teams but dummies to stock them. Nobody seemed able to abide by payroll guidelines that would encourage stability and on-the-field balance.

And yet some of what the USFL did was splendid. It was not a one-runner league, as the NFL insisted when Herschel Walker left Georgia after his junior year and signed with the New Jersey Generals. Lots of bright players and executives gravitated from the USFL to major roles with NFL teams.

Center Bart Oates and punter Sean Landeta were vital additions to a Giants team that beat the defending Super Bowl champions, the 49ers, in the first round of the playoffs last season. The best coach in the USFL, Jim Mora, is now charged with improving the sorriest team in the NFL, the Saints. One of Mora's aides, Vince Tobin, grabbed the job Buddy Ryan vacated with the Bears when Ryan became head coach of the Eagles.

Lack of leaguewide firmness encouraged a group led by Trump to attack the NFL, to sue in hopes of a merger, to risk a few million to reap the many millions a franchise in the NFL would be worth. USFL thinkers even botched the victory.

For them, winning wasn't everything. Or even the only thing. It wasn't anything at all. Give 'em a crooked W.

The USFL winners are the few players who already have made their fortunes. One of them, Walker, is making noises about possibly retiring rather than reporting to his NFL team, the Cowboys.

"I've never had the opportunity to be just Herschel," he said. "Real estate is an option."

Artificial real estate, in Texas Stadium, is more likely.

The NFL has signed few of its first-round draft choices. Look for that to suddenly change. With no alternative, those silent USFL rooters shortly will limp into their respective NFL camps. And possibly for a worse deal than was offered a few days ago. We're back to one football again.

So good riddance.

Good riddance to what the USFL became. Good riddance to Trump and his quick-buck buddies. Good riddance to all the lawyers, the only people in all of sport who never lose.

Goodbye to innovation. If fans may like the idea of Bryant, Walker, Jim Kelly and their peers adding quick quality to the NFL, they should brace themselves for more predictability. Goodbye to expansion, unless that were a tradeoff for antitrust legislation from Congress. Goodbye to roster increases, unless that was necessary in collective bargaining to bring about random drug testing.

The USFL was a nice idea greedy men destroyed when they got desperate and tried to bring down the NFL. The winners are loud and loose, as they should be. But glance around. Look at how few actually are celebrating.

The Race That Had It All

TRIATHLON

By *Lee Green*

From Outside Magazine
Copyright © 1986, Lee Green

He is standing *right there* in the relay transition chute, with slack-jawed spectators pressing in on both sides. The bolder ones lean over the railing, proffering hands and smiles and unconcealed idolatry. He is as compliant as can be, ricocheting his boyish grin and looking terrifically taut and aerodynamic in his skintight, logo-festooned, multicolored Lycra cycling jersey. Tour de France mystique radiates from him, and those up close are getting a little rush off it, for surely they will never again get so holy-gee close to Greg LeMond. Nor, for that matter, will any of the other riders in the chute once LeMond is set in motion by a tag from the aquatic member of Team Kahlua.

On this unseasonably cold, wet September morning, 203 swimmers (144 triathletes and 59 relay-team participants), most in wetsuits, are eggbeating along in Lake Tahoe's frigid waters, homing in on the beach while LeMond gets a last-minute briefing on the rules of his cheekily self-proclaimed World's Toughest Triathlon.

"You have to be *sure* to stop at the stop signs," Team Kahlua coach and manager Bob Augello warns urgently. By LeMond's reckoning this is an amusing mandate—like asking a purse snatcher to use the crosswalk. He has never before stopped at a stop sign in the middle of a bike race.

Augello presses: "Last year the woman who won didn't make a stop, and she was disqualified," he says. "She won by 30 minutes, but they didn't give her the $10,000."

LeMond is flabbergasted. "Jeez, I can't be-*leeeve* that! They should have just given her a time penalty—three minutes or something."

The disqualification occurred in 1984, the second year of the World's Toughest Triathlon, an event that seemingly had it all: a memorable name (will the hypemongers stop at nothing?); a challenging course (2.4-mile cold-water swim, 120-mile mountainous bike leg, 26.7-mile hilly run—all at altitude); a magnificent venue (picturesque South Lake Tahoe and the Sierra Nevada); big money (a $50,000 prize purse—unsurpassed in the United States—including $10,000 for first place, $5,000 for second, $2,500 for third); and a glamorous champion (Scott Molina, arguably the best triathlete in the world). Yet none of these features ultimately distinguished the race from the other 1,800 triathlons staged in the United States in 1984. It was the $10,000 traffic violation. That's what people started calling it. Even Charlie Lincoln, the race's executive director and the man who ultimately invoked the penalty. "Jacqueline Shaw will be back," he would boast when touting the 1985 race. "You know, the woman who committed the $10,000 traffic violation."

Shaw claims she was not the only one to barrel through a designated stop during the '84 race. She wants her $10,000, and she has filed suit against Charlie Lincoln.

Jacqueline Shaw, 29, is beamish and sprightly, dégagé and disdainful of regimented training. ("Usually I wake up and do whatever I want.") She views life as the dogged pursuit of good times. "That's what it's all about, isn't it?" she asks rhetorically while relaxing at her South Lake Tahoe hangout, a deli and soda shop. She sweeps her long, strawberry-blond hair to one side and smiles mischievously, blue eyes twinkling. Her clipped, vowelish, Canadian intonations are invariably gilded with lusty laughter. After an hour with her, you know she is the merriest soul in all of God's kingdom.

Until she races. When this woman competes, she turns into a hornets' nest of harnessed anger. She is McEnroe without the lip. And as Charlie Lincoln promised, she is back.

Shaw was the third woman triathlete out of the water, but the first onto her bike. She has surmounted Luther Pass, elevation 7,740 feet, and is coasting at mile 20 of the bike leg, slowing to heed the first of four stop signs. Who should be there to greet her, bracing against an icy wind at the desolate intersection of California state highways 88 and 89, but Charlie Lincoln.

Shaw would have given the whole ten grand to have seen LeMond arrive at this juncture. "That'd be my big thrill," she had impishly proclaimed before the race, "seeing Greg LeMond stop at a stop sign." But LeMond is many tortuous miles ahead, en route to a new bike-course record (5:16:33; old mark 5:29) and setting up Team Kahlua for the men's relay title.

Lincoln welcomes the women's front-runner with an unctuous smile. "Hello, Jacqueline!" he says cloyingly. Shaw halts and, as the 1985 rules require, touches a foot to the pavement—except she doesn't just *touch* the foot, she *stomps* it. Glaring at Lincoln, she asked sardonically, "Is this good enough?" On the far side of Highway 89 someone in a cluster of bystanders yells out, "Good stop, Jacqueline!" There's no escaping the notoriety of the damn thing.

★   ★   ★

Nor is there any escaping commerce at work here in South Lake

Tahoe. The South Lake Tahoe Marketing Council, controlled by the four major casinos in the community, has in three years invested more than a third of a million dollars in the World's Toughest Triathlon. Its visibility stokes the tourist fires, and tourism enables the area's 26,500 year-round denizens to stay in South Lake Tahoe instead of having to pack up the skis and sailboards and motor on down the mountain to a more plebeian existence in Reno or Sacramento.

Greg LeMond, who was paid $15,000 to interrupt his hectic European racing schedule to ride in the relay, is merely a tool in these marketing machinations. But it would be a mistake to let the mercantile elements obscure the fact that the World's Toughest Triathlon is a well-orchestrated race—a triathlete's triathlon—that lives up to its brassy name. Oh, sure, there will always be megamileage stage races: swim the Black Sea, cycle across eastern Europe, and then run 20 laps around Liechtenstein. But of the single-day, continuous-time, swim-bike-run triathlons, the Tahoe race is without equal, Hawaii's progenitorial Ironman notwithstanding—at least according to the pros. "The challenge of this course," says Scott Molina, "is that it's got *everything:* wind, heat, cold, hills, altitude."

★   ★   ★

Everything takes it toll. By noon, four and a half hours into the race, the leaders have begun trickling into the mandatory medical stop atop Monitor Pass (elevation 8,314 feet), 78 miles into the cycling leg. Ten racers never made it onto their bikes, cold-cocked by the 7:30 a.m. slog through the 59-degree lake. Several more will quit here at Monitor, and before the day has mercifully ended, fully a third of the field will grace the scratch list. In 1984 less than half of the competitors finished.

Monitor Pass summit is windy and bleak, a sagebrush plateau with only a copse of quaking aspen to suggest the surrounding Toiyabe National Forest. To get here, the cyclists have followed Highway 89 up the eastern slope of the Sierra on an 8 percent grade that rises 3,300 vertical feet in 11 miles of switchbacks. It's the sort of climb you'd avoid driving in a car.

Many of the riders arrive in ill humor, snapping irritably at the checkpoint volunteers, annoyed at having to stop for a precautionary check of body weight. "They weren't like this last year," observes a pleasant woman handing out newspapers for the riders to stuff under their jerseys as insulation against the benumbing downgrade ahead. It is cold, perhaps 48 degrees Fahrenheit, colder with the windchill, and there is no sun. "Last year they were calm and polite as could be," the volunteer continues. "This year they're so . . . intense."

LeMond was the first through the medical stop, of course, and six other relay cyclists came and went before triathlon leader Scott Molina pedaled in at quarter past 12. Molina was ahead of second-place Grant Boswell by six and a half minutes, a lead he would never relinquish.

★　　　★　　　★

Shortly before one o'clock, a leggy, very blond rider sporting the distinctive red-and-green racing jersey of 7-Eleven cranks in on a silvery Vitus and hurriedly dismounts. Julie Olson has taken the women's lead from Shaw, having caught her midway up the Monitor grade. "Hang in there," was all she could think to say to Shaw as she passed. The diffident 25-year-old from St. Paul, Minn., is anxious to get out of the checkpoint with her lead intact.

The race is no whimsical indulgence for Olson. She is one of a smattering of triathletes attempting to make a living on the evolving pro circuit. In 1984 she won all of $8,000. When she missed her charter flight back from Paris after the 1984 Nice Triathlon, she spent three nights sleeping on benches at Orly Airport in Paris because she had only $50 in her pocket. These days she is sponsored by 7-Eleven, but the support is modest and, so far anyway, slow in coming. Olson has had to borrow $3,000 from a friend to make it through the summer. The $10,000 in prize money—same as the men's prize—would be a godsend.

Weigh-in, cookies, two bites of watermelon, and Olson is gone in just 60 seconds. Four minutes later women's swim-segment winner Diane Israel blows in, followed 75 seconds later by Jacqueline Shaw.

The ear-popping descent from Monitor is long, steep in places, and serpentine. Shaw blitzes it, hurtling past a more cautious Israel in a white-knuckled plummet. By the time she has bottomed out at Markleeville (elevation 5,500 feet) and pumped over to the sylvan hamlet of Woodfords, she has made up more than a minute on Olson. Here the course completes its far-flung loop, part of which traverses the high desert of Nevada's Carson Valley, and begins to double back on itself for a return bout with Luther Pass.

Because this climb comes late in the ride (mile 93), many consider it the worst of the day. It is a relentless grade that ascends nearly 2,000 feet in nine and a half miles. You begin to get the feeling that the guy who laid out this course did so knowing he would never have to ride it himself. The run is no easier, a hilly sledgehammer of a route a half-mile longer than a marathon. Sub-2:15 marathoners starting fresh in the relay are hard-pressed to cover the route in less than three hours. Scott Molina will run it in 3:32:15. The more languid of those doing the full triathlon, after eight to nine hours on the bike, will take seven to nine for the run. The Puntous twins of Ironman fame, Patricia and Sylviane, reportedly arrived in the area two weeks before the race, took one look at the course, and left.

So it would appear that the architect of the World's Toughest Triathlon laid out the course and then sat back to see just how many fools would try it. But let the record show that race director Bill McKean, 36, is anything but the sort of sniveling mollycoddle who would build a gallows without testing the rope. The soft-spoken South Lake Tahoe chiropractor placed second in the 100-mile Western States Endurance Run in 1980; the next year he led the same race for 40 miles on a fractured ankle. He competed in the 1983 inaugural World's Toughest Triathlon just to make doubly sure he wasn't sending people out on a fool's errand, and he doubtless would be competing today were he not recuperating from a 1984 cycling workout that ended abruptly when a motorist turned in front of him as he was unwinding on a downhill. The impact jammed his right femur 10 inches into his stomach, shattered his right forearm, broke his nose, and inflicted gashes requiring 540 stitches. Thirteen months later he *looks* fine, but his body is held together by a menagerie of metal plates, screws, and wires. He thinks WD-40 is an elixir.

Any complaints about the course, see Dr. McKean.

★   ★   ★

At the top of Luther Pass, Shaw and Israel are together, but Olson has widened her lead to seven and a half minutes. Olson surprised everyone at the 1984 Hawaii Ironman when she established a bike-course record and began the run with a 13-minute lead. Though she finished third behind Sylviane and Patricia Puntous, notice had been served: The kid from Minnesota could boogie on a bike.

At the moment, though, Julie Olson has problems. Midway through the ride she became agonizingly cold, and she hasn't been able to recover. She thought the grunt up Luther would thaw her, but a chilling rain kept her muscles from regaining their suppleness; it hurts just to move her legs. She tries to conserve energy on the relatively flat last 13 miles to Harrah's Casino, where she will make the transition to the run. Don't push it, she tells herself. Save some for the run.

Invariably, during the running portion of an ultradistance triathlon, the heart and mind drive a body convinced its human rights are being violated. The mind, if it chooses to ponder the question, concludes that the world's toughest triathlon is whichever one the body happens to be doing at the moment.

Jacqueline Shaw managed to distract herself from this psycho-physical dichotomy for the first 12 miles of the run—an uphill grind along Lake Tahoe on U.S. Highway 50—by wearing stereo headphones. Springsteen. She trailed Olson by just two and a half minutes at the transition, having made up time, but by the time she reaches the point where the course leaves the highway for a precipitous climb on a forest jeep trail, the gap has doubled.

Israel was only a couple of minutes behind Shaw at Harrah's, but she has since fallen off the pace, the victim of abdominal cramps. After five long hours on her feet, she will gamely struggle in for the third-place money.

Olson's quarrel, then, is with Shaw. Picking her way through the dusk along a pocked and rutted dirt road on a ridge high above the lake, the leader casts an occasional glance over the shoulder. She can see her frosty breath, but can't see Shaw. Is she three minutes behind? Ten? Keeping the lead means $10,000; losing it means $5,000.

"I was hoping that she was hurting as bad as I was and that she would be walking," Olson later admitted. Only in the final few hundred yards, as she approaches the finish chute in Harrah's parking lot, does the daylight leader feel confident she has won. The resolute mind has shepherded the wayworn body home in 12 hours, 31 minutes; Olson is the first woman to finish and the 18th finisher overall, two hours and three minutes behind the victorious Mr. Molina (whose time was 10:28:29) and less than nine minutes ahead of the woman who committed the $10,000 traffic violation.

Within the hour Julie Olson and Jacqueline Shaw are seated together beside gas heaters in the first-aid tent. "You did a great job," Shaw concedes graciously.

Olson reflects for a moment. "I don't know if I'd ever do it again," she says. "But I guess this isn't a good time to think about it."

Certainly Shaw doesn't want to think about it. Before long she is saying, "It was fun. But I think I'm going to go out dancing."

Dancing, forgodsake! Well, why not? The night is cold, but it's still young.

Master of the Mount

COLLEGE BASKETBALL

By *Molly Dunham*

From the Baltimore Evening Sun
Copyright © 1986, The Baltimore Sun Company

Tuesday's snow wrapped College Mountain in a white shawl, and the stone buildings of Mount St. Mary's huddled against the hillside above U.S. 15 as if frozen in time.

Inside the airplane hangar that is Memorial Gymnasium, Jim Phelan was on his feet, berating yet another referee. Same wiry hair tousled every which way, same brush bristles for eyebrows, same snaggle-toothed grimace.

It could be a winter's night of four years past, when Phelan was approaching his 500th victory as Mount basketball coach. Or could it?

Since then, the deadly two-lane stretches of U.S. 15 from Frederick to Emmitsburg have surrendered to dual lanes. The Mount's 1,400 students have traded Topsiders for Reeboks. The town's Main Street, once an eight-block ride from West End Realty to the East End Garage, now extends west to the High's and east to the Super Thrift.

So, too, has Phelan changed. The temptation is to call him an institution and leave it at that. Let him while away his days in the comfort of the only head coaching job he has ever known, far from the madding crowds of Chapel Hill or Lexington or Westwood. How condescending.

"The thing that's so impressive is that he still *coaches,*" said Randolph-Macon Coach Hal Nunnally, who has played and coached against Phelan's Mount teams since the late '50s. "I've seen some people stay in the game 40 years, and all they're doing is taking a towel and running up and down the floor. I remember hearing him speak at a clinic in 1964, and he was one of the first people to play pressure man-to-man defense. Here we are 22 years later, and he's still changing his game to be effective out there."

Phelan, 56, is in his 32nd year at the Mount. Last night's victory over Liberty University brought his record to 598-268. He soon will become only the second active coach in the country to reach No. 600; the other is Clarence (Big House) Gaines of Winston-Salem State with 748. Like Gaines, Phelan has won all of his games in Division II.

"If he had a position in Division I, he'd have the same type of success," Gaines said. "The difference in Division I is you have more money; you can buy a faster horse."

Phelan says he always has believed he could make it in Division I, but the right offer just never came along. There were interviews with Rutgers and Lafayette and Virginia and the Baltimore Bullets and Georgetown.

"At Georgetown (in 1966), you were being interviewed by the players, to see how well you could fit in," Phelan said. "I wasn't particularly impressed with their selection process, and I withdrew my name."

He isn't particularly impressed about reaching No. 600, either.

"You're winding down, that's what it means," he said. "People talk legends, and any of the legends that you ever read about or know about are figures or feats that nobody's ever sure really happened, and certainly, all the people involved are dead. I'd like to try to avoid that if possible, being dead."

He winked, creating a few more creases in a face as crinkled as an oxford shirt straight out of the dryer. He'll leave the gushing, as always, to Dottie, his wife of 32 years.

★   ★   ★

It is three hours before game time Wednesday night, and eight cars crowd the driveway of the Phelans' brick rambler one mile from campus. Knock on the sliding glass door of the family room. Knock again. Goldie—a chubby part golden Labrador, part Irish setter—answers with feigned ferocity. Then Dottie Phelan appears, her arms beckoning.

"Come in, come in. I was just putting laundry away." She already had accomplished the evening's most important task—laying out Phelan's game clothes, ever-present bow tie and all—and she guided a visitor through the family room stocked with her husband's trophies and into the kitchen.

Dottie and Jim built the house in the early '60s. Once filled with their five children—Jim, Lynne, Carol, Larry and Bob—they now live there with Larry, a student at the Mount, and Bob, a senior at nearby Catoctin High. As the years went on they added an apartment for Dottie's mother and another for Jim's mother and aunt. Extensions for an extended family.

"You might not know the family at all, but you're there five minutes and you feel like you've known them all your life," said Bob Flynn, in his second year as Phelan's assistant coach. "As great a coach as Jim is, there are things in his life more important than basketball, and his family is the most important."

Jim Phelan was an only child. When he was six months old, his father left, and his mother raised him on her own until she remarried 16 years later. He learned how to fend for himself on the mean streets of South Philadelphia. Later, he learned to savor the joys of a large family.

Dottie and Jim Phelan met in Philadelphia in 1953, when he returned from a stint in the Marine Corps. She always has marvelled at how calm he remains after games, win or lose, and at how he remains so unaffected by the kudos that have come his way. One story demonstrates it best.

"When we were introduced, my friend said, 'This is Jimmy Phelan,' " Dottie said. "Well, I don't know Jimmy Phelan from Tom Smith. I lived near Villanova, and I had never seen LaSalle play. (Phelan was All-Philadelphia three years in a row as a star at LaSalle). At that time in Philadelphia, there was a big meatpacking firm called Felin's. When I told my girlfriends I was dating Jim, they were so excited because they thought I would marry into money."

Later, she went to dinner for the first time at Phelan's house, and his mother asked Dottie if she'd like to see Jim's bedroom.

"I thought, what's going on here?' " Dottie said. "Then I saw the trophies everywhere. I never even knew Jim played. He never told me."

Dottie is as gregarious as Jim is reserved. Before a home game, she hugs everyone in sight. Then she settles in for 40 minutes of screaming, fretting, cheering and imploring.

"I have wiped the three losing seasons (1970-71, 71-72 and 76-77) completely out," she said. "I don't know how I handled it. I must have died."

In 1959, the Mount finished 15-12 after going 86-27 in Phelan's first four years as coach. Dissatisfied students hung Phelan in effigy.

"I just remember he came home chuckling about it," she said. "It really doesn't affect him. I remember one night when the children were little, we came back after losing a heartbreaking game. I couldn't get the children to settle down and go to bed, and I started shouting, 'Don't you know what your father's been through?'

"Then Jim yells, 'Dottie, the children aren't bothering me at all, but you are.' "

In this age of coaching burnout, Phelan has mastered the art of resiliency. He has his outlets—the family, golf, tennis and betting the horses at Charles Town. And he convinces his players that they, too, need not let losses eat at them like acid.

★   ★   ★

"I'll find myself getting mad at a guy for a bad play," Phelan said. "But you've got to ask yourself: Is he trying to do that? The only guy I knew trying to do that were guys throwing games way back. Occasionally I'll say to them, 'If I didn't know better, I'd swear you guys were trying to throw the game. Except there's no line.' "

It is part of an approach that makes so much common sense yet is so uncommon.

"I promise them a couple of things," he said. "No. 1, I promise you you won't be guaranteed playing time, and No. 2, I promise you I'm going to try like hell to get somebody better than you to take your place."

He despises training tables, athletic dorms, and petty team rules. "I'll say what time's curfew, and they say 2 o'clock. I'll say what the hell do you mean, and they'll laugh and say 1 o'clock and I'll say OK. I really don't give a damn if it's 2 o'clock, 'cause I wouldn't want to check anyway. But when they make the rules, I expect them to keep them."

It works. "I think it helps us a lot as far as making us mature," said George Young, the senior point guard from Mount St. Joseph. "We're on our own. If we make bad decisions, he never says, 'I told you so.' "

Lynne Phelan Robinson, Phelan's daughter and the school's co-ordinator of women's athletics, also coaches women's cross country, indoor track and outdoor track.

"The one thing he always told me was that all you can ask of a coach is that a coach always be fair," she said. "He doesn't want to get involved in the players' personal lives, although they know he's there if they need him. He doesn't want to know what they're doing every waking moment or every sleeping moment. I think maybe that helps him remain fair."

Phelan's laissez-faire philosophy extends to the court. The team rarely runs drills in practice, but instead works on game situations. Thus they know what play to run when the need arises.

"Everybody makes a big deal out of it when Dean Smith comes out and says it's important to scrimmage in practice," said Flynn, Phelan's assistant. "Jim's been doing it for 30 years."

And how much longer will he do it?

"Tell Jim to keep on trying, but he'll never catch me," said Gaines, 63. "He won't live long enough. We're both about the same age, and I think both of us are planning to die in the saddle."

Dottie Phelan figures her husband will be going strong at 75. "And I'll be in heaven, looking out the window and praying him on."

Paul Edwards, the senior guard from Calvert Hall who leads the team in scoring and floor burns, had another estimate.

"I think he'll coach at least until I have a son who can come here and play for him."

A Straight-Arrow Addict

GENERAL

By *Armen Keteyian*

From Sports Illustrated
Copyright © 1986, Time, Inc.

The title of his biography was "Straight Arrow" and he was only 21 when it was published—an All-America quarterback and budding Heisman Trophy candidate at Ohio State. But even as the pages rolled off the presses, Arthur Ernest Schlichter was hurrying down a dark and crooked path that would lead him into a private hell, to be quickly followed by public humiliation.

As the world knows now, Art Schlichter was a pathological gambler, so hooked by the compulsion to bet on sports events that even he is not sure how much he lost—$1.5 million is considered a realistic guess. Because of gambling, he was suspended from the NFL for the 1983 season. Now he is out of the game once more, abruptly dropped last October by the Indianapolis Colts amid rumors that he had been gambling again.

Thus, at 25, Art Schlichter has been profoundly scarred, if not totally ruined, by his affliction. Dr. Robert Custer, the Washington psychiatrist who is considered the nation's leading expert in the field, has been monitoring Schlichter's progress for almost three years. He says, "Art has suffered the full effects of his disease."

Recently, Schlichter agreed to talk at length about himself and his addiction. He was without a job, low on money and living on his parents' 450-acre grain farm in Washington Court House, Ohio. The interview took place in the living room of the suburban Columbus home of Gilman Kirk, a businessman who is now Schlichter's advisor and unofficial agent. Despite the searing nature of his experiences, Schlichter was relaxed and looked more like a little boy than a desperate betting man.

Of course, he *was* a little boy when the psychological seeds of his affliction probably took root. Like most compulsive gamblers, he was a bright, tense child of whom his mother once said, "If he was still, he was ill." He was blessed with spectacular athletic talent (he

could dribble a basketball at the age of 4). He became a baby superstar: He once scored 47 of his team's 49 points in a junior high basketball game; his high school football team was 29-0-1 with him as an
All-America quarterback; and he was an all-state guard in basketball.

He was, in short, consumed by sports. "I regret that now," said
Schlichter. "The hype, the buildup, the headlines—it all beat me up. I
had no privacy." In a separate interview, Custer said, "Art had no
other recreation, no hobbies. Football was everything, and pressure
came from everywhere—family, coaches, fans, friends. The expectations when you are a straight arrow are immense."

Another likely influence on Schlichter was a terrifying accident
that occurred when he was in the eighth grade. He and his brother,
John, were using gasoline to remove roofing tar from a floor at home
when a spark from an oil burner caused an explosion and a fire that
badly injured both boys. Art's right side, from thigh to shoulder, was
severely burned. "It was torture," remembers his father, Max.
"They'd give him painkillers but they never quite took hold. He
screamed for me to let him die." But the elder Schlichter also recalls,
"When he was in the hospital, he would always repeat to himself, 'I
can play football this fall. I can play football this fall.' "

Custer said he had to dig this particular nightmare out of Art.
"Nobody had ever asked him before if he had had any close calls with
death. Incidents such as these set gamblers up psychologically. It's
something unresolved they need relief from."

Schlichter began gambling regularly while he was still in high
school. His family owned a harness horse and he was a frequent visitor to Scioto Downs, a racetrack 40 miles from his home. Usually, he
was a penny ante $2 to $5 bettor but once, when he was a senior, he
bet $20 on a long shot and won $150. More than the money, he liked
the anonymity of the track, sitting with the railbirds. "Nobody bothered me," he recalled. "There was no pressure on me because the
horses were the show."

Art had already come to see himself as more a product of other
people's expectations than of his own personality. Custer: "People
were telling him what to think, how to feel. He was trying to be a
number of different people for everyone else—except when he gam-
bled. Then he was Art Schlichter, his own man."

His years at Ohio State became a horrendous roller coaster. As a
sophomore, he led OSU to an 11-1 record—the loss was to USC, 17-16,
in the Rose Bowl. His coach, Earle Bruce, ticked off the attributes of
his straight-arrow quarterback: "Leadership, courage, toughness,
intelligence, quick feet, never gripes." From that high point came
the drop. OSU was picked No. 1 in Schlichter's junior year, but the
team went a disappointing 9-3. His senior season was worse, though
for different reasons.

He was considered a strong Heisman Trophy candidate early in
the season, but a minor scandal engulfed him. Three traffic tickets of

his had been suspended by friendly court officials and this was followed by a Columbus courtroom hearing in which 18 reporters and a TV crew turned up to see him fined $128 for the third offense, a speeding ticket. Then he hurt his ankle. He played bravely despite pain. But OSU lost to Florida State and then was upset by Minnesota, killing his chance for the Heisman. "By the end of the year," said Schlichter, "I was tired, sore, frustrated, worried about the NFL draft, and basically burned out. Once these things start to accumulate, you stuff them inside you. Pretty soon you're looking for an outlet for all that pressure."

He had been going to bet at Scioto Downs more and more often during his college years, upping his routine bets to $20 or $30 a race. When he was a junior, he began wagering on college basketball. It was quicker than going to a track; his bet was only a phone call away. He fell about $2,000 in debt. He didn't have the money himself, so he summoned his courage and went to his father. "He was shocked and angry, but he bailed me out," recalled Schlichter.

After that traumatic experence, Schlichter began betting more frequently than ever—$200 to $300 a college basketball game. By the end of his senior year, he needed another bail-out—$12,000 this time. The vicious pattern was set.

The Baltimore Colts had drafted him No. 1, in 1982. They gave him a $350,000 bonus, a salary of $140,000 and a $125,000 low-interest loan. But Schlichter was a physical and mental mess. He wound up third string. Another rookie quarterback, Mike Pagel, was named the starter. Schlichter was devastated. "It was like *whooooosh!*" he said. "All the air went out of my baloon and my world came tumbling down." The blow to his ego was tremendous and he felt a powerful sense of rejection. "He relieved it through gambling because that was the only thing he had found that could help," said Custer.

The NFL players' strike on September 20 also appeared to be a critical factor in his self-destructive behavior. Schlichter had never been without football to give him a sense of self-worth. The strike, in effect, cut his psychological lifeline. When he recalled those desperate months, he spoke in a faraway voice, as if he were reliving a nightmare. "I went home and got very heavily involved in gambling. I lost a lot, paid some money back, lost more. I never really won and I started chasing."

His bets were getting bigger. At first, he wagered $1,000 or $2,000 per college football game. When college basketball games began, he started dropping as much as $30,000 a night. Betting with a Baltimore bookie under the code name Fred, he often parlayed a dozen three-team bets at $1,000 or $2,000 a shot. He didn't always lose. He recalled one particularly bright night during his rookie year: "I won $120,000. It was a Friday and I had parlayed my ass off. I hit a whole bunch, nine out of 10, I think. It was the greatest night in the history of my life." His face lit up as he spoke, but then it grew cloudy. "I called the book to collect and they said they couldn't pay me until

Tuesday, because it wasn't the end of the week yet." Schlichter said that by Monday he had lost not only the $120,000 he had coming but also $70,000 more.

This madness went on for about three more months, until early February 1983. "I was living minute to minute," said Schlichter. "I was constantly, *constantly* worried, paranoid, sick to my stomach. I was up all night in my room at my parents' home thinking of ways to cover my bets." Food binges puffed his weight up from 202 to 222. He simply couldn't slow down. "It grabs you," he said. "You lose some money and then you start chasing. And you keep going and going and going. Your own mind is lying to you, telling you that your next bet is going to be better, that it's going to be the big winner. But it's not. It never is."

Schlichter tried to stop gambling by going into therapy. But he was in too deep. To keep betting, he borrowed $300,000 from banks just on his good name and signature. He hit friends, family, strangers, anyone who would give him a listen and a loan. He was betting $50,000 a pop on three-team college basketball parlays. He placed two huge bets one night in early 1983 in which he tried to win back $400,000.

"I just didn't give a damn," he said. "I knew I wasn't going to be able to pay my debts. I just fired, fired, fired, fired, fired. I kept lying. I said, 'I'll pay, I'll pay, I'll pay. . . .' But I didn't. *I couldn't.*" One night during that period, he fell to his knees in his room. "I've never come out and told anyone all that happened to me that night. I didn't want anyone to say I was using it as an excuse or to get sympathy. But I turned to the Lord. I prayed that he would make it all end."

Later, Schlichter found himself trying to con Kirk, whom he had met once, a year before during a pickup basketball game. Schlichter paced Kirk's living room, talking non-stop for 45 minutes about his "cash flow" problem. He finally got around to asking Kirk to lend him $65,000. "I about fell down," recalled Kirk. "I realized that he had just pegged me as someone to use. I told him flat no. I told him he had a gambling problem, not a 'cash flow' problem."

Schlichter left. He got money from another source, but he returned the next day, in tears. This time he begged for help instead of money. "Gil Kirk was the turning point," Schlichter said. "He told me I had a problem and that took some of the strain off me."

Of course, as far as the public was concerned, the worst of Schlichter's problems were only beginning. On April 8, 1983, the news broke that the FBI had arrested four bookies in Baltimore who had threatened to break Schlichter's passing arm and harm his family if he didn't pay the $159,000 he owed them. NFL Commissioner Pete Rozelle entered the case and ultimately suspended Schlichter for 13 months. At first Schlichter hid out at Kirk's home. Later he underwent an intensive 30-day therapy program at South Oaks Hospital on Long Island. In the last 15 days there, he says, "I finally found some inner peace."

The suspension ended in the summer of 1984. The Baltimore Colts were then the Indianapolis Colts and Schlichter was their starting quarterback. But last season he hurt his knee in the opener against the Steelers and Colts Coach Rod Dowhower let him stay on the bench behind Pagel. On October 7 it was suddenly announced that Schlichter had been waived. Rumors flew that he had been gambling again. He denied this vociferously. Dowhower insisted that Schlichter was dropped because "he didn't progress in practice." But Schlichter says he wasn't even allowed to take a snap in practice.

Schlichter is bitter about what happened in Indianapolis. He is broke and still deep in debt, but he claims his gambling problems are behind him, and he is burning with optimism. His weight is down to 204, and he is said to be close to signing with an NFL team. "I will prove myself again," he says. "I made a mistake, yes, and I paid for it. I am now 10 times a better player than I was before this all happened. I really believe that my best days are ahead."

Shoemaker Wins Kentucky Derby

HORSE RACING

By *Stan Hochman*

From the Philadelphia Daily News
Copyright © 1986, Philadelphia Daily News

He had roses in his lap and tears in his eyes and scuff marks on his left boot, the kind of ominous smudges the inner rail makes when you scrape against it going 45 mph with a 1,000-pound racehorse under you.

His horse had been battered at the start and herded back to last place. He had come from 30 lengths back, plunging through the narrowest of gaps in the homestretch, rumbling through the cramped alley that separates darkness and daylight.

Willie Shoemaker had won his fourth Kentucky Derby Saturday at age 54 on a colt named Ferdinand with a glorious ride that was a dazzling mix of patience, daring and skill.

"This was better than the rest," Shoemaker said, "because I'm in the twilight of my career."

Better than the first Derby victory, back in 1955?

"I was too young then," Shoemaker said bluntly. "I didn't know the difference."

For one golden afternoon, with 123,000 screaming witnesses, with millions more watching on worldwide television, Shoemaker's twilight was emblazoned with rainbow colors.

He is older now. He knows the difference now. He always has known his way around this lopsided race track, even if he misjudged the finish line once on Gallant Man.

And he knows the shortest path to the finish line when there are four horses careening in front of him, and a slender gap nearer the rail.

Even at 54, it does not take him long to decide, so he aimed Ferdinand into the dark alley at the eighth pole and came out the other side unscathed. Then he commenced to lash his horse lefthanded and he spurted away from the screeching traffic jam behind him to win by 2¼ lengths.

The safer path was going wide, around the wall of horses churning dust. The riskier route was inside. How long do you think it took Shoemaker to decide?

"One, two, three, boom," he said.

He estimated the elapsed time at "three seconds," but the euphoria had warped his memory, his sense of distance. It was more like a second and a half, three strides, long enough to go through the sliver of daylight and darken it for Pat Day on Rampage, who might have won it all if he had gotten there first.

"I could have gone to the outside," Shoemaker said bluntly, "but why go around three or four horses when you can save ground to the inside?"

And why risk life and 54-year-old limbs to ride cantankerous horses when you've got a gorgeous wife and a young daughter at home, and enough money in the bank, and a 12-handicap in golf that is deceptive.

"Nah, I don't worry about him being too old," said Charlie Whittingham, who trains Ferdinand. "You play golf with him, you better not bet against him if you're a hacker."

A whole lot of people bet against him Saturday, which is why Ferdinand went off at 17-1. Ferdinand was 1 for 4 this year and had wobbled home 7 lengths back of Snow Chief in the Santa Anita Derby.

The jockey was 54 and hadn't won the Derby in 21 years. The trainer was 73 and never had won the Derby. The breeder, Howard Keck, was 71, and never even had entered a horse in the Derby because he has billions of dollars and the patience that goes with that kind of bankroll.

Whittingham tried to tell people that his colt hadn't liked the "greasy" surface at Santa Anita that day, that his horse was improving, that he had said 26 years ago he would not be back to Churchill Downs unless he had a horse good enough to win the Derby.

Shoemaker is 4-11 and weighs 96, so you get 30 pounds of lead in your saddle when you hire him to ride a Derby horse. You also get 30 years of experience and 30 pounds of heart.

"Nobody," Whittingham said of Shoemaker, "can be as good at 54 as they once were. But he's got those great hands that let him do so much with a horse.

"He can do things that not even the best cowboy who ever rode a horse could do. He won't panic. He won't get you in trouble."

Saturday's race was cowboy-rough. Ferdinand had the inside post and when the gates clanged open, Shoemaker was in instant trouble. Wise Times thumped Mogambo. Mogambo thrashed Ferdinand and they thundered through the stretch the first time, with Shoemaker snug as paint along the rail.

"I didn't panic and I didn't try to rush him too soon," Shoemaker recalled. "I said, 'Well, I'm here . . . there's nothing I can do about it. I'll just take my time and gradually move him through the field.' "

Ferdinand began moving through the field down the back-stretch. On the far turn, the front-runners gasped. Favored Snow Chief's gauge flickered at empty and Rampage had to swerve to avoid him. The English horse, Bold Arrangement, surged to join Broad Brush and Badger Land on the lead.

"It was pretty tight," Shoemaker said blandly. "But when you've got enough horse you can get through."

Enough horse, enough heart.

Bold Arrangement held on to be second, three-quarters of a length ahead of Broad Brush, the quixotic Maryland horse.

Behind them were strewn 13 others, some with legitimate excuses that will provide vigorous conversation between now and the Preakness, two weeks hence.

The time was mediocre, 2:02 4/5, slowest in the last 12 years. The last half was a turtlish 53 seconds, the last quarter a lumbering 25 4/5.

The first two finishers were the only horses in the field of 16 running without medication (Bute or Lasix).

The ever-popular, complex Dosage formula that analyzes pedigree held up again. Favored Snow Chief didn't have the proper bloodlines to win at a mile and a quarter. Ferdinand did.

Day mourned his bad luck. Alex Solis, who may have moved too soon on Snow Chief, said his horse got tired. Jorge Velasquez, on Badger Land, said he "nearly got killed" in the bumper-car start.

The other jocks had excuses. Shoemaker had the roses in his lap and the tears in his eyes and his fourth Derby triumph, his sweetest.

Nobody's won more than five and Johnny Longden rode until he was 59, so there may be enough time.

"I can't think about next year," Shoemaker said. "I ride day to day."

Shoemaker knows that twilight turns to darkness in an instant. One, two, three . . . boom.

Unite, Fans of Boston Strugglers

BASEBALL

By *Mike Downey*

From the Los Angeles Times
Copyright © 1986, Los Angeles Times

Help me. Please, help me. I am suffering. I am in agony. The pain cuts to the bone and shoots to the heart. It lingers there and finally breaks it in two.

I am old, and respected, and refined, but when in need of help, no one is there for me. No one comes to my rescue at the last possible minute. No one soothes me with cold compresses and reassures me that everything is going to be all right.

I know that it is not going to be all right. It is never all right. I go on and on, hoping for the best, desperate for good news, yearning for relief, but the anguish continues. It never lets up.

I've grown accustomed to sad faces. For years I have borne the countenances of everyone around me, cheerful come springtime, miserable come fall, watching with hopeful eyes, then wiping the tears from their cheeks. My own cheeks are damp. They always are, this time of year.

I am not certain why no one is able to ease the discomfort. There is a perceptible sensation that I am never going to be able to shake this thing, that it will nag me the rest of my life, attach itself like a leech, never let go. I am destined for distress.

I am sitting here today wondering what I ever did to rate such a fate, why I deserve the unhappiness that the gods of the game have bestowed upon me. I am sitting here wondering why Fenway Park, our green-walled Valhalla, the place where we go to toast the souls of those who have fallen in combat, must strip away the ribbons and bunting and maintain a mortuary's gloom.

I am part of this country, same as anyone, anywhere, and older than most. I am richly American. I am the son of a farmer, who was the son of a statesman, who was the son of a poet. My ancestors were tea drinkers and revolutionaries. I have Olde England in me and New England in me. In my bones. In my blood.

★   ★   ★

I am the seafarers who docked at Plymouth Rock, and the colonists who ditched tea crates over the side, and the hoods who pulled the Brink's job. I am the gang practicing medicine at St. Elsewhere, and imbibing for medicinal purposes at Cheers.

I am Paul Revere, looking for a lamp in a steeple, or at least for a pitcher in a faraway bullpen who can get somebody out. I am the Kennedys of Hyannisport, asking not what we can do in the ninth inning for you, but what you can do in the ninth inning for us.

I am Henry David Thoreau, thinking this morning about plunging head-first into Walden Pond and ending it all. I am Julia Child, thinking about tossing my peanuts and Cracker Jack in the garbage disposal and putting my head in that oven.

I am Joan Benoit Samuelson, considering the possibility of running and running and running until I find myself hundreds of miles from the ballpark, safe at home. I am Charlie on the MTA, riding and riding and riding until I am absolutely certain that I am never going to get off.

I am Sweet Baby James Taylor, depressed by snow on the turnpike from Stockbridge to Boston, though the Berkshires seem dreamlike on account of that frostin'. I am Emily Dickinson, the belle of Amherst, wondering if, true to my word, a discerning eye can make the divinest sense out of this much madness.

I am George Plimpton, a Harvard man, ready to go out there and play if they need me. I am A. Bartlett Giamatti, a Yale man, not yet ready to rejoice for the league that I now run.

I am Tip O'Neill, reconsidering retirement, determined to speak one more time to the House about injustice. I am Ted Williams, prepared to go to war to fight for justice if necessary.

I am Rocky Marciano and Marvin Hagler of Brockton, and we will knock the block off the first person who makes a crack about this latest knockout. I am Howie Long of Milford, and I will personally attack and sack you, patriot or no patriot.

I am Stephen King, buried alive in Maine, wondering if this horror story will ever end. I am the Boston Strangler, bringing new meaning to the word *choking*.

I am Professor Kingsfield, still chasing paper, wondering if we will ever learn our lesson. I am J.D. Salinger, secluded as always, reluctant to agree with the world that we could use another catcher.

I am Capt. Ahab, setting sail at New Bedford, depressed that the big one always seems to get away. I am Hester Prynne, ready as always to take one, letter-high.

I am Ellen Goodman, wondering where I can write to complain about this. I am Cotton Mather, and when I preached to you about the virtues of Calvinism, it had nothing to do with young Schiraldi's ability to hold a lead.

I am Jeff Reardon of Pittsfield, and Steve Bedrosian of Methuen, and Mike Flanagan of Manchester, and I wish we could have been there to pitch in. I am Richie Hebner of Norwood, the gravedigger's son, and I wish I could be there today to assist with the services.

I am Oliver Barrett III, ready to write a check if you need money, and Frank Galvin, ready to defend you in court, and Thomas Banacek, ready to help you recoup all your losses, and Eddie Coyle, ready to beg, borrow or steal on your behalf.

I am Tom Yawkey, and Bud Collins, and Arthur Fiedler, and Jim Lonborg, and Ann Beattie, and John Kelley the Elder, and Doug Flutie, and Kevin White, and Tom Lehrer, and Haywood Sullivan, and Gordon Edes, and Charles Emerson Winchester III, and Hawkeye Pierce, for that matter.

I am Bunker Hill, and Beacon Hill, and Heartbreak Hill, and Calvin Hill, gaining yardage for Yale. I am jazz at Newport, and sand at Cape Cod, and lobsters at Bangor, and sharks at Amity.

I am a yelp from Oil Can Boyd's lips, and a limp from Bill Buckner's legs, and a teardrop from Wade Boggs' eyes.

I am Boston.

I am the Commonwealth.

I am New England.

Loser of the World Series once more.

New York City, have pity.

Let's play five out of nine.

All-Pro's Last Fight

PRO FOOTBALL

By *Ray Didinger*

From the Philadelphia Daily News
Copyright © 1986, Philadelphia Daily News

In his final days, Jerry Smith could not speak above a whisper.

The former All-Pro tight end, who played at 6-foot-3 and 210 pounds, was down to 140. He could not eat, he was kept alive by intravenous feedings the last four months. The pain, both mental and physical, was constant.

For a while, the ex-Washington Redskin talked about defeating AIDS, the deadly disease he was diagnosed as having in December 1985. But with each passing day, it became more apparent Smith was locked in a struggle he could not win.

He was dying at 43.

If Smith was afraid, he kept it to himself. When family and former teammates would visit, he told them what he thought they wanted to hear: "I'm doing all right. I'm not giving up." That was his nature.

Two months ago, Smith granted an interview to George Solomon, sports editor of the *Washington Post.* Solomon covered the Redskins in the days when the swift, sure-handed Smith was revolutionizing the tight end position in the NFL.

"I'm trying very hard to fight this," Smith told Solomon, "but I don't have many good days."

Smith did the interview, he said, in the hope that his suffering might serve a greater purpose, that Middle America might finally accept the fact that AIDS can strike anyone, even a pro football hero.

He thought his illness might help people understand the disease and hasten the search for a cure. It wasn't until then that the public knew what Smith was going through and now, after his death, in interviews with friends and former teammates, we get a clearer sense of who Jerry Smith was and why his fight touched so many lives.

"It took tremendous courage for Jerry to do what he did," former teammate Brig Owens said, referring to Smith's public disclosure of his illness. "But that's Jerry. He was a team guy right to the end."

Owens was Smith's training camp roommate for 12 seasons. When Smith retired in 1977, he said: "Of all the good things football has done for me, one of the best is my relationship with Brig." They remained best friends over the years.

Owens visited Smith almost daily the last few months. He was at Smith's bedside two weeks ago, along with Rev. Tom Skinner, the former Redskins' team chaplain, when Smith said he had made his peace with the Lord.

"He told us not to feel bad for him," Skinner said. "He said he had a great life and many wonderful friends. He said, 'When my time comes, I want you to tell everyone that. I don't want them to be sad.' "

Jerry Smith died October 15 in Holy Cross Hospital in suburban Washington. Skinner delivered the eulogy at the funeral service last week.

"Jerry had a knack for not giving up," Skinner said. "He would say it over and over again: Nothing should stand in the way of what we want to accomplish. That is what he would tell us today."

Smith is the first professional athlete known to succumb to AIDS, or acquired immune deficiency syndrome, a disease that has claimed more than 13,000 lives in the United States since its discovery in 1981.

AIDS afflicts mostly homosexual men and intravenous drug users. In his *Post* interview, Smith, who never married, declined to discuss his lifestyle or how he might have contracted the fatal illness.

Although that might have troubled outsiders, those who knew Smith stuck by him.

"A lot of people will judge Jerry Smith on the implications of him having AIDS," said Calvin Hill, who played in Washington in 1976 and '77, "but let those people remember the phrase, 'Let he who is without sin cast the first stone.'

"I'm not going to judge someone else's lifestyle as it affected them. In terms of how Jerry affected me, both on and off the field, it was very positive. He was an effervescent, helpful guy who was concerned when other guys were down."

No one summed up the organization's feelings better than Bobby Mitchell. Mitchell and Smith joined Charley Taylor and quarterback Sonny Jurgensen to give the Redskins the NFL's most explosive passing attack in the late '60s.

"If you love a guy, you love him. That's all there is to it," Mitchell, the Redskins' assistant general manager, told the *Post*. "Jerry's been a very dear friend for almost 20 years.

"He was always a very private person and everybody respected his privacy, but he had a lot of friends. One of the highlights in our house was having Jerry over to dinner. Around the people he knew, he was a very fun guy."

About Smith's decision to discuss his illness, Mitchell said: "He could have left it like it was, not said anything, and 99 percent of the people would have remembered him as a great All-Pro. But this is just like him.

"He was always our Mr. Clutch, the guy who'd make the tough third-down catch over the middle in traffic and never drop the ball. Maybe this will help people understand some things better."

★   ★   ★

Sunday, Jerry Smith will be posthumously inducted into the Washington Hall of Stars at RFK Stadium. The ceremony will be held before the Redskins-Minnesota game.

The decision to honor Smith was made early in the summer, long before the news of his illness became public. When Smith's mother saw the letter, she asked: "Do you think when they (the committee) find out, they'll change their mind?"

Smith told his mother not to worry. He said the committee would stand by its word, and it did.

As a player, Smith never cared for individual honors. He was courteous with reporters, but it was obvious he didn't enjoy the spotlight. He was considered "bad copy," a guy who spoke almost entirely in cliches.

A typical postgame session with Smith went like this: "It was a team effort . . . the guys hung together . . . we'll take 'em one at a time." A lot of athletes say those things. The difference was, Smith really believed them.

"The most unselfish player I've ever been around," said Ted Marchibroda, offensive coordinator under George Allen. "Most players want to know how much they'll be featured in the game plan each week. That didn't matter with Jerry. All he wanted was to contribute."

In 1974, Smith told an interviewer: "Some artists are called purists. They paint for themselves, their own satisfaction. I'm like that. I can go unnoticed and still be fulfilling myself. I understand what I'm doing for the team."

Smith was an All-Pro with a free-agent's ego. He played 13 seasons with the 'Skins and caught 421 passes, a total surpassed by only Taylor and Art Monk in club history. His 60 touchdowns is an unofficial record for NFL tight ends.

Smith was, in many ways, a pioneer at his position. When he came into the league, tight ends were a burly, plodding fraternity. They made their living in the trenches with the other offensive linemen.

Smith changed all that. A split end at Arizona State, Smith brought thoroughbred speed to his new position. When opposing teams doubled Taylor and Mitchell, Smith often had a linebacker in single coverage. It was no contest.

"Jerry was the Kellen Winslow of the '60s," said Rickie Harris, a defensive back who covered Smith at Arizona, then played alongside him in Washington.

Smith patterned himself after the Eagles' Pete Retzlaff, another wide receiver converted to tight end. He was a perfectionist who stayed after practice almost every day to work on his blocking.

The Peach from Long Beach, that's what his teammates called him. They teased him about his California roots and his shaggy, beach-boy-blond hair.

He was shy, painfully so at first. As a rookie, he showed up for a flight in a pair of bell-bottom slacks. Coach Otto Graham jokingly noted they were a little tight across the seat. Smith fled to the men's room and had to be coaxed out to board the plane.

When he was introduced at his first Washington Touchdown Club luncheon, Smith lowered his head and did not look up until the spotlight moved to the next player. He was bright and well-read, yet it often seemed he lived in a shell.

Smith was fond of a Rod McKuen line: "I'm just a man looking for that thing hardest to find—himself." That, Smith told friends, described him as well as anything.

Smith came to Washington as a ninth-round draft pick in 1965. Owens, a safety, joined the team the following year. They became roommates at a time when it was uncommon for blacks and whites to share quarters in training camp or on the road.

Smith was warned there would be talk. "So what?" he said. The issue died there.

Smith and Owens roomed together until they left the game in 1977. They developed a bond not unlike the one between Gale Sayers and the late Brian Piccolo in Chicago.

"We'd sit around talking, trying to solve the problems of the world," said Owens, who is married and the father of two children. "Jerry was a very sensitive guy. He cared a lot about other people.

"He took advantage of me, though. He'd order room service, give the waiter a big tip, then sign my name. I wouldn't know it until the controller took the money out of my next paycheck. I'd get pretty ticked off.

"We were fierce competitors, that's one thing we had in common. We went against each other every day in practice. At least twice a year we'd wind up in a fight. People would say, "These guys *like* each other?' But that's part of the game.

"I helped Jerry by pushing him and he helped me. I don't think we would have respected each other as much if we took it easy."

Smith was physically tough. He played under two coaches—Frank Kush at Arizona State and Vince Lombardi in Washington—who demanded it. Smith cracked four vertebrae one season and came back to play in the next game. His pain threshold was legendary.

That same toughness was evident in the way Smith battled AIDS. From the time his condition was first diagnosed—Smith was losing weight and feeling "sluggish"—he never complained. He never took his suffering out on those around him.

"As late as 48 hours before his death, he said he was doing all right," said Dr. Bernard Heckman, a staff physician at Holy Cross Hospital. "He was very stoic."

Smith was in the mortgage business in Washington when he was stricken. He spent the last 10 months living with his sister, Bonnie Smith Gilchrist, when he wasn't hospitalized. It was a difficult time, full of experimentation and disappointment.

Doctors tried a few anti-viral drugs on Smith but none was successful. When the drug AZT—the most promising yet in arresting the AIDS virus—recently became available, Smith was so weak the doctors felt he could not take it safely.

In the end, there was nothing anyone could do. Smith was heavily sedated and often fell asleep in the middle of a sentence. He died quietly, with his mother, sister and brother at his side.

The next day, his sister held a press conference and read a letter Smith delivered to an AIDS Project ceremony in Los Angeles last month:

"I am trying hard to fight AIDS the best way I know how, by letting people know how terrible it is.

"My best days have been hard, difficult, bad, but there is never anything so bad that something good doesn't come from it. My own experience with AIDS has shown me that life is important—every life.

"I've learned just how supportive and caring people can be. Relatives, friends, former teammates, doctors and nurses rallied (behind me). People I've never met wrote encouraging and thoughtful letters.

"All of these people showed me there is a reason to fight on."

Gilchrist also announced a fund was being established in her brother's name to build a Holy Cross Hospice, a home for the terminally ill in Silver Spring.

She said it was the way he would want to be remembered.

★   ★   ★

The Washington Redskins 1973 Super Bowl team was reunited on the steps of St. John the Baptist Catholic Church last Tuesday.

Many of the ex-players had not seen each other in a decade. They shook hands and embraced, then stood quietly while the casket containing Jerry Smith's body was lifted from the hearse.

Jurgensen, Taylor and Mitchell, the men with whom Smith rewrote the Redskins record book, were among the pallbearers. Roy Jefferson, the receiver who succeeded Mitchell in 1971, was another.

The other players, 23 in all, walked behind the casket as it was wheeled slowly down the aisle at the church. Several wiped away tears.

Jon Jaqua, a safety on the Super Bowl team, left his ranch in Oregon to attend the services. Dave Kopay, a halfback, flew in from Los Angeles. Special teamer Mike Hull, now a lawyer, came carrying his 3-year-old daughter.

Rickie Harris signed himself out of Holy Cross Hospital to attend. Harris, now a travel agent, was scheduled for knee surgery that afternoon. He told his doctor not to worry, he'd be back. The hospital wristband was visible under Harris's suit coat.

"It's an indication how the guys felt about Jerry that so many came back for this," Owens said. "We were all so close. A time like this, your mind drifts back. We had a lot of fun together."

There were about 250 mourners at the funeral Mass. Most sat with their heads bowed as Skinner spoke:

"Jerry loved crossing the goal line, then hopping back to the sidelines and jumping into the arms of his teammates. I believe if we could see Jerry now, he would be hopping and jumping happily into the arms of God."

After the service, the long procession of cars wound its way to the Gate of Heaven cemetery. There a few words were spoken at the gravesite and family and friends lined up to pay their last respects.

As Smith's former teammates walked away, they kept looking back as if they couldn't quite believe this had taken place. They had suffered losses before, but nothing like this.

"No matter how you try to prepare yourself for this," Owens said, "you never really prepare."

"I'm sorry I didn't take the time to see Jerry before he died," Harris said. "Partly it was my own ignorance about AIDS and what it can do."

For Kopay, Smith's death hit particularly close to home. Kopay, a nine-year NFL veteran who played with the Redskins in 1969 and '70, caused a stir in 1977 when he wrote a book acknowledging his homosexuality. No pro athlete before him had dared address this issue.

"Jerry definitely affected a lot of people's lives, especially mine," Kopay said. "I loved him as a brother and, although I haven't been able to see him much the last few years, I'll miss him.

"I last saw Jerry one year ago," said Kopay, who now sells linoleum floor covering in Los Angeles. "He seemed tired and different somehow. I didn't know (about his illness). We were going to meet for dinner but we never did.

"I learned he had AIDS the same way everyone else did (from media reports). I know what a private person Jerry was. It must have been an incredible burden for him to make that public, but he thought it would help people understand."

"Will it?" someone asked.

"I hope so," Kopay said softly.

Jurgensen was standing with his hands in his pockets, looking at the grave. He couldn't help thinking back to all the times he called the old 27-Y Corner. He knew Smith, the Y man, would never let him down.

"It started with a fake to (halfback) Larry Brown off tackle," Jurgensen said. "That left Jerry open in the corner (for a touchdown). It was our best goal-line play. We could run it in our sleep."

Someone asked Jurgensen if he could make any sense of Smith's death. Sonny smiled for the first time all day.

"Lombardi must have needed a tight end," Jurgensen said. "He went for the best."

As the mourners filed away, two cemetery workers began taking down the canopy at the gravesite. Owens watched for a while, then walked back alone.

He stood there a moment, then lifted a red carnation from the floral arrangement atop the casket. Before he left, Owens gently tapped the casket twice with his right hand.

When he looked up, there were tears in his eyes.

Jerry Falwell's Team

COLLEGE ATHLETICS

By *John Capouya*

From Sport Magazine
Copyright © 1986, Sport Magazine Associates

It was Sunday, Mother's Day, at the Thomas Road Baptist Church in Lynchburg, Va. The 11 a.m. service, the third of five, the one televised nationally as The Old Time Gospel Hour, is about to begin.

The church is octagonal, based on a design by Thomas Jefferson, made of red brick and fronted by white columns. About two-thirds full today, it seats 4,000 people and its membership of 22,000 (in a city of 67,000) is the second largest in the country. Thomas Road is the heart of the Jerry Falwell Ministries, including the Moral Majority, now known as the Liberty Federation, which claims a membership of 6.5 million families. The Gospel Hour's audience (there are no Nielsen ratings for syndicated shows) is somewhere between seven and 20 million. It is broadcast on more radio and television stations than any other program, sacred or secular, in North America.

Inside, the church walls are painted white, the floors covered in a light-blue carpeting. The plain brown wooden pews, downstairs and in the balcony, slant downward toward the pulpit. Because Thomas Road is also a television studio, there are no windows. The parishioners, well scrubbed but not formal, file in and then there is a song, "I Walk Today Where Jesus Walks," from the blue-robed choir. Mrs. Jerry Falwell is the pianist, as she has been for the past 30 years.

Now Falwell himself approaches the microphone. At 52, his neatly parted graying hair and the set of his prominent nose give him a facial resemblance to Lee Iacocca, and he projects the same mixture of confidence and combativeness. His trunk is big, dominating his body and adding a balancing resonance to his Virginia vocal twang. His arms are relatively short, their frequent, purposeful motions making him seem, at a distance, feisty rather than powerful.

The pastor's sermon for today is "Realizing Your Potential, or Deciding To Grow Up." Falwell describes what he calls "the two great tragedies of American society: the secularization of this country and the devaluation of this country and the devaluation of human life." He calls on the congregation to struggle with him. He talks about being "a dynamic Christian," physically and spiritually strong, a person, as he says, that God can use. "Our Father," Falwell invokes, hands grasping either side of the podium, "we don't want to be mediocre, we don't want to fail. We want to honor You by winning."

★   ★   ★

The man who started a church with 35 members in an abandonded Donald Duck bottling plant 30 years ago is now a confidant of the President, who shares his views on abortion and school prayer. (Asked by a member of the congregation if he will run for President in 1988, Falwell replies, "I'd have to step down to do it. I'm called to be your pastor.") The Southland Corporation, owners of the 7-Eleven convenience stores, has just agreed, under pressure from Falwell's and other groups, to remove *Playboy* and *Penthouse* magazines from its shelves. Falwell's notions of Family and Country, once considered extreme, are now mainstream, being used to sell beer and automobiles. It may be, as Falwell says, "hard to turn a ship this big around," but surely everyone can feel America either listing to starboard, or if you prefer, getting back on course.

Jerry Falwell has moved and he has shaken. And now, he is directing his energy, both his personal fervor and the force of his ministry, to sports, to creating a collegiate athletic powerhouse. "Brigham Young has won a national championship in football," he says, "and if you're a Mormon child in this country, you're probably thinking BYU as soon as you're thinking college. If you're a Roman Catholic, you think Notre Dame.

"In 1971 we started Liberty University (formerly Liberty Baptist College)," Falwell, the chancellor, continues. "We have a 4,000-acre campus here in Lynchburg on Liberty Mountain. Right now we have a student body of 7,000 and we plan to have 50,000 by the year 2000. Our goal is to become the Cadillac school for the evangelical young people of America. And before this century is history, Liberty will be on a par athletically with any university in this country."

He is speaking this time in the offices of the Old Time Gospel Hour in Lynchburg's Langhorne Plaza. Here he is casually addressed as "Doc," though his doctorate is only honorary. In person he seems bigger, more physically imposing. As always, he wears a dark suit ("I'm a conservative," he explains), with a gold JESUS FIRST pin in the lapel.

"We've had a very successful NCAA Division I baseball program," he says, "and we've played football, basketball, track, 15 sports in all, mostly at the Division II level. But by 1988-89 we're going Division I-AA in all of them."

Falwell was a fullback and captain of the football team at Brookville High School in Lynchburg, tried out for the St. Louis Car-

dinals baseball team when he was 18 and played basketball
(forward) at Baptist Bible College in Springfield, Mo. He admits to
reading the back of the paper first, and to rooting for the Yankees,
Celtics and Dallas Cowboys. "Here at Liberty," he smiles, "I attend
all the home games and I'm the loudest fan. I sit in the dugout for
baseball and I have prayer on the sidelines with the guys in football."

Liberty has put players in the NFL the past two years, Freddie
Banks of Cleveland and Kelvin Edwards, a wide receiver who was
the 1986 fourth-round draft pick of the New Orleans Saints. Cliff
Webber was the Celtics' third pick in last year's draft and the
Flames (the school motto is "Knowledge Aflame") have been to the
NAIA World Series three times in the last six years. The Pittsburgh
Pirates' Sid Bream is a Liberty alumnus. Their wrestling team was
fifth in the nation this year (Division II) and both the men's and the
women's cross country teams won their NCAA regionals. But that is
just the beginning.

"What I always tell our people in church," says Falwell, "is that
one of these days we're going to play Notre Dame in football, and
we're going to beat them. Of course, they have to schedule you first.
And if they agreed today, it'd be seven years before you played them.
But I'm going to guess that somewhere in the 1990s (Notre Dame
president) Father Hesburgh will decide to shut Jerry Falwell up."

★   ★   ★

From the top of Monument Terrace, a war memorial in Lynchburg's center, you see spires—there are over 120 churches in this city.
The Terrace is built on one of the steepest risings of the Seven Hills,
or original neighborhoods (the city now extends over 50 square
miles). Beyond them the Blue Ridge Mountains are softly but indis-
putably green.

Jerry Falwell is a topic of conversation and concern here, from
the men's room graffiti in Municipal airport ("The Moral Majority is
Neither") to the employment he provides for over 2,000 locals. But
Lynchburg is too big and too diffuse to be dominated by one man's
ministry, even his. Falwell's cousin, Calvin, businessman and president of the Lynchburg Mets minor league team, attends another
church.

From the Terrace, the Liberty campus is a 10-minute drive
south, five more during rush hour. Past the security checkpoint are
48 buildings, low and brickfaced like those downtown, but newer,
orange rather than red. All but a handful have been built since 1978.

Fresh from classes, the male students still wear the required ties,
the women skirts, at 3:30 on an April afternoon. No one wears black.
It's hot, in the high 80s, but there is no explicit tanning taking place.
There are couples, but no cuddling—that would be a "PC," or personal contact, a violation of the Liberty Way.

This student code of conduct is outlined in a 92-page blue booklet,
kept by every student. It begins with the admonition that "the student who is interested in 'doing his own thing' will not be happy in the

atmosphere of Liberty University." A detailed series of rules, warnings and reprimands ("reps") follows. Beards and tobacco are forbidden; among the infractions that warrant expulsion are using alcohol or drugs and visiting the room of a member of the opposite sex. Secular music is taboo, and that definition extends to include Christian rocker Amy Grant. Finally, ominously, "No one is to enter or leave campus the back way."

Prospective students are required to make a profession of faith: "Have you received Jesus Christ as your personal Saviour? Explain in detail your salvation experience." Thomas Diggs, Dean of Academic Services, admits that "some people con us. But it's very difficult for a non-believer to make it here." Diggs, 33, with brown hair and metal-framed glasses, is sitting in his office in the new B.R. Lakin School of Religion. Behind him on the painted yellow cinder block wall is a sign that declares, "I Like You—You're Weird."

"I've been here for 13 years," Dr. C. Sumner Wemp, Vice President for Spiritual Affairs, admonished the student body at the final chapel session of 1986, "and every year there are some students who play the fool for one night of pleasure." Athletes are at least as susceptible and, it seems, equally punishable. During the 1984-85 season two starters and the sixth man on the basketball team were expelled for drinking on New Year's Eve.

Liberty's religious and behavioral requirements obviously limit its recruiting possibilities. The coaches say they have a "recruit for retention" policy. "I make sure all these kids know exactly what they're getting into," says football coach Morgan Hout. "I tell them that if they're not a true, devout Christian, these rules will be just like a hammer constantly hitting you in the head."

Race is another obstacle. Parishioners say they see fewer black faces at Thomas Road since Falwell's trip to South Africa last summer and his subsequent, highly publicized remarks, which were interpreted as supporting the system of apartheid. Donations to the ministry also fell off as a result. Are black athletes, who dominate college sports, wanted at Liberty and will they want to attend? Will their parents remember the things that Falwell said and did during what Southerners call "the seg days?"

Falwell responds that "We have the highest percentage of minorities of any predominantly white private or public school in the state. (Actually, James Madison and Virginia have slightly higher black and minority enrollments; the University of Richmond, slightly lower.) In South Africa, I support President Reagan's policy of constructive engagement to bring an end to apartheid.

"As for my being a segregationist, there wasn't a church or a school from Virginia to the Gulf of Mexico at that time that wasn't. It's a generation ago for all of us; the only difference is that I still recall it and talk about it publicly, and tell of the osmosis whereby the Thomas Road Baptist Church and I have long since repudiated any separation of the races. As a matter of fact, the black Christian families, from where these athletes must come, are among the main supporters of our ministry."

Black students at Liberty see themselves first in the minority of born-again Christians and say they don't feel tolerated or exploited. "Except they say they don't mind interracial dating here, and they really do," says Kelvin Edwards. "I don't think it's the people here, though, as much as the parents. A lot of them would be upset."

As for Lynchburg itself, he adds, "there's places you can go and places you can't go." He shrugs. "That's the South."

"I know Dr. Falwell loves me as much as he does any other person here," stresses Michael Goode, a black junior (non-athlete) from Landover, Md. "He's always hugging me, calling me 'buddy,' and you can tell who's sincere and who's not. Really, there's no problem here with any of the professors or administrators. It's just that socially, some people ... but that's not Liberty, that's society."

★   ★   ★

"I feel like I have a 50,000-pound weight over my head," says Hout, "and it's hanging by a spider web. Every day when I get up in the morning I say, 'Lord, give me the strength, give me the courage to do what has to be done.' I want to be the head coach here when we play Notre Dame."

Hout handled the wide receivers for Jerry Claiborne at Maryland, where they went to five bowl games in six years. He plays the passing game with the Flames as well; after his first two years, his record is 8-10-1. He knows that, as Falwell says, "football is the key," the sport that requires the most athletes, attracts the most attention and is potentially the most lucrative. It is also, reminds Brian Boulac, assistant athletic director at Notre Dame, "the area where you usually get into trouble with the NCAA."

This fall Liberty will begin a two-year probationary period in order to qualify for Division I-AA by 1988. To meet scheduling requirements, it is seeking affiliation with two regional conferences, the Southern and the Big South. Only 50 percent of its games must be against Division I (A or AA) opponents; proposition 48, the new NCAA academic minimums, will be harder for Liberty to meet.

Plans for a new football stadium, as well as a basketball/convention center, have been discussed but not drawn—Liberty football games are now played at Lynchburg's Municipal Stadium, where they averaged 6,562 fans last year. Liberty football has already survived The Flood; their practice facility was swept away by the James River this spring, leaving only one usable ball and one helmet. And the athletic department has recently undergone sizable budget cutbacks, part of an overall austerity regime in the Falwell ministry.

Over $5 million was slashed from the $100 million annual expenditures (the ministry spends $300,000 a week on air-time alone) and over 300 employees were laid off. Falwell explains that $14 million worth of construction had to be done at Liberty in 18 months for the purposes of reaccreditation by the state of Virginia. Other ministry sources say they were also hurt by gay activists and others running up enormous bills on Falwell's 800, or toll-free, telephone lines.

Twenty-five percent of the athletic operating budget, $140,000, was cut. The department's overall budget is $2.1 million, of which one-third is funnelled to football. A Division I-A power like the University of Michigan will spend $14 million a year on its athletic program. Virginia spends $2 million annually, Liberty's entire athletic budget, just on scholarships.

The position of full-time sports information director was eliminated. "It hurt personally," says the banished Lawrence Swicegood, "and I also thought it was bad for the ministry. Ninety percent of having a Division I program is pushing your school with the media." When the visitor's statistics suddenly disappeared at a baseball game this spring, one observer joked that the top half of the scoreboard had been laid off.

"Maybe I just don't have the vision or know enough about their situation," says Notre Dame's Boulac. "But I would think that if they could duplicate the kind of success that we've had or that BYU has had, in the same amount of time, that *that* would be a spectacular achievement. After all, we've been playing football here for nearly 100 years." So he's not quaking in his Roman Catholic boots? "Not yet."

★   ★   ★

But finances and facilities aren't everything. Liberty has faith, their belief that the Lord has blessed and will continue to bless their efforts. If it moves mountains, surely it can move a few linemen downfield.

Falwell insists that no full-time coaches have been laid off, no scholarships lost and points out that former Yankee great Bobby Richardson came on as baseball coach in the midst of the reshuffling. Under Richardson, South Carolina was second in the country in the 1975 (Division I) College Baseball World Series. This past season, he was at Coastal Carolina College, where he won the Big South Conference Tournament and was named Coach of the Year.

"A year from now," Falwell promises, "we're back on track." Falwell asked his Old Time Gospel Hour followers for a Seven Million Dollar Miracle to make that happen. Says Swicegood, "I've seen it happen before."

Already Liberty has been blessed by a minor miracle—that of Dave Williams and his weight room. Five years ago the former Little All-America nose guard thought the Lord had led him to the perfect job: head strength coach at football-crazed Texas A & M. But one day Williams found himself looking out his big picture window and wondering, "Why are we doing this?" A few phone calls and a substantial pay cut later, he found himself at Liberty.

Then Atlanta insurance magnate A.L. Williams (no relation), a frequent contributor to the ministry, honored his wife's parents in

1986 by donating the Hancock Athletic Center. At the dedication, he sprang for another $200,000 to fill the empty weight room. Machines are still arriving, but the room's 8,200 square feet are fully carpeted and mirrored; a fierce Liberty eagle holding a barbell is painted on one wall. Furnished to Williams' specifications, it is as good a facility as Oklahoma, Alabama or most pro teams have—at a religious school of 7,000.

Williams tells his players, "The Apostle Paul said that the body is fearfully and wonderfully made, and it is. But it's funky because of the Fall. That's why we want to lie around in front of the television eating cookies and getting fat. But if you push and work and strive, it'll change."

He sees no conflict between the violent nature of football and Christian precepts. "I ask the kids, 'What if Jesus were a football player today at Liberty University. How would he play? I bet he'd knock you flat, doing it clean, within the rules. And if he got behind, would he quit? I don't believe he would. I think he'd try harder."

★　　★　　★

Eventually, Liberty's religiosity may prove more of an asset than a liability. In her book "Redemptorama: Culture, Politics and the New Evangelicalism" (1984), Carol Flake points out that athletes and born-again Christians tend to come from the same geographic and economic sectors. "Growing up in a lower middle class family in a small town in the South, Southwest or Midwest," she writes, "increases the odds that one will become either an athlete or an evangelical or both."

Private Christian academics and high schools are also proliferating. At the beginning of this decade, there were more than 14,000 of them and three new ones opened each day. They may come to sustain Liberty athletically as the parochial schools have Notre Dame.

Most important, Falwell has just purchased a national cable television network and began transmitting from Liberty Mountain in midsummer to over one million homes. "We're on Sat-Com 4, Transponder 7," Falwell rattles off, "and we'll be televising all major sports home games. It's a great recruiting tool."

Liberty people also believe that being or dealing with born-again Christians has inherent athletic advantages. Presumably, their players don't abuse their bodies with the substances and the zeal that secular athletes do. Christian athletes respect their elders and authority ("Yes, sirs" resound across campus); they are eminently coachable material.

They're closer, Liberty athletes believe, because of the built-in solidarity of their faith. And they may be more consistent. "A secular player may get all worked up and go out and use alcohol after a bad game or two," says Liberty alumnus Sid Bream. "We Christians will pray, stay in our rooms and read the Bible. I think there's a greater peace there."

"There's definitely less tension," says athletic director Al Worthington, who was saved at a Billy Graham crusade in 1958 while pitching for the San Francisco Giants. "We know we have a home in Heaven and we're going there."

Worthington, 57, leans back in his chair and brings his hands together in front of him. His dark-blue suit and gold rimmed glasses say businessman, but his build and his tan still say baseball man. "You see," he says, "God and Man were once together." He holds up his right forefinger and middle finger, side by side. "But sin"—he separates the two fingers, forming a V—"drove them apart. Now Jesus"—he brings his other forefinger across, into the gap, forming a solid rectangle of flesh—"brings them back together." And he smiles.

Brigham Young athletic director Glen Tuckett talks casually of $300,000 guarantees for playing an away football game. Is money a motive at Liberty? "If we're winning in football at the Division I level and drawing 15,000 people to a home game, we'll be making money," says Falwell, but all agree that is years away. What other appeal does sports have for the Falwell ministry?

"To me," Falwell says, "athletics are a way of making a statement. And I believe you have a better Christian witness to the youth of the world when you, competitively, head-to-head, prove yourself their equal on the playing field."

Diane Winston of *The News and Observer* (Raleigh, N.C.), who has written often about Falwell, suggests that "Manliness is a big part of the whole Falwell package. It's real important for him to have good teams because that proves you're not a wuss." And certainly, there's conscious image-breaking at work at Liberty.

"When people think of Christians, they think of some guy in polyester clothes, with glasses and greasy hair," says Pat Sipe, who broke Sid Bream's school record with 20 home runs this year. "So when I get to the plate, I like to look the pitcher right in the eye to let him know a Christian can still have aggression. And when I shake a guy's hand after a game, I shake it kind of firm."

Falwell the capitalist naturally feels that "Competition is good. Paul in the New Testament often speaks of running the race of life, that many run but only one wins the prize." And the absolutism he sees in sports appeals to Falwell the fundamentalist. "When the game's over and you've won or you've lost," he says, "you know something you didn't know before you started."

But if, as Falwell says, ours is the terminal generation before the return of Jesus Christ, should He come back to find us playing games? "No man knows the day or the hour when the Son of Man comes. I believe that you have to deal with the nasty now-and-now while looking forward to the sweet bye-and-bye."

★   ★   ★

To this point in the Mother's Day service, Falwell's audience has been attentive, but not rapt. The atmosphere is one of comfort and community rather than catharsis. Falwell himself is moderate, constantly smiling. He makes a few jokes about "the liberals," but today he doesn't denounce, he regrets.

But the air is suddenly charged, and the congregation falls silent as the service closes with The Invitation. Falwell requests that no one leave except in case of emergency, and that the parishioners bow their heads and close their eyes. Falwell asks if any present feel a spiritual need and would like to be prayed for, and hands are raised. Falwell blesses them and invites them to come forward and be counseled in private afterward. He asks if there are any who want to join the Thomas Road Baptist Church, and they too are invited to come forward.

Finally, Falwell asks how many would like to be born-again Christians, to embrace Jesus Christ as their personal Saviour. "Lord," Falwell invokes, "I know I'm a sinner and I deserve to go to hell. And I believe that Jesus Christ died for our sins. Come into my heart, Lord, and save my lost soul."

Rain, Rain Go Away

by Karl M. Ferron of the Baltimore Sun. An unscheduled visitor to
the Broadneck-Severna Park high school soccer game was Mother
Nature, who said hello to Broadneck's Matt Howard with about
five minutes left to play. Copyright © 1986, the Baltimore Sun.

Getting His Kicks

by Boris Spremo of the Toronto Star. With his body parallel to the
ground, Manuel Negrete of the Mexican National Team blasts a
shot that results in Mexico's second goal in a World Cup Soccer
victory over Bulgaria. Copyright © 1986, Photo by Boris Spremo,
Toronto Star.

Down and Out

by Smiley N. Pool of the Austin American-Statesman. A disappointed Baylor runner and a loose baton tell the story of missed connections during the 4X100 meter relay at the Texas Invitational track meet. Copyright © 1986, Austin American-Statesman.

The Sad Odyssey Of Jason Burleson

HIGH SCHOOL FOOTBALL

By *Jan Hubbard*

From the Dallas Morning News
Copyright © 1986, Dallas Morning News

If some of the more unpleasant aspects of Texas high school football had been apparent when the saying was first uttered, there might have been a twisted footnote to the declaration that winning isn't everything, it's the only thing.

Last year in Hamilton, Tex., winning wasn't everything, the only thing that mattered was who got the glory.

Football divided the town of 3,200, and caused the resignation of the head football coach and his wife, who was the head girls' coach. It caused the subsequent suspension of their teaching certificates. And it led to their response of a lawsuit against the school district.

Football caused the coaching couple to send their son, a star quarterback, to four schools in a year. Football caused them to spend their retirement money, and forced them to borrow more money using land they owned as collateral while they fought legal battles. Football led to the school district spending $15,000 to have the couple's teaching certificates suspended.

Football was the root of a lot of evil in Hamilton.

★   ★   ★

"The problem started in the eighth grade," said Hershel Burleson, the coaching father. "The problem starts, I guess, in any small town when you have a basketball game, your team gets beat, 54-53, and he scores 51 points. Or when your eighth grade team averages 37 points a game and he averages 33. Or when you go to a junior high track, he enters five events and scores 50 points."

Or when your son is obviously the best quarterback on the team as a sophomore. If Jason Burleson, the son, had been born and raised in Hamilton, or if his father had not been a coach, perhaps there never would have been a problem. If Jason Burleson had been 5-foot-5 and weighed 120 pounds as a sophomore, perhaps there never would have been a problem. Perhaps he still would be the starting quarterback in Hamilton, which is 150 miles southwest of Dallas, rather than in Sherman.

But by the time Jason started his sophomore year, he was 6-5, 220 pounds, and an accomplished athlete.

As a freshman, he averaged 40 points per track meet. He had high-jumped 6-5½, thrown the shot put 53-8, and the discus 166 feet. He had bench pressed 300 pounds, played center and averaged 27.5 points on the basketball team, was a member of the *Waco Tribune-Herald* Super Centex basketball team and had advanced to the regional tennis semifinals, where he lost to the eventual state champion. In the summer of 1985, he set a national decathlon record for his age group at The Athletics Congress meet in New York.

"You don't find many like him," said a football recruiter at a major college. "We've known about him since he was a freshman."

Jason also was considered a good kid.

"He's too good to be true," said one Hamilton resident. "He doesn't spin out his tires, doesn't drink, smoke, chew or mess with the girls that do. It's hard to imagine a kid that good, and that physically accomplished."

His father, who had been a coach for more than 20 years, had planned to help Jason became a great athlete. Hershel and his wife, Jane, even held Jason back a year in the seventh grade and Jane said, "We did that on purpose, for athletic reasons."

Hershel forced his son to work hard, and Jason did. Citizens in Hamilton still talk about how Jason and wide receiver Charles Gonce would work on their passing game during the summer for hours at a time. "The other kids never even looked at a football until two-a-days started," said one resident.

The work paid off. In the first four games of the 1985 season, Hamilton won three times and scored 16 touchdowns. Jason was a part of every TD—passing for nine, running for six and catching one scoring pass.

During the last game at Hamilton on September 27, 1985, Jason completed 10-of-15 passes for 281 yards and five touchdowns. He also ran for three touchdowns and caught a pass for another. Hamilton hammered Hico, 61-18.

Nine days later, Jason Burleson left town.

★   ★   ★

When Hershel Burleson walked into the Hamilton fieldhouse Tuesday afternoon after the Hico game, he was unaware that someone had told Jason at lunch, "Well, I guess we know how to spell team in Hamilton. It's J-A-S-O-N."

Hershel was unaware that the normally mild-mannered Jason was ready to fight at lunch, but Jason knew if he was caught he would be suspended for three days and would miss the next football game.

Hershel was unaware that members of the team were going to call a meeting to ask that the offense, the touchdowns and the glory be spread around.

What shocked Hershel was that Jason had another player pinned against the wall and, according to Hershel, "was going to do some violent harm. I thought it was over some little ol' girl."

Hershel separated the players, and then the team meeting began. It ended with Hershel telling the players he was going to coach the way he wanted.

A few minutes later, Jason emerged from the fieldhouse with tears streaming down his face. It had been years since Hershel had seen his son cry, and the sight of it unnerved the father.

"I can't play," Jason told his father. "I can't play with these guys no more."

Hershel made an instant decision.

"I don't know," Hershel said. "Maybe it was years of coaching and just being tired. I could have kicked seven or eight of them off the team, but that wouldn't have helped anything in Hamilton. I really thought at the time, and I told my wife, that I thought we were doing the best thing for Hamilton and us just by leaving."

Hershel took Jason to see Clyde Raibourn, the Hamilton school superintendent. He told Raibourn he was resigning immediately and that the family would leave town.

Later, friends and players came by the Burleson house, some to express sadness, others to plead with them to stay. One sight remains vivid to some who saw Jason, a 16-year-old boy in a man's body.

"I have never seen a young man so devastated," said one citizen. "He was absolutely in shock. He thought the guys were his friends, but they had banded together and said some really cruel things."

Five days later, the Burlesons moved to Mertzon, 30 miles southwest of San Angelo.

★   ★   ★

The Burlesons' abrupt departure caused an immediate hardship for the school. Besides being the head football coach, Hershel taught a physical science class and a physical education class. Jane was the girls' volleyball coach, taught three classes of English, one of drama and one period of athletics at the junior high and another period of athletics at the senior high.

"I just had to find some warm bodies," said Raibourn. "One of the positions was not too hard to fill because a man in town was looking for a job. The other one, I was just flat lucky."

Despite the inconvenience, the Hamilton School Board voted, 6-1, on October 7 to accept the Burlesons' resignations, but that was before a quote in a newspaper story was attributed to Hershel, who allegedly said that there wasn't much talent in Hamilton. Hershel denies he said it.

On the field, the players were struggling. After Jason left, Hamilton lost to DeLeon, McGregor, Clifton and Glen Rose by a combined score of 146-53.

On October 28, three weeks after accepting the Burlesons' resignation and a month after Hamilton won its last football game, the Hamilton school board met and, by a 4-3 vote, decided to seek the suspension of the Burlesons' teaching certificates.

"I don't think the fact that they lost had anything to do with the board's decision," Raibourn said. "I can't tell you what goes on in people's minds, but I don't think it did."

Others disagree, but it is such a volatile issue that those who live in Hamilton and side with the Burlesons ask not to be identified.

"It was a personal vendetta (by the school board)," said one citizen. "I don't know whether it will be proved or not. I was absolutely floored when they had that second meeting. They had accepted their resignations. A lot of people were there to protest them trying to take their certificates. If they felt like it needed to be done, they should have done it in the first meeting. They said later that that wasn't why they had the first meeting, but everybody in the community knew that it was."

W.N. Kirby, the state commissioner of education, sided with the school district. Kirby said the school district had no choice but to accept the Burlesons' resignations in the first meeting because the Burlesons had resigned without seeking the board's approval. The commissioner said the board "accepted the resignations for the purpose of enabling it to find replacements for the positions vacated by the respondents."

Therefore, the commissioner ruled, the board was within its rights to pursue suspension of the Burlesons' teaching certificates and he delivered a stinging commentary on their decision to leave, saying, "There are no other cases in which the level of immaturity and pettiness displayed by a teacher abandoning a contract has risen to the level demonstrated in the present case."

The hearing officer in the case recommended that the certificates be suspended for the 1986-87 school year, but the commissioner ruled that the one-year penalty was retroactive to when the Burlesons abandoned their contracts. They will be eligible to begin coaching and teaching Wednesday at Sherman High School.

Some in Hamilton are not satisfied with the penalty.

"I think it was a farce," said Hamilton school board president Dr. George Tolbert, who cast the deciding vote when the board decided to seek the suspension of the certificates. "The punishment was for a month (September). It looked like to me that if he (Kirby) is going to do something, he ought to do it."

It cost the school district at least $15,000 to pursue the suspensions, which is irritating to Jane Burleson. Two years ago, she organized a drive in Hamilton to raise $10,000 to build a weight room and buy weights.

"If I'd known the school board had extra money to throw away,"

Jane said, "I wouldn't have bothered."

★   ★   ★

The Burlesons say they abandoned their contracts for the purest of reasons—they were protecting their son.

"Right or wrong," Jane said, "Jason was our main concern."

Yet they admit making mistakes.

"We were wrong by leaving," said Hershel.

"We would have left anyway," said Jane. "The thing we probably should have done is when we went and saw the superintendent, we should have requested that he call a school board meeting and we should have asked the school board to be released from our contracts. Had they released us, great. Had they not released us, we still were going to leave."

Others in Hamilton, even some who say they like the Burlesons, note that the coaches were not perfect. While some defend the way Burleson used his son, they say that Burleson intentionally ran up the score against Hico. It was 54-18 after three quarters, but Jason continued to play, and he scored the last touchdown.

★   ★   ★

The Burlesons certainly have paid for their decision to leave Hamilton, and perhaps no one has paid more than Jason. He is in his fourth school in a year with his fourth group of teammates and friends, and his parents say he worries about getting too much good publicity. At a time when he should be celebrating his successes and looking forward to the recruiting war that major college recruiters say will surely take place, Jason, now 6-6, 232, is reluctant to talk to the press. He would not consent to an interview for this article.

His parents have suffered, too. When the school board sought the suspension of their certificates, they had to send the certificates to the Texas Education Agency until the process was complete. That meant they could not stay in Mertzon because they could not work in Texas.

They then moved to Newark, Ark., where they were offered jobs during the spring semester. But when the Burlesons went to Newark, what they did not know was that the school had gone through five football coaches in two years. It was not a good situation, and the Burlesons wanted to get Jason in a AAAAA school.

Burleson then applied for an assistant's job in Sherman and was hired by G.A. Moore, the new coach.

"And we certainly didn't come here because of their success on the field," said Hershel. "They were 0-10 last year."

In Sherman, the Burlesons live in a new apartment complex that offers the attraction of one month's free rent on a six-month lease. They say the free month was needed.

"We have no more retirement," said Hershel. "It's gone. We have land that we borrowed some money off of until we get back on our feet."

After moving to Mertzon, Jason had to sit out 30 days before becoming eligible to play for Irion County High School, a Class A school. In Arkansas, he played basketball and ran track.

Now at Sherman, he is the starting quarterback, which irritates some of the people in Hamilton.

"There was always a comment that if Jason went to a AAAAA school, he'd never get to play," said a resident. "Now that he's going to a AAAAA school and playing quarterback, that just infuriates them."

★   ★   ★

And the controversy shows no signs of dying soon. The Burlesons have filed suit against the Hamilton school board in state district court in Austin, claiming that their First Amendment right of free speech had been violated. The basis of the suit is a comment allegedly made by Tolbert after he cast the deciding vote as the board sought the suspension of the Burlesons' teaching certificates.

In Hamilton, it has been suggested that Tolbert said he would not have voted that way had Hershel not been making derogatory comments to the press about the school's lack of talent. Tolbert denies the charge.

"That is not true," he said. "That's not why I voted how I did. . . . I didn't change my mind. I was more or less wanting to be through with it, and we could get on about our business. When it came to a vote of whether he did wrong or not, I think he breached his contract."

Some citizens in Hamilton wish the controversy would end, but because of the Burlesons' suit, it will not. And the school board has requested that the trial on the suit be held in Hamilton, which is likely to re-open painful wounds.

"It brought out the worst in everybody," said one citizen, "and they just won't let it die."

Last Friday, Jason threw a 66-yard touchdown pass with 1:05 left in the game to direct Sherman past Weatherford, 17-13.

After four games, Sherman is 3-1, and Jason has been superb—34 completions in 67 attempts for 452 yards and four touchdowns.

On the same night, Hamilton lost to Glen Rose, 29-0.

"We won't get this whole thing turned around for at least two years," said a Hamilton citizen. "We could have gone to state this year and we could have gone last year if we had just all worked together. But there still is bitterness now. We got tromped Friday night."

No matter how ugly it was on the field, it did not compare to the ugliness off the field the last year in Hamilton. There have been no winners. It has been a case of Texas high school football at its worst.

The Americanization Of Frantisek Musil

HOCKEY

By *Jerry Zgoda*

From the Minneapolis Star and Tribune
Copyright © 1986, Minneapolis Star and Tribune

The first phone call was the worst.

Frantisek Musil, who had lived almost all of his 21 years at home, slipped away on a summer's night without saying a word to his family or friends. He already was an ocean away when the postcard arrived at his parents' home in Czechoslovakia, telling them their son had left everything for a hockey career in North America. A few days later, Musil picked up a telephone at his lawyer's house in Edmonton, Alberta.

"I call the number, say, 'This is Franti' and my mother starts crying," Musil said. "We talk 30 minutes and she cry all the time. She say she never see me again, and then my father say he want to come to North America and bring me back to Czech. I must explain that she never lose me. It was terrible."

Musil tried to explain to his father, a worker in a chemical factory, why he walked away from a tour group in Yugoslavia and shut the door on his past.

"I say, 'I want to play hockey, I want to win the Stanley Cup,' " said Musil, the North Stars' second-round draft choice in 1983. "He is a sportsman; he tell me always to be the best, to win. So I think he understood. He lose me, too, but he tried to help my mother understand. I explain to them that I have a good deal here."

★   ★   ★

Musil ran his hand over the roof of a new $15,000-plus Cadillac Cimarron, which he is leasing from an Edina dealer. "It is American, yes," he said as a smile burst across his face.

It is American, yes. As American as Big Macs and football and credit cards and Walkman stereo headphones, a few of his other discoveries. Musil still fumbles sticking the key into the ignition and unlocking the steering wheel, but the automobile—white with blue interior and, of course, with stereo sound and air conditioning—is symbolic of a wealth and a lifestyle that he had never known before he followed North Stars General Manager Lou Nanne off the plane at the Minneapolis-St. Paul International Airport. The time: 11 p.m. The date: July 18, 1986.

A year ago, Musil was earning $18 a game for his club team, but was paid only if his team won. Today, Musil, who had played on the Czech national team since he was 18, is owner of a six-figure NHL contract, a closet full of Levi's jeans and his own destiny.

"Czech was free, too, but there's more freedom here," Musil said. "Whenever you want to go to a football game, why not? Florida? Yeah, why not? In Czech, you must make a lot of stuff, get a visa, if you want to travel much."

Musil, who was joined by his new teammates Saturday for the start of training camp, is expected to step straight into the North Stars' lineup; many NHL scouts say he is a Can't-Miss prospect. Nanne says that, given time to adjust to the North American style of play and the smaller ice surface, he can become one of the best defensemen in the league.

But in his first two months here, Musil has had so much to learn away from the ice. He studied English for years, in preparing for the day he'd move to North America. He bought workbooks, took them home and studied them at night. He put his English to use when he played in the 1982 World Junior championships, at Met Center, and in the 1984 Canada Cup. But that didn't fully prepare him for what he would see and hear every hour of every day of every month.

Musil spent Week One in Edmonton with Rich Winter, his attorney and the man who helped Nanne get Musil out of Yugoslavia. The idea was to break Musil slowly into the North American way of life. While Winter worked during the day, Musil found his way around town; he went to the gym, to McDonald's, to the West Edmonton Mall. On a Friday night, Winter and Musil stopped at an instant cash machine so that Winter could get money for the weekend.

"He'd never seen anything like that before," Winter said. "He thought, 'You put card in the wall, money comes out, it's a great thing.' He wasn't sure how you got billed."

Winter sat down with Musil and explained credit cards and cash machines and tax planning and investments. Musil knew nothing about any of them. Back home, he was paid in cash.

"In Czech, they give you money, you put it in bank and it stays there," said Musil, whose yearly income was about $7,000, nearly $1,000 more than that of the average Czech worker. "Here, you take your money, invest it and you can make more money. I had never heard of it. It is a good idea."

Said Winter: "It's just like if you and I went to the outback of Australia and had to learn the day-to-day transactions of the aborigines. Well, here the aborigines use Visa cards and money machines."

Musil has learned to like fast-food and pizza and football; he says he cannot learn to like American beer.

"He came in one day and said how much he liked Big Macs," said Mark Baribeau, a North Stars equipment manager who helped show Musil around the Twin Cities. "I said, 'That's really good, but you can't eat that all the time.' I figured if he was going to eat junk food, he better go someplace where he could at least get something half-way decent. So I showed him Arby's."

Musil liked it, almost as much as Big Macs and football. He decided he liked football almost as much as hockey after he went to both Vikings preseason home games and an Edina High School game.

"If I don't do so well in hockey this year, maybe I try football next year," he said with a smile. "The players are strong. They want to win so bad. There is so much emotion, I like it very much. It is not boring; baseball is boring."

Musil almost always is smiling and laughing. He laughs when he shows off his new car. He laughs when he talks about getting lost on the highway. He went to lunch the other day with Baribeau and North Stars Tim Coulis and Dirk Graham and he laughed because he was eating beer cheese soup.

"I don't think he had ever had it before," Baribeau said. "He was just sitting there, laughing his tail off and saying, 'It is good, it is good.' The only time I ever see him get really serious is when he is talking about his family."

Said Musil: "Why be sad? I'm so happy to be here. I worried about my parents at first, but then I felt good that they start to understand. Now I have a very good life. I worry only about hockey now."

★　　　★　　　★

It has been one adventure after another since Musil arrived.

There was that first day in the new world. Musil had brought with him only a small sports bag that held two shirts, a pair of trousers and a toothbrush. Nanne, a man of extravagant means, and Winter took him shopping at Southdale.

"It was like a scene straight out of 'Moscow on the Hudson' (a movie about a Russian musician who defects in Bloomingdale's)," Winter said. "Louie is going, 'Try this, try this,' and Frantisek is saying, 'Maybe only need two shirts and a pair of pants now; I get rest when winter comes.' His parents taught him well. He buys only what he needs."

There was the first time Musil tried to throw a football. He is an athlete who has achieved everything he has ever wanted—he won a spot on the Czech junior national team and then the national team; he played in the Canada Cup and the World Championships and then became a world champion when the Czech team won the 1985 tournament. His results went right off the scales when he was tested by the North Stars last week for oxygen consumption and cardiovascular endurance.

There was the time Musil flew to Detroit to visit his friend and former teammate, Petr Klima, who defected from Czechoslovakia in the summer of 1985 and joined the Red Wings. Musil stayed at Klima's huge house and saw the swimming pool and the fancy sports cars and played with Klima's three dogs. Then they took the Porsche and ran it out at a deserted race track.

"Petr, he likes to drive fast," Musil said. "I don't like to drive so fast. But we got on the track and, sitting in that deep chair, it was wonderful. On the outside, it looks dangerous. Inside, it looks not so dangerous. In that car, in that deep chair, you *must* drive fast. But do not tell Mr. Nanne that."

There was the first time Musil tried to drive himself to the Stars' training facility at Eden Prairie Community Center. It was the first day of pre-camp a week ago and Musil was scheduled to go on the ice with his group at 9. It was almost 9:30 before he showed up.

"I take the wrong way and end up on (Highway) 169," Musil said. "I didn't know where I was, so I stopped and asked a man. He make me a map and I find my way. I don't get lost the next time."

And then there was the time he went to the AC/DC concert at Met Center. Musil had been to a Kenny Rogers concert in Edmonton and met Rogers backstage, but that was a long way from AC/DC, a heavy-metal band that plays such teen anthems as "Highway to Hell" and "If You Want Blood (You Got It)."

"AC/DC very popular in Czech, so I want to see them," Musil said. "But it was too noisy, too crowded. I had earplugs in my ears and when I hear a good song that I know, I take them out. But only for half the song; then I put them back in. They don't have concerts like that in Czech."

Said Baribeau: "He couldn't believe it. He was, well, he wasn't scared, but he was shocked. He wrinkled his nose and said, 'What's that smell?' I said, 'Marijuana.' He just looks at me and says, 'AC/DC gets them crazy.' "

★   ★   ★

Musil has heard the story before. It goes like this: His countryman Jiri Poner came to the North Stars' training camp in 1984, and, as Musil did last week, shot to the top of all the conditioning tests. He was labeled Can't Miss by many observers, but couldn't adjust to the physical play in North America and spent his first season in the minors. The next year Poner came to camp and was below-average on most of the tests. The conclusion was that he was too Americanized. He had found too much junk food and he was too soft.

Musil shakes his head and says it won't happen to him. "I know I must be smart and not be too fat," he said. "I am watching my weight. I don't worry about that."

Winter also says he doesn't worry about luxury getting the better of Musil. "He is as mature as any client I've ever had," Winter said, "and he's only 21. You can't compare him with Poner because he has so much more playing experience. But this is something so different for him and he has handled it so well, much better than I would have done had you just thrown me into Czechoslovakia."

Overnight, Musil found that he could have just about anything he had ever wanted. He was whisked out of Yugoslavia to London, jumped on the Concorde to New York and was taken in a limousine crosstown to another plane that took him to Minnesota. Less than a week later he was in Edmonton, where Kenny Rogers, who also is famous in Czechoslovakia, rushed up and said he had seen Musil on television the night before.

"Kenny says, 'Wow, what a great story!' and Franisek is there going, 'Hello,' " Winter said. "I was worried that he was getting a distored picture of life here. I was worried he might be thinking that this happens all the time."

Winter's worries might have started to ease when he asked Musil how he planned on getting around the Twin Cities. Musil said he would take the bus, of course. Winter said he probably would need a car, but suggested he buy a used one. Musil agreed, until he met someone from the Cadillac dealership and worked out the deal to lease the Cimarron. Musil said he does not like big American cars, but he liked the Cimarron, the smallest in the Cadillac line, because it was more like Czech cars, only nicer. It is rumored around the North Stars dressing room that Musil is getting the car for little more than $100 a month.

"He did better on that car than I've ever done," Winter said.

Musil probably could afford a big house and fancy sports cars, like Klima, but he said he doesn't want a house, nor does he want to buy a car right now. Instead, he is paying room and board in the Edina home of a family of Czechoslovakian descent. He is expected to live there through his first NHL season. When asked if he planned to buy a stereo, he said he had a radio in his car. "Why do I need a stereo?"

"For him, a big investment is going out and buying a Walkman," Winter said. "We go shopping and he goes for good, solid buys: a couple pairs of pants, a few T-shirts. He didn't want to buy the Polo shirts because they were too expensive. I told him, 'You're paying for this little label here,' and he said, 'That's stupid,' which it is."

Musil has splurged on occasion. Such as the day he saw a Sears advertisement for Levi's, went out and bought $200 worth of jeans. Or the day he decided, without telling anyone, to fly to New York City for the weekend.

"Maybe everybody changes if they have a lot of money, but I want always to be like I was in Czech," Musil said. "I know that I must save for after hockey. I like America, but I always want to be Czech—be smart and save money."

★   ★   ★

The second phone call was much better. Musil picked up a phone in a Minnetonka ice rink and dialed the number overseas. He said,

'This is Franti,' and his mother didn't cry.

"He went nuts," Baribeau said. "He was talking 100 miles a minute in Czech. We were in an office and people were looking in to see what was going on. He was so happy. He was so excited because he felt his mother finally understood."

He had explained that he hadn't defected. He said he was only in America to play hockey. Winter is drafting a letter to the Czech Ice Hockey Federation, offering Musil's services, if possible, for world tournaments and the like.

"Czech very nice country, very beautiful," Musil said. "I had a very good life there. But I did everything I could in hockey there."

Musil said that because he doesn't know when or if he can ever return home, he hopes his parents will visit him here next summer.

"We walked through this Safeway (grocery) superstore in Edmonton and he said, 'Wow, wait 'till I show my mom this. She'll never believe it,' " Winter said.

The hard part may be over now for Frantisek Musil. He occupied himself for two months, when his mind probably wanted to wander and ask, "What am I doing here?" Now, all Musil has to do is play hockey.

"Frankie should fit right in," Stars Coach Lorne Henning said, using Musil's new American nickname. "His teammates already love him. Who can't love him? He's an upbeat type of guy; he's always kidding, always having fun. And all you have to do is watch him skate and watch him move to tell he has talent."

Said Baribeau: "You can tell he is so much more comfortable. Before, he was nervous about maybe ordering something the wrong way. Now, it's 'I'll have a bowl of soup, a bacon double-cheeseburger and a malt.' No problem. He doesn't have to worry about the off-ice stuff so much anymore. Now, all he's talking about is, 'I want to show them I am a good player.' "

Said Winter: "Ever since the day I met him, he has been on the straight and narrow. 'I want to play hockey. I am leaving. We are going. I'm not looking back.' He made the decision and he understands that decision."

Three Seconds

PRO FOOTBALL

By *Kevin Lamb*

From Sport Magazine
Copyright © 1986, Sport Magazine Associates

From the snap to the interception, the play took 3.1 seconds. Blitz plays don't take very long. That's the idea. "We were pouring in so fast," Bears defensive end Dan Hampton says, "he was just throwing the ball up for grabs."

Gary Hogeboom, the Cowboys' quarterback, threw the ball directly to Bears cornerback Mike Richardson. As he let it go, linebacker Otis Wilson clobbered him from the right. An instant later, Richard Dent tagged him from the left. The hard work was all done by the time Richardson returned the interception for a 36-yard touchdown.

That touchdown was the backbreaker. It gave the Bears a 17-0 lead on the way to their shocking 44-0 rout of the Cowboys last November. It was the most one-sided defeat Dallas had ever suffered. It was the 11th straight victory of the season for Chicago and seemed to slam the door on the rest of the NFL for 1985.

Like all plays this blitz had a history, a number of overlapping histories, in fact. Compressed into these three seconds were the circumstances of the series, the game and the season to this point; the history of recent Cowboys-Bears matchups; and within all of that, the personal stories of the key players involved.

Nearly a year later, the outcome of this play makes it a good one to dissect, to see the anatomy of every play. It's a chance to examine the decisions football players must make faster than most people can decide to call for a decision-making conference.

The blitz didn't go the way the Bears had planned it. They left Hogeboom with an escape route. A linebacker never came close to the receiver he was supposed to cover. Richardson didn't bump his man at the line of scrimmage, like the playbook said he should. Even the alignment, a 3-4 with Dent at right outside linebacker, was one the Bears seldom used or practiced. A good blitz can cover up a lot of mistakes.

But these missed assignments were not mistakes. They were choices. They were reactions to a play that had hurt the Bears repeatedly in Dallas' victory a year earlier. They were reactions to events that took place as suddenly as a car accident.

"The blitz caused all the problems," says flanker Mike Renfro, the intended receiver on the play. "The pressure made him throw in a hurry and the blitz created confusion. But the bottom line is, the Bears executed very well."

They made the right decisions. That doesn't happen often. Players on both teams had to make dozens of decisions. "And all this is happening, mind you, in two or three seconds," Cowboy halfback Tony Dorsett says. There were barely two seconds before Hogeboom unloaded the ball. "You're thinking on the move," Dorsett says. "It's like they say when you're dying, your whole life passes in front of you. It's that fast. You're reading and digesting all this and making decisions."

★　　★　　★

THE SITUATION

Hogeboom had entered the game only one offensive play earlier, after Wilson laid out Danny White on another blitz. The Bears had just punted and Dallas had a first down on its own 30, trailing 10-0 with 5:49 left in the first half.

The game was closer than the score in one sense. The Bears had only four first downs. Their defense had scored their lone touchdown. But the Bears were beyond reach in the sense that the Cowboys' running game was already on cement blocks. Their last nine plays had been passes. This one probably would be, too.

Most defensive coaches are wary of blitzing in the other team's territory. Blitzes foster big plays, one way or the other, and the Cowboys had room for 70-yards worth of fireworks. But under defensive coordinator Buddy Ryan, now the Eagles' head coach, the Bears blitzed from anywhere. And from any formation. With Hogeboom still getting his game legs under him, it was a good time to dust off the old 3-4. Give next week's opponents something else to practice for.

The blitz was a relatively safe one. The Bears called it SAM-WILL BLITZ, SINGLE FREE. That meant both outside linebackers rushed, five men in all. Everyone else had single coverage except the free safety, who guarded the deep middle. It wasn't the all-out 59 BLITZ, a seven-man rush from the 46 defense that worked so well for Chicago in the Super Bowl. Under new defensive coordinator Vince Tobin the Bears are apt to use SAM-WILL much more this season.

The Cowboys' play was called 16 WING ZOOM. Renfro, the wing, ran a zoom pattern, going six yards upfield before crossing to the opposite sideline. He was to cross slightly higher than parallel to the line of scrimmage, but not as high as a post pattern, where he would angle toward the goal post.

Renfro lined up near the right sideline and ran in motion toward the ball. The tight end and fullback were on his side, too. They were key players. They would get in the way of Renfro's defender, Richardson, while they ran routes toward the right sideline.

"In '84, I bet I got 60 yards out of that play," Renfro says. Seventy-two, to be exact. On four catches. The Bears remembered it well. Richardson and middle linebacker Mike Singletary had talked about it the night before. They were waiting for it.

★   ★   ★

THE FIRST DOMINO

Everything started with Hampton's pass rush. He was at left end, nose-to-nose with right tackle Jim Cooper. The standard blocking against a SAM-WILL BLITZ is for the tackles to block the defensive ends and for the guards to pull out and cut off the linebackers. Five on five. "With a quick pass play," says Renfro, "your backs usually don't need to stay back."

On the Bears' right side, the guard, Glen Titensor, caught a piece of Dent and slowed him down. But on their left side, guard Kurt Petersen couldn't get to Wilson. Hampton didn't let him. Hampton's first step was smack into Petersen.

"A lot of times on a blitz," Hampton says, "we try to get their offensive linemen to double-team us. If we force a double-team, then the blitzer comes free.

"You do that a lot on stunts, too. You'll give yourself up. You collapse inside a hole and you hook the offensive lineman with your arm and hold him so the guy he's blocking can come free."

Petersen couldn't leave Hampton, or Hogeboom would have been dropped in his backpedal. Wilson had farther to go. At least Hogeboom would have an extra half-second before Wilson could knock on his helmet.

But no longer. Hampton not only tied up Wilson's blocker, he also collapsed the pocket. Hogeboom couldn't step up inside. That's important on an outside blitz. If there isn't a strong inside rush to go with an outside blitz, Singletary says, "The quarterback can step up just one step and the guy from the outside can't reach him." Wilson would have been running too fast to change direction.

Hampton's inside charge might have left Hogeboom an out. He could have circled back toward Hampton's sideline. He would have had plenty of time then; he may even have made a long gain. But he would have had to notice the opening. He would have had to look there first. The play wasn't a rollout and Hogeboom's not a scrambler. The inside charge was no more than a mild risk.

"On a blitz, we try to force the pocket right back into the quarterback's lap," Hampton says. "What that does is he starts looking at the line to see if anyone's running free. He takes his eye off the receiver and the DBs. A lot of times he throws an interception."

Hampton knew he was tying up Wilson's blocker. He had seen

the Cowboys' blocking schemes on film. But he couldn't have been sure that Hogeboom would stay put, or that the offensive tackle wouldn't switch over to Wilson. It is often hard to distinguish fortune from design.

★   ★   ★

THE BLITZER

With Petersen out of the way, Wilson was a bomber underneath enemy radar. He was going to get to Hogeboom. The only question was, would Hogeboom still have the ball?

Most blitzes aren't this easy. On most blitzes, the blitzer has to beat a blocker. On a lot of them, he doesn't even know he's blitzing until after the snap. For Wilson, sometimes it depends on whether the tight end starts his pass route inside or outside. Sometimes it depends on a running back. It's his man to cover, but if the back doesn't go out into the pattern, it's his man to beat to the quarterback.

"Either you just run it through him or you take a side, inside or outside," says Wilson, who prefers the outside. "You just get out of his way and get to the quarterback in the same process. That's when you have to use your skill. You keep him off balance. Like a wide receiver faking."

The finesse approach gives Dorsett more trouble, even though he's small for a blocking back. "A lot of guys want to be bullies, try to overpower you," Dorsett says. "I don't mind that. If they're going to come right at you, you just cut 'em."

Chop their legs out from under them.

Wilson had no such trouble this time. Renfro was the only player in his way, right at the snap. "I jumped over him," Wilson says, exaggerating, "and went on through." The QB Express. But when he got there, the ball was gone.

★   ★   ★

THE OUTLET

A back's decisions are all prescribed in the playbook. In this situation, do this. In that, do that. The tough part is telling this situation from that. Dorsett has to check both linebackers on his side. Four different situations. Maybe four different responses, considering whom to block and which pass route to run. "And a lot of times, they'll disguise what they're doing," Dorsett says.

He's reacting to the defense. Usually, it's the other way around. A blitz puts a defense on the offensive. Now the back has to wait for the linebackers' moves. Who's coming? Do I have to stay back? If I do, should I screw in for a head-on charge or stay on my toes for a feint? All things considered, Dorsett would rather go out. Most linebackers outweigh him by 40 or 50 pounds. They come at full speed. "It's not fair," he says.

A lot of times, a running back can nullify the pass rush more by going out than by staying back to block. First, if he goes out, he may take a blitzer with him. Second, he becomes an outlet, a quick and easy target for unloading the ball.

That's why both backs went out on this play. The Cowboys knew the Bears would send extra blitzers for every back who blocked. Dallas liked five-on-five better than six-on-six. Besides, the backs gave Hogeboom a chance for a safe pass. While Wilson and Dent were closing in on Hogeboom like alligator jaws, Dorsett was curling from the backfield toward Hogeboom's left sideline, two yards upfield. Timmy Newsome, the fullback, ran the same route to the other side.

Hogeboom never found them. He probably didn't think he had to bother checking out the backs. After all, his primary receiver was running a quick route.

★   ★   ★

THE RECEIVER

Maybe the Cowboys would have been better off if the call in the huddle had been a longer-developing pass play. Then Hogeboom might have looked for a receiver besides Renfro. Or Renfro might have changed his route to something even quicker than the zoom.

In this case, it would have been a quick post. That's not only a fast route, but a short throw for the quarterback. Renfro would have run three steps upfield instead of six, but he would have cut across at a deeper angle. He would have wound up in about the same place. It would have saved a step, maybe a step and a half.

"When you have a very short pattern already called and you see a blitz," Renfro says, "you have to decide, 'Do I run the quick post or stay on this same pattern that takes about the same amount of time?' " With Hogeboom new in the game, Renfro figured it was best not to muddy the issue. He stayed on the zoom.

The first thing Renfro had to determine was whether it really was a blitz. That looks easy enough from the 50-yard line. If five or more men rush, it's a blitz, right? But they aren't always blitzing just because they barge across the line. "Sometimes the linebacker comes running up, but all he's doing is pressuring the guy he's covering," Renfro says. "To us as wide receivers, it looks like a blitz. He may be just taking two or three steps forward, but that's all the time we have to look at, two or three steps."

The receiver can't wait around to see where the linebacker's going. He can't turn around and watch him. He can't ask him. He does have an idea from the defense's formation. He knows the other team's tendency at that down and distance. But if he guesses wrong, the quarterback will look bad. The receiver may be running a quick post because he saw that linebacker charging, but the quarterback saw the linebacker pull up with the fullback, so he throws the deep square-in he called in the huddle.

★   ★   ★

ANTICIPATION

Richardson had Renfro's route pegged two steps after the ball was snapped. When he followed Renfro in motion, he narrowed the possibilities to two. The Cowboys might still have sent Renfro back to the sideline from that formation. He hadn't quite reached the tight end at the snap. But when Renfro went behind both the fullback and the tight end, Richardson knew it was the zoom. He knew he would have to fight traffic to beat Renfro to the middle of the field.

"He uses the tight end as a shield," Richardson says. "The tight end releases straight up the field and tries to block me off. So when I saw the receiver was trying to get inside, I went where he was trying to run."

He circled back quickly, so he would cross tight end Doug Cosbie's path near the left hashmarks before Cosbie got there. Now the congestion around the hashmarks worked to Richardson's advantage. Renfro couldn't get open until after he cut inside.

Usually, it's important on a blitz for the cornerback to bump his man at the line of scrimmage. Slow him down. Make him take 2.5 seconds to run his route instead of 2. Then if the rush men force a pass in 2 seconds instead of 2.5, something good should happen.

Richardson didn't bump Renfro. That looked especially risky because he had started the play close to the line, in bump-and-run position. If Renfro had changed his route to a fade, sprinting downfield under the ball, he could have blown right by Richardson. But Richardson knew Renfro was going inside. He couldn't bump Renfro and beat him inside both. The other cardinal rule for corners on blitzes is to take away the receiver's inside. That's the short throw the quarterback looks for.

"Mike did a good job of recognizing what has happening," says Jim LaRue, the defensive backfield coach and the Bears' only assistant returning from Ryan's staff. "That's about as good a job as you can do in single coverage with that much traffic. He had to go underneath or over the top. Against a wide receiver, you better go over the top or you're going to be trailing him."

★   ★   ★

THE CONVERSATION

Mike Singletary had thought about that zoom play all week. Saturday night at the hotel, he talked about it with Richardson. They had the same problem on the play. Singletary, the middle linebacker, had to fight through traffic to follow the tight end outside. Singletary told Richardson, "Instead of you trying to run with the receiver all the way across the field and me trying to run with the tight end out there, let's just switch up."

The Bear linebackers are all proud of their speed. Singletary and Wilson begged Ryan to let them run with wide receivers. On a short route against a slower wideout, Singletary says now, "I felt I could get a hit on him and run with him. It worked out perfectly."

"We talked about switching," Richardson says. "But usually in man-to-man, the corner tries to stay with the wide receiver. So I just stayed with the wideout."

Huh? But Singletary switched. He covered the wideout, too.

"I guess the tight end wasn't covered then," Richardson says matter-of-factly.

He wasn't. But it didn't matter. Cosbie's job on the play was not to get open, not quickly anyway. His first responsibility was to get in Richardson's way. It's technically called a clearing route. All teams have them, although it is difficult to tell clearing apart from basketball-style picking, which is illegal.

Cosbie ran about six yards straight upfield before angling toward the sideline. He wound up 12 yards deep on the field numbers, wide open. If Hogeboom had had time, Cosbie could have gained 20 yards before free safety Gary Fencik caught up with him from the deep middle. But if Hogeboom had had time, he could have done a lot of things better.

★   ★   ★

PAYDIRT

Renfro was confounded by a coverage pattern he had never seen before. Of course he hadn't. The Bears hadn't seen it, either. They hadn't even drawn it up in the dirt. It just happened. And as a result the only receiver who could hurt them was double-teamed. With Singletary in his way, Renfro says, "I had to slow down."

"He tried to adjust to the guy covering him," says Dick Nolan, the Cowboys' receivers coach last year. "He was trying to find an open spot. He didn't know Gary was in trouble."

"The receiver adjusted and the quarterback didn't," Richardson says.

"He threw the ball where he thought the receiver was going to be," Singletary says. "But he wasn't there. Mike Richardson was there. He threw it right to Mike."

The ball was in the air before Renfro even made his cut. He turned inside at the 36-yard line, on the defense's left hashmark. Singletary was two yards upfield, facing him. Richardson was across from them on the right hash, straight upfield from Hogeboom.

"It's unusual for me to be looking at the quarterback that late in the pass route," Richardson says. But Renfro wasn't closing in on him. And how about this? The ball was. All Richardson had to do was catch it.

"It was about six guys to one after he caught the ball," Singletary says. Dorsett, the only Cowboy ahead of Richardson to his right, never had a chance. The touchdown was so anticlimactic, Richardson raised the ball over his head at the 15-yard line to celebrate his first NFL score.

"We'd worked on that play all week," LaRue of the Bears says. "We didn't work on it against this particular defense, but we'd seen the pattern enough. Mike recognized it. It doesn't matter what defense you're in if you recognize the play and pressure the quarterback. Sometimes things just work out right."

Belated MVP

GENERAL

By *Randy Giancaterino*

From the South Philadelphia Review
Copyright © 1986, Review-Chronicle Inc.

Life's good friends are hard to find and now one of mine is dead and things I should have said . . .

—songwriter **James Taylor**

The holiday season wasn't a time for dying, Ben Simpson thought at the time. And Ben didn't care much for ceremonies. That's why he never attended Stevie's funeral. But last year he took a cab to Holy Prayer Cemetery as he did today to visit a lonely corner of the graveyard, where Stevie is buried.

With one hand shoved deep in the pocket of his jeans and the other awkwardly clutching a paper bag, Ben stared down the headstone that was inscribed, "Steven 'Sticks' Antigone: 1961-84." He read it, moving his lips as a priest does when reciting prayers.

Ben often wondered whose idea it was to put Stevie's nickname on the headstone. Ben gave him that name one day after Stevie cut four of his mother's mops to play stickball.

It began to snow. White flakes flickered down and melted against Ben's jacket. But the chilling weather meant little today; it was December 11, two years since Stevie died.

Ben remembered Stevie when both were growing up together playing sandlot sports. Ben always threw harder and hit farther than Stevie. But Stevie, a wiry, almost frail kid, was so damn competitive with Ben that his lack of talent was no barrier. It seemed to bring out the best in him.

They played baseball in the Pat Lani League when sports caps were adjustable and uniforms were flannel. Stevie, with his chalky face and curly brown hair, always squeezed into his cap, making a crease in his forehead. He said a tight cap made him more intense. Pride, though, is what set Stevie apart.

In 1975, when Ben won the league's most valuable player trophy, beating Stevie in the coaches' voting by one point, Stevie was furious. Especially when Ben's mother displayed the award in the window of their home. One day, Ben saw Stevie standing below the Simpson's window, staring at the trophy. Tears had gathered thickly in Stevie's eyes. When Stevie saw Ben walking down the street toward him, he ran off.

They didn't speak to each other for nearly a year. The two didn't renew their relationship until that day when Stevie broke up those mops. Ben pursued a job, while Stevie took refuge in the wrong places. He somehow found more highs in the corner bar than he had on the playing field.

His penchant for reckless friends and a good night's drinking consumed him. It finally ended one desperate night in his bedroom when he pressed a revolver to his skull and squeezed the trigger.

For this confused kid, suicide seemed to be the answer. But for his survivors, only questions remain. Did he realize the void it would leave in his own family, the restless nights? His brother was to marry in two months and Stevie was to have been best man. Wasn't that worth living for? Why did he have to pass so passionately into the other world? Maybe Stevie's failure to find the right outlets for his competitive spirit killed him. Nevertheless, for sure the only certainty in life is uncertainty.

Stevie's life was short but his memory lingers. To Ben, though, Stevie was a true innocent, a child in a man's body.

The wind kicked up as Ben watched the flurries fade into the ground; the cold air crept into the sleeves of his jacket. Holding the bag, he knelt and removed a dusty trophy from the bag, and then gently leaned it against the white stone. The marble on the award was chipped.

Tears snaked down his cheeks. Ben looked up and peered hard at the snow as it fell faster on the crooked crosses, headstones and on the tops of the gate nearby, where a cab driver waited.

"C'mon, the meter's running, buddy," the man said curtly. "I got fares to make before I go to sleep." Ben started toward the narrow gate into a gray world, where his friend tried so hard. He would have won too, Ben thought.

He just ran out of time.

The Revolution Started With the Shot He Fired

BASKETBALL

By *Malcolm Moran*

From The New York Times
Copyright © 1986, The New York Times Company
Reprinted by Permission

Beyond his 70th birthday, the man appears taller and sturdier—if a little grayer—than the one in the pictures that were taken in his youth. Fifty years removed from the basketball revolution he began as a junior at Stanford University, Hank Luisetti was talking about the consistency of his game.

"Basketball has not changed," he said. "The plays haven't changed. Attacking a zone defense in college is the same. Man-for-man, that's always been the same. Nobody's come up with some sure-fire idea. The fundamentals in basketball are still the same. The only change is the jumping. And better shooters."

Luisetti had overlooked one of the most significant developments in the evolution of the game, of any game: his resourceful means of putting a ball into the basket. He did not modernize basketball single-handedly, just one-handedly. Fifty years ago tonight, long before athletic reputations were made or broken by the presence of television cameras, Luisetti's performance on a New York stage forever altered the structure of the sport.

Years later, when he conducted clinics in the Bay Area, Luisetti discovered a result of his innovation. "When I grew up," he said, "we were taught dribbling, passing, fundamentals and footwork—running backwards on defense. The kids didn't want that. After the first couple of years, they all wanted to shoot. They're all shooters now."

Luisetti's simple one-handed push shot led, in recent years, to the graceful deception of Earl Monroe, the showmanship of Julius Erving, the long-range consistency of Larry Bird and the acrobatics of Michael Jordan.

The game took place at the end of an eventful year. The Berlin

Games had politicized the Olympics. Joe DiMaggio, who had grown up in the North Beach section of San Francisco, not far from where Luisetti was raised, had played his first season with the New York Yankees. In a little-publicized decision after a meeting held in New York on December 27, a special committee at the National Collegiate Athletic Association convention determined that colleges would be allowed to benefit from the sale of the radio rights to their games.

And on December 30, the Stanford Indians trotted onto the court of the old Madison Square Garden on Eighth Avenue between 49th and 50th Streets. Their opponent, Long Island University, had won its previous 43 games. In their 10 victories that season, the Blackbirds had won by an average of 28 points. Stanford had not confronted a mobile player as tall as Art Hillhouse, the 6-foot-8 LIU center, and the Indians had never experienced a game in a place as big as the old Garden.

As the crowd of 17,623 gathered, Art Stoefen, the Stanford center, looked up into the smoky haze made silver by the bright lights. The people were stacked on three levels, seemingly straight up to the roof. When the houselights dimmed, Stoefen saw dozens of tiny lights. "It was like fireflies," he remembered. "We thought, 'What were all the lights?' "

★   ★   ★

They were cigarettes being lit high above the court. "I'll never forget. Art Stoefen looked up and said, 'That's a lot of people,' " said Luisetti, the player the crowd had come to see. "We were just so amazed that people could watch a game from where they were."

The Indians had watched the LIU players during the warmup. They had seen the accepted form of the time—feet planted, heels together, two hands pushing the ball upward to the basket.

"It's easy to guard a man that does that," Luisetti remembered, "because he has to put his feet together. I learned that when I was a little kid. I was small, playing against high school kids. I was only in grammar school. The only way I could shoot was to throw the ball up with one hand. I couldn't shoot with two hands. They'd block it."

He was the only child of a dishwasher who eventually came to own an Italian restaurant in downtown San Francisco, on Market Street. Luisetti, a child of the Depression, was taught that basketball could provide a way to a college scholarship. He would regularly leave his family's home on Russian Hill, just above North Beach, and travel six blocks to the Spring Valley playground where he would play until lunch and again until dark.

Luisetti once high-jumped 6-6, but at the top of his leap to release his new shot, he was only three to four inches off the floor. No matter—defenders found it difficult to stop a shot released on the move. And if the shot failed, Luisetti's momentum often carried him forward, toward the ball and into rebounding position. The new approach was unorthodox, but the thought behind it was sound.

★   ★   ★

Against LIU, Luisetti began the game as a forward. He soon became a 6-foot-2 center, moving to the post and freeing Stoefen to the wing, where the taller Hillhouse would be lured outside into poor rebounding position.

Occasionally, Luisetti would move to guard, where he could use his ball handling and passing skills. Long before defensive plans were defined by complex terminology, the Indians played what they called a team defense, an aggressive zone that gave Luisetti the freedom to gamble.

He was guarded by Leo Merson, who used the accepted technique—placing a hand on the offensive player. "He always had a hand on me, really kind of holding," Luisetti said. "So you push it down. That's street basketball; you learn that in a hurry."

When Luisetti pushed too hard he was called for a foul by Pat Kennedy, the flamboyant official. Luisetti remembered: "So I said: Mr. Kennedy, may I ask you a question? He has a hand on me all the time. On offense, am I allowed to put a hand on him?' He said, 'What do you mean?' I said, 'Put my hand there so I can keep him off me.' He said, 'As long as you don't hold him, I guess it's all right. Nobody ever asked me that question.' "

Clair Bee, the legendary LIU coach, protested that Luisetti was holding, but Kennedy said he did not see a violation. Eventually, Bee would say, "I can't remember anybody who could do more things."

"The Coast sensation surpassed everything that had been said about him," *The New York Times* reported the morning after. ". . . It seemed that Luisetti could do nothing wrong. Some of his shots would have been deemed foolhardy if attempted by any other player, but with Luisetti doing the heaving, these were accepted by the crowd as a matter of course."

★   ★   ★

The coaches were unconvinced. "That's not basketball," said Nat Holman of City College. "If my boys ever shot one-handed, I'd quit coaching."

Five years later, Joe Lapchick of St. John's said, "I can't be persuaded that two hands on the ball doesn't make far superior shot control and a greater percentage of hits."

But the inevitable had happened. As Stanford built a 22-14 halftime lead, Stoefen felt the New York crowd beginning to appreciate the Indians. Near the end of the 45-31 Stanford victory, when Luisetti left the game with 15 points, the spectators stood and cheered.

In an era when teams often plodded along, slowed by a center jump after each goal, Luisetti passed and handled the ball behind his back. A decade before the emergence of Bob Cousy, Luisetti was making judgments to pass or shoot while in mid-air. More than four decades before Earvin Johnson's creative versatility helped Michigan State win an NCAA championship one season and the Los Angeles Lakers win the National Basketball Association playoffs the following season, Luisetti played three positions on one historic night.

He was the college Player of the Year in 1937 and 1938, as Stanford won 46 of 51 games. Fifteen years after his career ended, he finished second to George Mikan in a poll for the best player of the first half-century. The year after Luisetti's senior season, an Oregon team that Stanford had beaten twice won the first NCAA tournament.

Luisetti never played in the tournament and he never played as a professional. He joined the Navy, developed spinal meningitis and after his recovery turned down a $10,000 offer to play in Chicago.

He became a regional president of a travel firm until his retirement four and a half years ago. He has occasionally gone to shoot with his grandson, Tommy. When he went beyond the foul line, Luisetti shot with two hands. "The brain is there," he said, "but the body isn't there."

On February 22, a statue by Phil Zonne, a substitute guard on the 1937 team, will be dedicated on the Stanford campus. Nearly all the old posed pictures show Luisetti in a defensive stance, but the statue captures him as history does, with his right arm extended and a ball leaving the tips of the index, middle and ring fingers of his right hand.

Just as it did 50 years ago tonight. "At the end of the game, Pat Kennedy came up to me," Luisetti remembered, "and he said, 'Are you lucky?' I said, 'What do you mean?'

"He said, 'Well, you shoot the one-hand shot.' I said, 'That's the only thing I know how to shoot.'"

LeMond Packs Up Tour de France

CYCLING

By *Randy Harvey*

From the Los Angeles Times
Copyright © 1986, Los Angeles Times

With the Arc de Triomphe at his back and the end of the rainbow ahead of him, Greg LeMond coasted across the finish line Sunday, more relieved than elated to have become the first American to win the 83-year-old Tour de France.

His victory was all but assured before the 23rd and final day of the 2,543-mile bicycle race began. LeMond, who is from Reno, Nev., was 44th in a pack of 132 survivors to ride under the yellow-and-white "Arrivee" sign at the end of one of the world's most famous boulevards, the Champs Elysees.

But with his three-minute, 10-second lead in the overall standings over runner-up Bernard Hinault intact, LeMond, 25, was immediately mobbed by photographers and tour officials, one of whom had the responsibility of handing the winner a Coca-Cola.

Oh, to be an American in Paris.

An estimated crowd of 200,000 was lined 10-deep along the Champs Elysees, many of whom arrived early Sunday morning even though the cyclists were not due to arrive until 4:30 p.m. The crowd was reserved in the reception for LeMond.

That was not so much because he is an American but because he conquered the French hero, Hinault, a five-time winner of the Tour de France. His finish, in contrast to LeMond's, was greeted with a tremendous ovation and gushing banners, one which read: "Bernard, France still belongs to you."

But not the Tour de France. Hinault, who will be 32 in November, has announced he will retire at the end of the year, although virtually no one believes him. But in what he proclaimed would be his last Tour de France, his French fans wanted him to become the first six-time winner. Jacques Anquetil and Eddy Merckx also won five before they retired.

It was not to be, but no one will ever convince LeMond that Hinault did not attempt to deliver. He contended until Friday and finished a close second, well-ahead of third-place Urs Zimmermann of Switzerland and fourth-place Andrew Hampsten, another American who, like LeMond and Hinault, rides for the La Vie Claire team. Hampsten is from North Dakota.

Longtime observers said this was one of the most dramatic of the 73 races, which have been run annually since 1903 except for years when interrupted by world wars.

It certainly was one of the most treacherous. Of the 210 cyclists who started on July 4, 78 were swept up by the broom truck, which each day collected riders who could not continue.

One of them was France's two-time champion, Laurent Fignon, who limped down the Champs Elysees Sunday as the crowd cheered and blew him kisses.

Even in defeat, the temperamental Hinault was the focus of the world's most prestigious bicycle race.

His pursuit was the source of tension between him and LeMond, who sacrificed his chance for victory in 1985 so that the Frenchman could win and expected the favor returned this year. On the victory stand last year, Hinault promised no less.

On this victory stand Sunday, there was no such camaraderie.

Hinault, the first cyclist on the podium, ignored LeMond when he joined him. It was not until LeMond leaned over and kissed Hinault on the cheek that he shook the American's hand.

Later, when Zimmermann joined them, he raised LeMond's left hand and tried to coax Hinault into taking his teammate's other hand. Instead, the Frenchman sat down, apparently bored with the ceremony.

From the victory stand, LeMond said: "Wonderful, it feels just wonderful. I was nervous, but everything went perfectly today. To win, you've got to be one of the great champions."

Afterward, LeMond was rushed to City Hall, where he was toasted by Jacques Chirac, the mayor of Paris and the prime minister of France, but the American told family and friends that he was in no mood to celebrate.

"It hasn't sunk in yet," said Ron Stanko, LeMond's Philadelphia attorney. "He said he felt like a load had been lifted from his shoulders. There was a lot of pressure, so much to overcome."

Stanko said that even though LeMond is in the second year of a four-year contract with La Vie Claire, he probably will exercise his option to resign from the team at the end of 1986 and wants to form his own team, ideally with a U.S. sponsor. The United States had its first entry this year, the 7-Eleven team, but it finished far behind the leaders.

With the 10-man La Vie Claire team divided into Hinault and

LeMond supporters, with the team's manager publicly pronouncing his preference for Hinault, and with Hinault fans taunting LeMond on the road to Paris, the American worried until the final three days of the race that the victory would be stolen from him.

"I'm very paranoid, I tell you," he told CBS last Thursday. "I've had some sleepless nights. I'm afraid someone will push me off my bike. I'm afraid someone will poison my food. I just hope everything goes all right Sunday."

The final leg began 158 miles from Paris in Cosne Cours Loire, a farming village that was the vacation home of King Louis XIV's mistress.

LeMond's mother said last week that La Vie Claire might give him a rotten bicycle. It was intended as a joke, but LeMond had to wonder when his brakes locked early Sunday.

After a momentary delay, LeMond received a replacement and proceeded without further difficulty, riding conservatively to avoid a disabling accident, the only occurrence that could have prevented his victory.

That was not LeMond's first difficulty with his bicycles. Huffy, the Dayton, Ohio, company that supplies him, sent him four new bicycles two months ago, but they never arrived. LeMond used his only Huffy for the first three weeks of the tour but had to discard it last week and began using a French brand that was unfamiliar to him.

When a reporter jokingly suggested that LeMond's missing bicycles might be victims of sabotage, a Huffy spokesman said: "Don't laugh. We've been checking that out."

Italy's Guido Bontempi finished first Sunday in 6 hours 51 minutes 55 seconds. The other finishers crossed the line in a pack and, as customary on the final day, were given the same time as the leader. LeMond's composite time was 110 hours, 35 minutes and 19 seconds.

"Greg told me when he was 16 that he wanted to win the Olympics, the World Championships and the Tour de France," said LeMond's father, Bob, a Reno businessman. "He's been living with this dream for a long time."

LeMond's father was overwhelmed by his son's achievement.

"With Greg being the first English-speaking winner, I think the sport's going to explode in the United States," he said. "I think it's going to become bigger than running."

LeMond was unable to compete in the 1980 Olympics because of the boycott but won the World Championships in 1983. He was third in his first Tour de France two years ago and finished second last year before winning Sunday, a remarkable progression for someone who was not raised on the sport.

LeMond's ambition initially was to become an acrobatic skier. Even though his father was an amateur cyclist and still rides in senior events, LeMond did not become interested in the sport until a ski instructor told him it would help him build up his muscles for the slopes. LeMond was 14.

Two years later, disillusioned with skiing because of a drought that left Reno with no snow in the winter and inspired by the cycling movie "Breaking Away," LeMond began racing competitively.

He was a natural, becoming, at 19, the youngest captain of a U.S. cycling team for the 1980 Olympics. But when the United States boycotted, LeMond turned professional and moved to Europe. He now lives for eight months of the year in Kortrijk, Belgium, and spends the other four months in Sacramento.

After LeMond's third-place finish in the 1984 Tour de France while riding for the Renault team, Hinault encouraged La Vie Claire's financial backer, Bernard Tapie, to buy out LeMond's contract.

Whether he now regrets his support for LeMond, only Hinault knows. As precocious a newcomer as the sport has ever seen, LeMond would have won the Tour de France last year if La Vie Claire's team manager, Maurice Le Guilloux, had not insisted that the American, who was in the lead through half the race, allow Hinault to catch him. Hinault was the victim of an earlier accident, which had left him shaken and bloodied.

While LeMond tried to grin and bear it, Hinault expressed his gratitude, pledging that he would ensure that 1986 was LeMond's year.

It is a matter of interpretation whether Hinault kept his promise.

There is no question that after LeMond earned the yellow jersey, traditionally worn by the overall leader, last Sunday, Hinault spared his teammate a certain amount of strain the next day by leading him through the Alps. The leader takes the brunt of the wind, creating a drag effect for the man behind him.

But the truce lasted only 24 hours, after which Hinault said LeMond was on his own.

"He made promises to me he never intended to keep," LeMond told the *International Herald Tribune*. "He made them just to relieve the pressure on himself. I'm positive, 100 percent sure of it. I have kind of bitter feelings about him."

Hinault told reporters he wanted to keep LeMond off balance in order to make the American a better competitor. LeMond has been accused by other cyclists of lacking a champion's heart.

"I've pushed him as hard as I can and spared him nothing, not words, not action," Hinault said.

"If he didn't buckle, that means he is a champion and deserves to win the race. Next year, maybe he'll have to fight off another opponent who will make life miserable for him. He'll know how to fight back now."

Hinault's gesture in the Alps, however, was all the French press needed to declare their favorite son the true champion.

"Everyone knows Hinault is the moral winner despite Greg LeMond wearing the yellow jersey," the Paris newspaper, *Le Journal du Dimanche,* told its readers Sunday.

But it was LeMond who rode away with $25,000, the deed to a resort apartment worth $17,270, a porcelain vase, a diamond-studded trophy valued at $46,153, and his place secure in cycling history.

Tension Personified

by Steven Wayne Rotsch of the Associated Press. The five expressions leave no doubt that the Shady Spring High School girls basketball team was involved in a tense struggle late in the West Virginia Class 2-A state high school championship game. Copyright © 1986, Steven Wayne Rotsch.

Full Cycle

by Bernard Brault of La Presse newspaper. Just the right angle and some scenic surroundings were enough for this photographer to create an interesting picture during competition in a cross country race on the Mount-Royal in Montreal. Copyright © 1986, Bernard Brault, La Presse.

Cosell Leaves 'Em Fascinated

PRO FOOTBALL

By *Stan Isaacs*

From Newsday
Copyright © 1986, Newsday

Some of the most famous trials in 20th century American history have been argued in the courtrooms above those long steps leading down to Foley Square. And on Wednesday, Howard Cosell, ex-lawyer, would-be senator, incomparable sportsvoice and cub sportswriter, gave a virtuoso performance that hinted what a loss it may have been to American jurisprudence that he chose to pursue glory in the bubble-gum world of sports rather than in the halls of justice.

Harvey Myerson, the lawyer who had called Cosell to the stand as a star witness for the United States Football League, said: "He was all that I would have wanted him to be. I also found him very entertaining."

A New Jersey Generals official said, "I wouldn't have missed this for the world."

Al Davis, the owner of the Los Angeles *nee* Oakland Raiders, said: "You get different reactions from different people. He's my friend, so I react to him accordingly. He's brilliant."

A National Football League owner said, "I kept thinking that we were hearing a man giving a terrific imitation of Howard Cosell."

Cosell was, all at once, witness, prosecuting attorney, defense attorney and even the judge (he referred to Judge Peter Leisure as "my honor" at one point).

He rode high, playing that imitable baritone voice like an instrument, speaking softly, loudly. He shouted when pressed, he postured, he lectured, he played the teacher, the clown. For a man who has faded from the limelight he once reveled in when working great sporting events, it was something of a last guffaw.

"For a time I thought I was becoming the chief eulogist of the

NFL," he said of his many eulogies for deceased NFL figures. Laughter.

Reciting his early career on television, he said: "I was supposed to be a six-week replacement for Kukla, Fran & Ollie. But I lasted longer than Kukla, Fran & Ollie." Laughter.

After one of his colorful digressions showing off his phenomenal memory, he said with a broad grin, "That is irrelevant, but it is colorful." Laughter. He called New England Patriots official Charles Sullivan "Chuckeroo." More laughter.

And when defense lawyer Frank Rothman asked him if he understood a question, Cosell answered, "If you ask a question I don't understand, you will have the biggest story of the century."

Alas, poor Rothman. Cosell soared with flights of fancy as if he were in front of his microphone. He ridiculed Rothman. He painted himself as the white knight of sports journalism, recited in lush detail a litany of his many awards, and declared anew that the great trinity of American television consisted of himself for sports, Johnny Carson for entertainment and Walter Cronkite for news.

Cosell pictured himself as a patriot defending the American public against the evil forces in sport. He looked purposefully at the jury and said he dealt in "issues related to each and every point of your lives, like the Constitution, things like eminent domain." In one of his monologues detailing a slice of recent sports history, he mentioned "the years of inflation curtailed by the Reagan administration."

He went on and on in exaggerated detail almost unchecked by Rothman or Leisure. The judge has logged so much time listening to dreary legal nitpicking in his court that he wasn't about to muzzle a man providing entertainment that a Broadway show costing $40 couldn't equal. At the end he told Cosell: "Thank you very much. We enjoyed having you with us."

Trumpeting his own virtue, Cosell defined his journalistic credo to "tell the truth" and "not take sides." Here was exquisite irony, because the underlying thrust of Cosell's testimony was of a man who has boldly taken the side of the USFL, which appropriately had called him as its star witness.

He has for some time had a vendetta with the NFL. His rancor eventually distorted the high journalistic purpose of his show "SportsBeat" and hastened its demise. In his fall from grace at ABC, he lashes out against his former bosses now and sees NFL conspiracy at every turn.

Rothman tried to exploit Cosell's partisanship toward the USFL. When he approached sensitive territory, Cosell's voice rose into a semi-bellow as he ridiculed the questions. When the lawyers shouted less vehemently earlier in the trial, the judge had asked for some decorum; here he let the courtroom shake with Cosell's thunder.

In the midst of it, one might have conjured up the long ago when Sen. Joe McCarthy rode roughshod as the dominant figure in an adversarial hearing against a client of lawyer Joseph Welch. McCarthy played the patriot, the defender of the republic, until he overreached himself and the gentle Welch delivered a reproach that echoed across the land and started McCarthy's downfall.

It seemed in this courtroom, as Rothman forsook objections, allowing Cosell to dominate, that he was playing the low-key Welch to Cosell's bombast. When Rothman asked if he was making himself clear and Cosell said, "So far you have an expressive lucidity," he let it pass. Once he told Cosell, "I'm not as smart as you." Cosell said, "You learned that a long time ago."

Years ago, Rothman defended Cosell in a case in which Philadelphia columnist Stan Hochman sued Cosell for assault. He had been tough, getting the case dismissed in pretrial hearings. Now he spoke haltingly, fumbling in his attempts to show that Cosell's closeness to Donald Trump makes him the unofficial backscratcher to the USFL.

Cosell seemed vulnerable when he said ABC forced his appearance before Congress because of NFL pressure. He had testified in favor of a bill the NFL did not want, so the argument that he was sent there by ABC to appease the NFL seemed fallacious and ridiculous.

Between Rothman's hesitancy and Cosell's bluster when trapped, however, it is questionable whether the jury of five women and a man, none of them particularly knowledgeable about football, grasped Cosell's inconsistency. It is just as questionable that the jury will take anything out of the courtroom other than the memory of having witnessed a consummate showman.

Afterward, as Rothman collected himself and his things, he was asked if it was a tactic to allow the famous witness to dominate the courtroom that way.

Rothman said, "What I wanted to do was to have the jury understand the kind of man he is."

"Did you succeed?"

"I don't know."

The Odd Couple

COLLEGE BASKETBALL

By *John Feinstein*

From The Sporting News Basketball Yearbook
Copyright © 1986, The Sporting News

At first glance, the name Alford is anything but a tongue twister. Nice and simple. Two syllables. But the Al is not what it seems to be. The name, if you ask, is Steve ALL-ford. Not AL-ford. The problem is the young man in question is much too polite to correct anyone who says the name wrong. Only when asked will he say, softly but firmly, "It's All-ford."

Bob Knight knows how to say the name. After all, he's known the kid for 12 years, known him since he first started coming to Knight's basketball camp at Indiana at the age of 9. And yet there still are moments when Knight opens his mouth and says, quite clearly and quite incorrectly, "AL-FORD!"

Often a torrent of words not nearly as polite as that one follows. It's almost as if Knight is subconsciously saying, "If you can't play defense like I want, then why should I be able to pronounce your damn name."

Knight has never said this—and never would—but this pronunciation lapse, coming from a man who prides himself on his ability to use the English language, almost seems a symbol of the tempestuous nature of this coach-player relationship.

Steve Alford represents everything Bob Knight has stood for in 21 years as a college basketball coach: He is a great competitor. He is tough. He is smart. He is a good basketball player, but a better person. He goes to class and to church. He is articulate and unfailingly polite. He is a hard worker. He *is* Indiana basketball as defined by its creator, Robert Montgomery Knight.

Someday, Knight may even tell Alford all these things. But not this year. From October 15 until he plays his last game for Indiana in March, Alford is going to hear that piercing voice again and again: "Al-FORD, can't you guard anybody?"

★   ★   ★

In the last three years, Alford has given Knight a lot to be proud of. He was a brilliant freshman, capping that season by earning a spot on Knight's Olympic Team, then playing superbly in Los Angeles. He was Indiana's leading scorer as a sophomore, averaging 18.1 points per game. And as a junior he was a consensus All-America, taking over the leadership role on a team that desperately needed it and keying Indiana's comeback 21-8 season.

And yet, no player in those three years has given Knight more grief than Alford. None of it intentional. Like all of Knight's players, Alford tries mightily to do everything his coach asks of him. But when you are gifted, Knight's demands are often extraordinary. If you are good, he wants you to be very good. If you are great, he wants you to be the best. If you are the best, he always thinks there is a way to get better.

It is that trait that draws a player like Alford to a coach like Knight, the knowledge that for four years you will always be pushed, that more will always be demanded, that you will never satisfy the coach. That way, you will always keep improving. And players like Alford always want to improve.

Of course, that is easy to say sitting in a comfortable restaurant during the off-season. When one is on the practice court, feeling bone-tired in the middle of a winter workout and your name is being screamed over and over again, it is not so easy to take.

And yet, Alford has taken all this for three years and, in spite of the pain he has felt—most of it emotional—he has achieved most of what he and Knight wanted him to achieve when he first came to Indiana. At 6-foot-2 and 170 pounds, he is never going to be big enough or quick enough to be a great defensive player. A lifelong shooter—he averaged 37.2 points as a high school senior—he is never going to be an instinctive passer. Quiet by nature, he will never be a natural leader.

But he has improved immensely in all three areas, largely because he has been pushed, cajoled, yelled at and insulted by Knight. One of the more vivid memories of a season spent with the Hoosiers comes from the first Purdue game. With Indiana trailing by two and less than two minutes left to play, Alford placed his frail body right in front of 6-9, 235-pound Melvin McCants and did something that Knight had sworn he would never do—he took a charge. Not just any charge, but a charge from a player 65 pounds heavier than him at a crucial moment. Indiana won by a point.

Knight could hardly ask for more. But he did and he will. And, in all likelihood, Alford will respond. Alford likes to joke that his father, Sam, who coached him in high school, has thrown him out of practice twice more lifetime than Knight. Don't bet on that record to hold up this season.

★   ★   ★

At first glance, the Knight-Alford relationship is one of the strangest in college basketball. The coach has always had to fight his temperament, whether dealing with his players, officials or the media. The player never seems out of control in any way, always calm on the court, always saying the right things to the press.

And yet, if one looks a little closer, Knight and Alford are alike in many ways—more ways than either one would probably care to admit.

Start with ability. Knight was never a natural as a player. He was a star in high school but never was able to overcome his defensive deficiencies at Ohio State. He was a good shooter, but because he got in foul trouble and was a step slow on defense, he always came off the bench for Fred Taylor's brilliant teams of the early 1960s.

Alford can do one thing better than almost anyone: Shoot the basketball. He is not quick, and that makes defense difficult for him. It is no coincidence that Knight harps on Alford's defensive troubles. He honestly believes—and has his own past to prove it—that to be a complete player, one must be able to, as he puts it, guard somebody.

Alford tries. In fact, he tries very hard. Just like Knight used to try very hard. Sometimes, he succeeds. One night last season during a scrimmage, Alford made three straight steals. Knight called him over.

"You been reading books on how to play defense?" he asked. It was almost a compliment.

Knight and Alford have one other thing in common, and more than anything else, it's probably what keeps them together: Competitiveness. Knight's aversion to losing is well documented. Alford's is not so noticeable because he does not wear his emotions on his sleeve the way Knight does. But as a competitor, he is just like his coach. He cannot stand to lose and that is why, in spite of his quiet nature, Knight turned to him last season and demanded that he become the team's leader. It was not just that Alford was Indiana's best player; it was that he also was the most competitive.

"I've always played on winning teams, ever since I was a little kid, and Coach has always coached winning teams," Alford said. "I think that's the bottom line in our relationship. We may seem different in some ways, but when it comes to basketball, we're a lot alike."

The adjustment for Alford to Knight's style has not always been easy. At Chrysler High School in New Castle, Ind., Alford played in a zone defense most of the time, largely because Sam Alford knew he had to keep his son out of foul trouble if the team was going to be successful. Unlike most freshmen who come into a program like Indiana's, Alford did not have any time to learn by watching when he arrived. He was a starter from the beginning, a starter who was the team's leading scorer, the star of the team right away and also someone who struggled to learn Knight's man-to-man defense.

After the Olympics, Knight worried that Alford's sophomore year would be a struggle.

"The kid was 19 years old and he had an Olympic gold medal,"

Knight said. "He was the hero of an entire state. I don't care how level-headed you are, that's tough to deal with."

In other years at Indiana, it might not have been that tough for Knight to help Alford deal with it. But 1985 was a nightmare for Knight, who sparked a statewide furor by starting four freshmen in a defeat at Illinois. Knight later explained that he was upset with the performances of his regular starters—Alford included—and wanted to light a fire under them. Be that as it may, the rabid Hoosier faithful were alarmed that Knight, who preached the gospel of excellence and perfection, seemingly conceded defeat in an important Big Ten Conference game.

A few weeks later, when Indiana was hosting Illinois, Knight kicked and cracked a chair in a fit of anger. He made headlines again after the Hoosiers' next home game when, enraged by an official's call, he tossed a chair across the court. The Hoosiers ended that turbulent season with a 19-14 record and finished in the second division of the Big Ten for the first and only time in Knight's 15 years at Indiana.

Being the best player, Alford bore a good deal of the burden that season. He was not alone: Forward Mike Giomi was thrown off the team; forward Marty Simmons was benched and eventually transferred; and swingman Winston Morgan also was chained to the bench. But the player Knight kept coming back to, pleading for, demanding help from, was Alford.

Alford wanted to help. But because he is limited physically, there was only so much he could do. Last season, with a smaller, quicker team that pushed the ball up the floor, Alford got more shots. And he created more shots for himself. The result was a superb season—a 22.5 scoring average while connecting on 55.6 percent of his field-goal attempts—as the Hoosiers, directed by a slightly calmer Knight, jumped from seventh to second in the Big Ten. Offensively, Knight cannot ask for much more from Alford this season.

But he will ask for more. He will ask for more defense. He will ask for more good passes. He will ask for more leadership. Alford improved in all those areas last year and will do everything he can to keep getting better this season.

Knight knows this. Late last season, when he would talk about Alford in the evenings, his tone would soften and he would talk almost glowingly about Alford's improvement. Once, when All-America teams were being discussed, Knight forgot himself for a second and said, "How could you not vote for Steve?"

That may be the greatest irony of this Odd Couple relationship. Both men, player and coach, have suffered at times in dealing with each other. Knight's anguish last season when Alford had to sit out the Kentucky game because of a holier-than-thou NCAA ruling after he posed for a charity calendar was quite genuine. He was angry, first with Alford, later with the NCAA. As the season progressed he softened, realizing that even though Alford had been careless, there was no malice in his mistake.

There also are moments when watching Alford struggle defensively will almost drive Knight to distraction. But overall, Knight understands that Alford is exactly the kind of person he wants to represent Indiana basketball. And he understands how hard Alford has worked to improve and to try to overcome his deficiencies as a player.

For his part, Alford has had more than his share of miserable moments at Knight's hand. He has been yelled at, screamed at, called names and, especially last year, often was held responsible when things went wrong for the Hoosiers.

And yet, through it all, two things have happened: Alford has become a much better basketball player. He has improved himself in all the areas where Knight has been critical of him and, thanks in large measure to his coach, enters his senior season as a legitimate national Player of the Year candidate.

The second thing is not as noticeable to the outside world but perhaps equally important. By making Alford his whipping boy, Knight has seen to it that the other Indiana players have never once resented Alford's star status. They have all watched Alford deal with Knight's tirades and never once back down, never once complain. Because of that, they respect Alford. On a lot of teams, a player who has been showered with honors and attention—not to mention the screeches of teen-age girls—like Alford has would be the target of a lot of jealousy. Not at Indiana.

And so, as Knight and Alford enter this final season together, there undoubtedly will be moments when each will drive the other a little bit crazy. Alford will lose his man on defense, Knight will lose his temper. It will go on from October 15 until the moment when Alford shoots his last shot as a Hoosier—and exits as Indiana's all-time leading scorer.

And when Alford is gone, bet two things: Bet that when people ask him years from now whom he credits for his success, the name Bob Knight will be out of his mouth in no time. And bet that when people talk about Steve Alford years from now, Knight will lean back in his chair and say with a smile: "Now let me tell you about All-ford. There was a kid I really enjoyed coaching."

SMU Lets Collins, Hitch Quit

COLLEGE FOOTBALL

By *Doug Bedell*

From the Dallas Morning News
Copyright © 1986, the Dallas Morning News

Somehow, into the body of an ailing football program, SMU leaders must now try to breathe new life.

None of their resuscitative measures will be a panacea. Nothing the Board of Governors can do will completely swab away the damage from the latest allegations of NCAA rules infractions. No blue-ribbon committee, no set of recommendations can wipe out the pain of the last 21 days, a tumultuous three weeks that have seen the university president, the athletic director and the head football coach resign.

But other schools have been in similar straits, and in their remedial efforts, SMU may find some guidance.

In simple terms, the university could press on with a revamped, high-profile program, much as the University of Maryland has done with its basketball team after the cocaine-induced death of Len Bias.

Or it could choose the course taken by Tulane University, which disbanded its basketball program after the team was rocked by a point-shaving scandal.

Or, last, SMU could simply drop down a level in competition—out of the Southwest Conference and into a division with less performance pressure.

"It's a sad day for all of us," Mustang Club board member David Lott said Friday. "Everybody wants to say this is the death of SMU football. But it's not. It's time to pull together and make something positive happen."

What comes next for SMU—for its players, faculty, coaches, boosters, students—is the key to any recovery, according to those who study such situations for a living.

"SMU has got to really make a statement now in its selection of new leadership," Richard Lapchick, head of Northeastern University's Center for the Study of Sport in Society, said Friday. "In Maryland, they chose a high school coach with no college experience. A guy who was highly respected, but really had an anti-Maryland perspective because of the things that had gone on.

"That was a strong, strong statement. It might take a selection of a coach at SMU that, in your conference, might seem really off the wall. But if they want to straighten things out right, they've got to make a strong statement with their selection."

Harry Edwards, sports sociologist at the University of California at Berkeley, agreed: "You're down to personal integrity now. You've got to bring in someone whose integrity is unassailable. He's got to be someone who at least gives the hope that things are moving in a different direction."

"Finding someone to put the program back on track won't be easy, but it's not impossible," said Lott. "Whosoever comes here will be coming into the situation that can't get much lower."

A combined position of athletic director/head football coach would undoubtedly make the job more appealing. But the university is already on probation and stripped of most of its available football scholarships. Should the latest allegations of extra benefits to football players be proved by the NCAA, the Mustangs could be the first major college to suffer the so-called "death penalty"—a mandatory halt to the program for up to two years.

And, without a coaching staff, recruiting will prove to be even more difficult for the new coach. Instead of signing up high school seniors, someone in the SMU athletic department said, the program could simply save the available scholarships until a new coach is selected, then allow him to bring in junior college transfers of his choosing.

But, still, the doubt surrounding the future of Mustang football will most likely take a toll on returning varsity players, who include 15 starters from the 1986 squad. Seniors have already talked among themselves of the need to call a team meeting to dissuade underclassmen from departing.

The alternative of dropping from major college competition into the Division 1-AA ranks seems unlikely at SMU. Holy Cross did so in 1981—although not out of any scandal. "We're now where we should be, competition-wise," said Jeff Nelson, spokesman for the Holy Cross athletic department. "We still think we can compete with some 1-A schools, but we just didn't have the resources to compete regularly with them.

"If SMU did the same thing, it would just seem very drastic to me," Nelson said. "Maybe SMU people are very serious about this thing. I don't know. But it's Texas, and football is king. It just strikes me as hard to figure."

Reaction from Mustang Club members was similar. Executive

director Doug Smith's response: "Definitely not. I want SMU to compete for the SWC championship and the national championship. This school deserves that much."

That leaves the Tulane approach, or a version thereof. In March 1985, the university president chose to kill the basketball program completely after John "Hot Rod" Williams was arrested on five counts in a sports bribery scheme. All scholarships for basketball were rescinded and the players enrolled at other universities.

"At first there was reaction from the students, but that really has settled down since then," said Tulane spokesman Jeff Seal.

Meanwhile, as in the Maryland and SMU situations, a blue-ribbon task force has been formed to examine the role of athletics at Tulane. Already, policies have been changed. Admissions requirements for athletes have been stiffened.

"There had been a wide gap for a long time between the faculty and the athletic department," Seal said. "The basketball scandal widened it even more. But now the relationship between the academic community is closer than it's ever been."

And, Seal said, most within the athletic department believe basketball will return to Tulane. "The president never did really rule out basketball for life," he said. "We don't have a timetable, but we'll have it back here in a couple of years, we think."

Whatever measures SMU's leadership chooses to employ to repair its damaged program will no doubt be tested severely, according to Lapchick and Edwards.

Said Lapchick: "The SMUs and the schools who have the problems have been kind of cynically . . . been saying for years that in order to maintain the competitive edge, you have to do these wrong things. Well, you don't. I can name you 20 great schools who run clean programs and never are going to see this type of thing. It's a matter of will."

Edwards: "There's something to be said for coming clean from past transgressions and being very public about the direction you're heading, especially as the collegiate athletics scene gets filthier and filthier and filthier. SMU is just the first wave of what we're going to see in this regard.

"Oftentimes the press is like vultures circling a herd of sickened wildebeests. The first one whose knees buckle, they're on him, and that's it. All that's happening with SMU is that SMU's knees are buckling."

Fighting the System

COLLEGE ATHLETICS

By *Randy Harvey*

As Jan Kemp reclined on the sofa in her living room after another tiring day in court, her mother talked about her ability to see into the future.

"Mother's psychic," Kemp said.

"I'm not proud of the fact," her mother said.

Four years ago, the future came to Margie Hammock in a dream and startled her out of a deep sleep.

"It was h-e-l-l," she said, genteelly spelling the word.

She said she saw her daughter's depression, the nervous breakdown, the suicide attempts, the trips to the hospital, the financial drain as medical and legal bills mounted, and eventually the trial that would force Jan Kemp to live through it again.

She got out of bed and wrote a letter to her daughter.

"It was like someone was telling me what was going to happen to her," she said. "I wrote it down and mailed it to her. I told her I would prefer for someone else to do this."

"I was crushed," Kemp said.

"It's the first disagreement we've had," her mother said.

"I thought you were being unsupportive," Kemp said. "You didn't sound like my mother. After telling me all of my life to stand up for what I believed in, you wanted me to take the easy way out."

"I was scared," her mother said.

"I was scared, too," Kemp said.

★   ★   ★

Her detractors can say what they will about Jan Kemp, and the words they have used to describe her run from abrasive to disruptive to vicious, but she never has been one to take the easy way out. That was true as far back as high school in her hometown of Griffin, Ga., about 30 miles south of Atlanta, where she was the president of a youth group at the Methodist church.

In the interest of hearing both sides, she once invited an atheist to speak to the group. When her offer was discovered by the elders of the church, they raised h-e-l-l. She was forced to withdraw the invitation. But she did not go down without a fight, invoking the principle of freedom of speech. In another time, in another fight, it is an issue that she again has embraced.

"Basically, I'm shy," Kemp said in her Southern drawl, a voice so soft that it does not seem to go with her 6-foot-2 body. "In school, I was terrified about having to give a book report. But if I thought something was immoral or unethical, I summoned up courage to speak about it. I have strong convictions. I want things to be done right.

"I'm like Rosalynn Carter. What did they call her? The Iron Magnolia. I'm an Iron Magnolia."

That does not mean she is invulnerable. She twice tried to kill herself in 1982. Even Iron Magnolias get the blues. But there is no questioning her resiliency. Three days after she was released from the psychiatric ward of Atlanta's Peachford Hospital for the second time, she filed a suit against the two University of Georgia administrators responsible for firing her, Dr. Virginia Trotter, vice president for academic affairs, and Dr. Leroy Ervin, director of the developmental studies program. Kemp contends she was fired for speaking out against preferential treatment for athletes who were enrolled in developmental studies. Now an adjunct professor at Southern Technical Institute in Marietta, Kemp, 36, seeks reinstatement, less than $100,000 in actual damages and an undisclosed amount in punitive damages.

She said her husband, Bill, who is chairman of the social studies department at Atlanta's Therrell High School, has remained supportive, even though the legal fees have exhausted their investments and retirement funds. They live with their two children, Will, 3½, and Margie, 20 months, in Acwater, a middle-class suburb about 25 miles north of Atlanta.

"If it hadn't been for the J.C. Penney's charge card, we couldn't have had Christmas at all," she told the *Atlanta Journal-Constitution* in early January. "We haven't missed a meal, but we've put some strange things on the table. If we lose, we'll go bankrupt."

Now being heard in the U.S. District Court of Northern Georgia, the trial begins its fifth week today.

Six days into the trial, a white-haired woman in a purple shawl approached Kemp and placed $5 in her hand.

"We'd all go to hell if it wasn't for people like you," said Margaret Bridges, a retired teacher and a 1933 Georgia graduate. "This is a widow's mite toward your lawyers' fees."

Later, outside the courtroom, Bridges said: "All I happened to have was $5. If I'd had $100, I would have given it to her. It's shameful what's going on at the university. I'm embarrassed. When I was in school, Georgia wasn't a great school. There was so little money that the teachers were paid in scrip. But it was an honest school."

★   ★   ★

Asked why she filed her suit, Kemp said, "Because I love the University of Georgia."

From 1976, when Kemp returned to her alma mater to begin work on her doctorate degree, until 1983, she was associated with the developmental studies program, first as a teaching assistant, then as an instructor before her promotion to English coordinator.

Georgia law requires that all of the state's colleges and universities offer developmental studies, non-credit remedial courses in math, reading and English for students who are not prepared for regular curriculum. Of the approximately 250 students that the University of Georgia admits into its developmental studies program each year, about 10 percent are scholarship athletes.

In 1981, Kemp complained to her superiors about preferential treatment for athletes within the program. The most blatant example was Trotter's decision in December 1981 to promote nine football players into the regular curriculum so that they would be eligible for the 1982 Sugar Bowl, even though they had not met the requirements in their developmental studies courses.

In a tongue-twisted admission that has brought her considerable ridicule, Trotter said, "I would rather err on the side of making a mistake."

There have been other questionable practices. Evidence has been presented that standards for gaining admission to the university are lower if an athlete participates in a revenue-producing sport such as football or basketball, that some athletes are admitted even if it is believed they have little chance ever to graduate and that they remain eligible by enrolling in non-demanding courses. One athlete whose transcript was read in court took First Aid, Tumbling and Personal Communications in Health during one quarter.

Oddly enough, one of the most damaging indictments of the university's policies came from Ervin in a speech he made to the developmental studies faculty in 1983. His comments were tape-recorded by one of the instructors and presented during the trial.

"I know for a fact that these kids would not be here if it were not for their utility to the institution," he said. "There is no real sound academic reason for their being here other than to be utilized to produce income. They are used as a kind of raw material in the production of some goods to be sold as whatever product, and they get nothing in return."

Other faculty members within the program also objected, but Kemp was the least diplomatic. She threatened to go public with the information. In April 1982, Kemp was demoted from coordinator to instructor. Four months later, she was fired by Ervin. Trotter approved the firing.

Kemp contends that the dismissal was a violation of her civic rights.

Presiding over the trial is Judge Horace Ward, who has been involved before in litigation with the University of Georgia. In 1950, he was prevented by state and university officials from becoming the first black to attend Georgia. As a crusading civil-rights attorney a decade later, he was instrumental in gaining admission for the university's first two black students.

During a break in the trial last week, Ward said: "I'm amazed by the amount of bitterness involved (in this trial). I'm bothered by that. Bitterness does sometimes cloud the truth."

Testifying on Kemp's behalf, Teresa Timmons, a former instructor within the developmental studies program, said, "You don't have to be a scholar to figure out that the people who spoke out strongly were gone within a year."

Another former colleague, Ruth Sabol, said Kemp had an "extraordinary amount of moral courage."

The defendants, on the other hand, contend that Kemp was fired because she did not participate in scholarly research, a requirement for professors at the university, and because she was insubordinate and unable to get along with other faculty members.

"She would belittle others in meetings if they did not agree with what she said," said one former colleague, Rebecca Galvin.

Galvin, the university's tutoring coordinator, said Kemp once threw a piece of candy at her. At least Galvin said she thought it was candy. When she opened the wrapper, she said she found a condom inside.

"Mean, vicious, abrasive, aggressive, intimidating, caustic, combative," one of Kemp's attorneys, Hue Henry, said one afternoon while cross-examining a defense witness, who was critical of Kemp. "Did I leave out any adverbs?"

Proving that you can take the professor out of the classroom, but not the classroom out of the professor, Kemp leaned over to her attorney and corrected him.

"Adjectives," she said.

"Pardon me," Henry said. "I went to the University of Georgia."

★   ★   ★

Trotter and Ervin may be co-defendants in the U.S. District Court of Northern Georgia, but the University of Georgia is on trial in the court of public opinion.

"The issue is bigger than the case," Henry said last week. "Everybody on our team, including Jan, wants it that way. We want the verdict real bad. But no matter which way the verdict goes, we feel that we have achieved our objective."

The university has virtually conceded that point. In his opening remarks to the jury, Hale Almand, the lawyer hired by the state attorney general's office to defend Trotter and Ervin, admitted that the university will enroll an athlete even if it realizes he has little chance to graduate. His defense of the practice further embarrassed the university. "We may not make a university student out of him," Almand said, "but if we can teach him to read and write, maybe he can work at the post office rather than as a garbage man when he gets through with his athletic career."

As Kemp said, "In one sentence, he managed to insult postal workers, garbage men and athletes."

The relationship between academics and athletics at Georgia has been the subject of controversy before. An 18-part, Pulitzer Prize-winning series in 1984 by the *Macon Telegraph* revealed that over a 10-year period the university graduated only 17 percent of its black football players and only 4 percent of its black basketball players. Since black athletes began attending Georgia in 1969, as few as 30 from among 200 have graduated. But no university's policies in regard to student-athletes have ever been placed under such a microscope as Georgia's have been since this trial began.

So far, Georgians do not like what they have seen.

"People are shocked," said Pat Nelson, another of Kemp's attorneys. "They thought that these things were going on at Auburn and Clemson but not at Georgia. They know better now. About the only thing people can say in Georgia's defense is that this is happening everywhere."

In a letter to the *Atlanta Journal-Constitution,* Tommy Lawhorne, a co-captain of the 1967 Georgia football team and now a vascular surgeon in Columbus, Ga., wrote: "During the last few years, my love (for college football) has begun to fade. Too much business and too little scholarship has cooled my zeal. . . . It is common for colleges to display TV vignettes of laboratories and libraries during halftimes of games in which illiterate students represent these same institutions. The irony of this is equaled only by the hypocrisy of it all."

Another reader, Tom Brewer of Decatur, Ga., wrote: "Keeping the athletic teams well-stocked with talented jocks is important, but not important enough to compromise the integrity of the university."

Bill Shipp, an editorial page columnist for the *Constitution,* wrote: "The Jan Kemp case is a disgraceful mess not only as it relates to the school for gladiators, but to the entire administration of Georgia's higher-education system and to the regents who are supposed to set policy. It's time somebody called for a broom."

An editorial in the newspaper asked, "Sheepskin or fleece for athletes?"

Armed with their answer to that question last week were about 250 students on the Georgia campus in Athens, who, despite a temperature of 12 degrees and a wind-chill factor of minus 20, participated in a protest march from the office of university President Fred Davison to Sanford Stadium. Upon arriving, they had an auction for an imitation diploma. It went to the lowest bidder for a nickel.

The demonstration was organized by a newly formed group

called Students Against Campus Corruption. As they marched, students chanted, "SACC Trotter/SACC Ervin."

In reference to athletic director and football coach Vince Dooley, some of the students also chanted, "SACC Dooley."

At a hastily called press conference the following afternoon, Kemp said: "I am pleased that there was a student response. It's the first time since the early '70s there has been a student demonstration. I'm pleased it's for academic integrity.

"However, I am somewhat disappointed that some of the people were chanting, 'SACC Dooley.' From all the dealings I've had with Coach Dooley, I have known him to be a man of utmost dignity."

Kemp was asked about a letter that had been introduced into evidence earlier. In the 1982 letter to Trotter, Dooley asked that an outstanding track athlete be admitted to the university, even though he did not meet required standards. The athlete was allowed to enroll.

"I saw that for the first time along with you guys," Kemp told reporters.

Dooley said Thursday that he has been notified that he will be called to testify this week as a witness for the defense.

"I don't think he will hurt me," Kemp said.

Despite everything that has transpired, Kemp said she and her husband are as devoted Georgia football fans today as they were as undergraduates, when they met in the Bulldog Room in the student center at Georgia.

"I didn't miss a game for 15 years," she said. "I didn't miss any games the national championship season. I went to all 12 games, including the Sugar Bowl. We followed them around like groupies. Everything I had was red and black. We still follow the Dogs, even though we can't afford to go to the games.

"I still want Georgia to win. But I want them to do it honestly."

★   ★   ★

Testifying on Kemp's behalf, one former football player, Ronnie Stewart, said: "There is no finer person. If there was any preferential treatment that I got as an athlete, it was from her, because there was no time she wouldn't get out of her bed and come to the dormitory to help me. I remember one Sunday she came to the library and we sat for 10 hours while I wrote a paper."

Even witnesses for the defense concede that Kemp was an excellent teacher, whose evaluations from students generally were good except for occasional complaints about her moodiness.

Kemp admitted she sometimes was "not as pleasant as I could have been" to her students.

"I think it's related to my unwillingness to let them coast," she said. "I wanted them to do well at the university. I stayed on their backs. I don't want athletes knocking on my door five years from now offering to rake my leaves when they could have had an education."

During an interview at her home, Kemp said she did not always want to teach. She received her undergraduate degree from Georgia in 1971 in journalism. But when she could not find suitable employment, she accepted a job as secretary to the president at Georgia State in Atlanta. When her boss was appointed by Gov. Jimmy Carter to the state Board of Pardons and Paroles, she went with him as an assistant, meeting regularly with Carter's administrative assistant, Hamilton Jordan, to discuss cases.

She took advantage of her journalistic background by writing free-lance articles, most of them dealing with education. Inspired by her research, she taught in public schools for four years before accepting an offer to return to Georgia in 1976 to work on her doctorate and teach in the developmental studies programs.

"I love the challenge of developmental studies," she said. "There is nothing more satisfying than taking someone who hasn't learned the power and effectiveness of the language and teaching them to use it. Friends of mine prefer honors courses in English. But there's no challenge. The challenge is taking someone who can't read or write and teaching them to be an accomplished writer. Left alone, we can do that."

She said she came to that conclusion that she would not be left alone in April 1981, when she said Ervin requested that she ask another instructor within the English department to change the grades of five scholarship athletes from failing to incompletes. She said that when she protested, Ervin told her: "Who do you think you are? Who do you think is more important at this university, you or a very prominent basketball player?" Ervin has denied he made such a request.

In December 1981, Trotter promoted the nine football players who had not completed their developmental studies requirements.

According to testimony, most of the faculty members within developmental studies objected to Trotter's decision. "We are outraged because we felt the athletes were being exploited to produce revenue," said Dr. William Diehl, a former reading instructor within the program who since has left for another university. "Their primary purpose wasn't to graduate." But as it was Kemp who objected the most vigorously, she was chosen to draft a letter to Trotter. When the other faculty members refused to sign the letter because they felt it was too vitriolic, they say she accused them of cowardice.

Kemp said that was not her intention.

"I said, 'Silence is golden, but sometimes it's also yellow,' " she said. "They asked me if I was calling them cowards. I said, 'No, but if the shoe fits, wear it.' "

In April 1982, Kemp was demoted from coordinator to instructor.

On a leave of absence while pregnant with her first child, Kemp said she learned that Ervin was attempting to build a case against her by soliciting negative comments from students who had failed her courses. After she filed a libel suit against Ervin, she said he attempted to blackmail one of her best friends, a homosexual instructor, by threatening him with exposure unless he would agree to testify against Kemp. She said the instructor resigned. Under instruction from his attorneys, Ervin has not commented on the charge.

"As long as I was the only one being hurt, I was making it beautifully," Kemp said. "But when others became involved, that's when the depression set in."

Kemp earlier suffered from depression in 1974, but she said that was a "mild case of the blues" compared to her state of mind in 1982.

"I lost my ability to contribute," she said. "I had insomnia. I had nosebleeds. I couldn't read. I couldn't dress myself. I couldn't cook breakfast. I couldn't do the laundry. I thought I was a burden to my family and that the best thing to do was get out of their lives. It was irrational, but depression makes you irrational."

She said if she had not been pregnant, she would have committed suicide then.

"I owe Will my life," she said of her son. "I planned to commit suicide in April. I was rational enough to do it then. But I didn't want to do it before Will was born. When he was about two months old, I went ahead with it. But I couldn't find my heart. I stabbed myself in the chest with a butcher knife. I kept stabbing myself in the chest.

"All the way to the hospital, Will was crying. My mother and my husband were telling me to breast-feed him. This is the most vivid memory I have, one that I will never forget as long as I live. Will was crying because he hadn't been fed all day, but I thought my milk was poison. I wouldn't feed him. Mother and Bill were begging me to feed him. I finally said OK. As I was feeding him, the blood from my chest was running down in his face. I'll never forget that as long as I live.

"When I woke up in the hospital, I thought I had succeeded in committing suicide, and I thought I was in hell. I was in the psychiatric ward, and the patient next to me was a drug addict. I thought she had Will."

While she was in the psychiatric ward, she received notice from the university that her contract would not be extended beyond 1983. A month later, Kemp's doctors approved her for release. Three days later, she again tried to commit suicide by taking an overdose. She was readmitted to the hospital for two more months.

She still takes medication for depression but said she believes the worst is behind her.

"I was spiritually healed in a faith-healing service at the Living Faith Fellowship in Watkinsville," she said. "The Good Doctor and the Good Lord got me over it. The first thing I did when I got out of the hospital was file another suit."

When her daughter finished telling her story, Margie Hammock was asked if she could see far enough into the future to reveal the verdict.

"It doesn't matter," she said. "Jan has already won."

Even though she has asked to be reinstated at Georgia, Kemp said she probably will remain at Southern Tech even if she wins her suit. She has applied for a full-time position in developmental studies next fall.

"There's nothing that I would like more than to go back and be a part of the new Georgia, after it's swept clean," she said. "But more than likely, I'd stay at Tech because it's such a fine institution, such an honest one."

Mauch's Eyes, Not Words, Say It All

BASEBALL

By *Jerry Green*

From the Detroit News
Copyright © 1986, the Detroit News

The door opened after a decent interval and Gene Mauch was standing behind the desk. His eyes were rimmed with red. They were moist. He snuffed out a Marlboro cigarette in the ashtray on the corner of the desk.

"I hurt like hell for those players," he said. "I hurt like hell for Gene Autry.

"They played their hearts out out there. It got stepped on."

He spoke his sentences in a slow monotone. He was behind the desk. He still was dressed in his road-gray Angels uniform top and a pair of baseball player's undershorts.

Nobody dared ask him the hard question.

"Eight months of hard work," Mauch said. "Eight months of hard work. We feel like we got the job done. It got away."

It got away, the pennant got away, and this was the third time it had happened to Gene Mauch. On Sunday, the Angels were one strike, one pitch, from the A.L. pennant.

Mauch pursed his lips against the agony that tortured him inside. He is 60 now, still fit. He has been a major-league manager for 25 years. He is the dean of those in this business. And he has never won a pennant.

Somebody asked him about John Candelaria, who lost Wednesday night's seventh game to the Red Sox.

"He threw a helluva lot more than this game," Mauch said. "I don't want to talk about it."

There was pain in his voice. Then there was silence. He broke it himself.

"I'll say this, I was very comfortable with him going out there."

There was more silence in the small room used by visiting managers as an office in Fenway Park. But the blast of horns and the thunder of cheers crashed into the quiet room.

Mauch was left for a moment with his memories, the bitterness of other pennants that got away. He is to be remembered as the manager of the '64 Phillies. They led the National League by 6½ games with 12 to play—and lost 10 games in succession. They lost the pennant. He is to be remembered for the '82 Angels. They won the first two games of a best-of-five playoff with the Brewers. They lost the next three and the pennant.

Now this, the worst for Gene Mauch. One strike from the pennant in the ninth inning Sunday. Losing that, losing two games in Boston, losing another pennant.

Mauch lit another cigarette. He stared ahead through the reddened eyes. Now he was asked about his plans, his future, his feelings.

"Well, my situation is obviously something a lot of media enjoy," Mauch said.

"So let them take care of that. Wonder how I feel. Wonder what I'll do."

Next spring? somebody asked.

"That's all I got," Mauch said. "That's all I want to say. There's no use discussing a game like that. Get beat that badly."

Bobby Brown, the American League president, slipped into the office.

"Sorry, Gene," said Brown.

"That's it boys," said Mauch. The room emptied and Brown closed the door.

Gene Mauch had showered and was dressed in a blue blazer when the door opened again 30 minutes later.

"I never made alibis," he said. He was more composed now. "We had it won."

Then a question about his feelings.

"A lot of them have a lot of fun, I'm a failure," he said, his voice now sarcastic and mocking. "You can assume anything you want. Do you think I should quit?"

Nobody answered.

"You can read my mind," said Mauch. "You can read my heart." He stood there again in silence.

"Why don't you give the Red Sox credit for the way they played?" he said. "They played like hell.

"The Red Sox ran into an undermanned team that was in a bit of shock at the game that got away."

Gene Mauch will skip the World Series again. He will not be a spectator, there to explain how another pennant got away. He will not be there to defend himself against the charge of overmanaging. He won't have to answer the hard questions about why he took out his finest pitcher, Mike Witt, in the ninth inning Sunday—and allowed himself to be beaten by his own bullpen.

It is all conjecture, this cruelty of second-guessing.

"All I can go by are facts and logic," Mauch said.

The facts are that Gene Mauch lost another pennant he had won. There is no logic for it.

Mixing It Up With the Guys

PRO BASKETBALL

By *Franz Lidz*

From Sports Illustrated
Copyright © 1986, Sports Illustrated

After Nancy Lieberman made her United States Basketball League debut early last week as the first woman to play in a men's professional league, the game ball was taken off to be displayed in the Boston Museum of Science. They might as well have displayed Lieberman's folding chair. The Springfield Fame's 27-year-old rookie point guard entered the game with 3:40 left in the second quarter and her team ahead of Staten Island, 54-40. In the second half, despite the chants of the 2,187 spectators in Springfield, Mass., she didn't play.

During her historic—if limited—time on the court, Staten Island players tended to buzz by Lieberman like speedboats passing the Statue of Liberty, but she made up for her obvious handicaps with a twitchy, foxy cunning. Beneath a squall of apricot-colored curls, Lieberman got off some of her trademark passes, crisp, hard and at times so deceptive that her teammates couldn't handle them. She didn't miss any shots—but then again, she didn't take any, either.

All the time she spent on the pine didn't sit well with Lieberman. "I accept my role with the team," she said after the Fame's 122-107 victory. "I just wish I'd been in long enough to break a sweat."

"I wanted to break her in gradually," explained Fame Coach Henry Bibby, whose perimeter-prowling style during a nine-season National Basketball Association career was not so different from Lieberman's. "She showed she could compete against physical play without backing down."

Lieberman's asphalt arrogance and Bird-like intensity had made her a three-time All-America at Old Dominion (1978-80). "She plays like a man," her opponents used to say. Now she's just one of the guys—almost everybody plays like a man in the USBL.

"I want to stick around long enough to stay embedded in people's minds," says the 5-foot-10, 155-pound former Olympian. "You can't force-feed them to remember your accomplishments."

Not that she's above dropping a few hints. Her publicist has assembled a press kit packed with facts, figures and testimonials. Besides book and film deals, she has a personal secretary, three cars, two sporting goods stores, real estate holdings in Texas and St. Croix and promotional contracts for everything from health food to fur coats. What other athlete is wealthier than her team owner?

Lieberman isn't the USBL's first odd attraction. Last year, in the league's inaugural season, the Rhode Island Gulls hired 7'7" Manute Bol and 5'7" Spud Webb. Still, Springfield led the league and won the title when officials canceled the playoffs because half the players abandonded their teams for NBA tryout camps. In a ceremony before the game with Staten Island, the four Famers left over from last year's championship squad were honored with certificates. Second-year starter Michael Adams showed his gratitude by exhorting his teammates: "O.K., guys, let's go out there and get another certificate!"

After scraping up enough money last season to pay Bol $25,000, with only press clips to show for it, the USBL put a $10,000 cap on salaries this year. That doesn't leave much room for attracting stars, though Lieberman is getting top scale. "Nancy's bigger than Manute," offers Springfield forward Oliver Lee, "at least publicity-wise. She's gonna save our franchise! She's gonna save our *league!*"

Lieberman knew what she would be up against in the USBL, having often scrimmaged with NBA veterans in summer pro-am leagues. The Fame could afford to try her out as a project because they have the league's best frontline. In Adams, who played in the NBA with the Sacramento Kings last season, Springfield also has the slickest and quickest point guard in the USBL.

"Nancy's a great gimmick," says Al Lewis, who has been scouting basketball players for more than 30 years but is better known for playing Grandpa on "The Munsters." "She's always been a pugnacious s.o.b., but she doesn't have the speed or strength to compete with these men. It's genetics." And who knows genetics better than a guy whose son-in-law was assembled in a basement lab?

The Brooklyn-born Lieberman once spoke in an accent that would have lent authority to a subway cop on the BMT Brighton line, but she now favors the drawl of her adopted hometown of Dallas. Before catching on with the USBL, Lieberman played in two women's pro leagues, both of which went broke. The defunct Dallas Diamonds, in fact, will pay her $60,000 this year on a guaranteed contract that expires in 1987. Between Lieberman's forays into pro basketball, she was housemate, conditioning coach and psychic booster to Martina Navratilova. She moved out of Navratilova's house when she joined the Diamonds three years ago. "I was losing my identity," she says. "I don't want to be remembered as Martina's coach. I want to be remembered as a great basketball player."

Her greatest basketball achievement so far has come in the not-yet-released movie "Perfect Profile," the story of a woman who accidentally made an NBA team because the owner thought she was a guy. Two weeks after she finished shooting the film, the Fame called. Ironically, her new team took its name from the local Basketball Hall of Fame, which inducted its first women in 1985 only after feminists picketed.

Lieberman's first appearance with the Fame was in Springfield's lone exhibition game, a 135-115 rout of Westchester's rotten Golden Apples, on June 6. Bibby used the occasion to showcase her for nearly 25 minutes. At first Lieberman appeared listless. She was tentative, dribbled into traps, and was stationary on defense. She missed all four shots she took in the first half but swished an open jumper with 9:28 to go in the fourth quarter and finished four for 12 with 10 points and two assists.

Lieberman blamed her shaky start on nervousness caused by the presence at the game of her father and mother, who hadn't seen each other in 15 years. She said, "I envisioned a *New York Post* headline that read: WOMAN MAULS EX-HUSBAND IN GYM."

As a kid, Nancy dreamed of playing in the same New York Knick backcourt as her idol, Walt Frazier. She now wears Clyde's number—10—and endorses his brand of sneakers. Maybe someday an NBA team looking for some attention will sign her to a 10-day contract. "Then I'll know there is a God," says Lieberman. But she also says, "The party's just starting, and I'm ready to dance."

One Who Didn't Make It

BOXING

By *Alan Goldstein*

From the Baltimore Sun
Copyright © 1986, The Baltimore Sun

They were such good friends, Sugar Ray Leonard and Derrik Holmes. Only in those days, the early 1970s, it was Derrik Holmes and Sugar Ray Leonard.

They were two precocious, brash teen-aged fighters from the same lower-middle class suburban Washington neighborhood of Palmer Park, who traveled around the world stockpiling amateur boxing medals and trophies and dreaming of winning the gold in the 1976 Olympic Games.

"Derrik was my main man," said Leonard, 30, now a millionaire. "We were really like brothers. We dated together, played ball together, hung out together, and fought each other hundreds of times in the gym.

"Everyone knew Derrik. He had a real persona at an early age—extremely confident in himself and wearing flashy clothes—while I was basically shy, content to hang back.

"We both went to Kent Junior High and then Parkdale High, and everyone knew Derrik could fight. He really didn't have to. He was a smooth talker and always tried to avoid a confrontation unless someone backed him into a corner.

"When we were 14, he talked me into joining the boxing team at the Palmer Park Boys Club. I weighed about 118 pounds, and he was 112, but at first, he knocked the living hell out of me. He was just so slick and always had that beautiful left hand. He could spin me every which way and box my ears off. I just tried to get by on strength. I kept growing, but he kind of stayed the same, so we quit sparring. He was the one with the most skill and pizazz."

In December of 1975, as the American boxers counted down to the 1976 Summer Olympics, it was Holmes, not Leonard, who was considered America's best amateur boxer and was singled out for special praise by Col. Donald Hull, the Amateur Athletic Union's boxing administrator, who wrote this personal letter:

Dear Derrik:
As we near the end of 1975, it is time to again thank you for your tremendous contribution of time and effort in representing the U.S.A. in international competition. Your success has been unsurpassed by any other athlete representing us in our sport.
Your victories against the Hungarians and Polish boxers proved your capacity as an international competitor. When you won the 1975 North American Championships, you became the only boxer to win that three consecutive times. You have not only contributed time and sweat, but as in any tough contact sport such as ours, you have also contributed blood in representing the U.S.A. and we hope that you continue activity in our sport in the year 1976.
Sincerely,
Donald F. Hull.

Leonard recalls that triumphant tour through Europe.

"We were a couple of 18-year-olds with our heads in the clouds," he said. "Everywhere we went, we were treated like visiting royalty. After we polished off the Poles, we decided to have a private party. We bought ourselves satin dressing gowns, king-sized cigars and a fancy chess set. Derrik was close to being a champion. Me? I couldn't tell the king from the queen. But we had ourselves a ball. We were sitting on top of the world."

Ray Leonard still is sitting on top of the world. In 1984, he retired from the ring after winning the welterweight and junior-middleweight crowns and having earned an estimated $50 million. He still makes a reported $300,000 as a boxing commentator for Home Box Office, but his gilt-edged bonds and investments permit him to live a life of relative leisure at his custom-built home in Potomac, Md.

Derrik Holmes, who earned a top purse of $30,000 for his unsuccessful challenge for Wilfredo Gomez's junior featherweight title in 1980, is prisoner No. 175462 at the Maryland State Penitentiary in Baltimore, facing a minimum of 30 years for attempted first-degree murder of his "good friend," Roswell Howard, an itinerant Kentucky coal miner with whom he was working as a salesman in a Clinton, Md., Christmas tree lot in the winter of 1983.

Holmes maintained his innocence and had three witnesses offer alibis at his trial in Prince George's County Circuit Court. The jury deliberated for 15 hours, but finally could find no reason for Howard, who was shot five times with a .25 caliber pistol, to fabricate the name of his assailant. An appeal to reduce the length of Holmes' sentence is scheduled in September.

Today, Holmes spends his days preaching religion, taking college courses and teaching fellow inmates how to box, hoping that one day they will be able to display their talents outside the prison.

"Everything was pre-destined," he said recently. "For some reason, I was meant to be here.

"There's no such thing as 'would've, could've or should've.' I got involved with some devilish devices I shouldn't have. I could have been just like Sugar Ray, but I abused my talent. I have no one to blame but Derrik Holmes."

How did these best friends take such divergent paths, Leonard using his lightning fists to find fame and fortune, while the equally gifted Holmes found only frustration?

★   ★   ★

In the course of several weeks, the *Sun* talked to friends, fellow fighters, trainers and managers who were a big part of Holmes' life in and out of the ring. Almost all talked of his sentencing and imprisonment as a "real tragedy," but in different ways. They somehow understood how the dreams of glory became a nightmare for a star-crossed boxer once proclaimed by an admiring French sportswriter as "Holmes, Sweet Holmes."

Most agreed that it was in the 1976 Olympic trials when Leonard and Holmes reached crossroads in their celebrated amateur careers. Leonard survived his tests and ultimately joined Leo Randolph, Howard Davis and Michael and Leon Spinks in winning gold medals in Montreal.

Holmes lost a close decision to his Palmer Park neighbor, Charles Mooney, a setback so damaging to his psyche that he wouldn't fight for more than a year. The more Leonard progressed, the more Holmes regressed.

"Derrik couldn't stand to be in another man's shadow," said Dave Jacobs, who trained Leonard and Holmes in their formative years. "If he couldn't be out front, he didn't want to be there at all.

"Talent-wise, there was no one better or any gamer. I remember when I took him to the North American Championships in Milwaukee in 1974. Both of his hands were hurting and I wanted to pull him out of the tournament, but he begged me to let him fight. He said, 'Don't worry, Jake, I'll knock all these guys out. And if I really hurt my hands, then the AAU will have to pay to get them fixed.' And, you know, he did just like he said. Knocked 'em all dead."

The "father-son" relationship that existed between trainer and fighter began to sour after Holmes' loss to Mooney, a fighter he had beaten twice.

"When we came back from the 1976 Olympics, Derrik had in the back of his mind that I was favoring Sugar Ray," Jacobs said. "He was jealous, but there was no basis for it. And I just don't think he had that same motivation to succeed anymore."

Jacobs said that Holmes "got caught going in too many directions" after being offered a scholarship to the University of Maryland by D.C. delegate Walter Fauntroy.

"Leonard got the same scholarship offer, but decided to devote all his time to winning an Olympic gold medal," Jacobs said. "Derrik tried to do both. He spent two years at College Park taking pre-law courses, but he was also working to help support his mother, who was ill. It became a terrible burden, and he finally dropped out of school.

"But when he lost to Mooney, it was like his whole world fell apart. He acted like he wanted to die. I tried to tell him that everyone goes through disappointments in life, and that he could fight his way back, but he seemed to lose his spirit. And when he left me, it was like losing a prodigal son.

"Derrik started going from trainer to trainer. He worked with Adrian Davis in Washington and then with George Benton in Philadelphia, where all the fighters throw hooks and want to be another Joe Frazier. That wasn't Derrik's style. He was a boxer, not a slugger.

"I'm convinced that, if he had stayed with me, he would have beaten Wilfredo Gomez and won the title. When we were still together, he was the only one to knock Gomez out as an amateur. Derrik was a big part of his life, and that's why what happened is a shame, a crying shame."

Leonard says the loss to Mooney should never have happened. "Making the Olympic team should have been a formality for Derrik," he said. "He'd easily beaten Mooney twice. But when he lost in the trials, everything kind of snowballed.

"We kind of went separate ways after that, but after I became the welterweight champion, I had Derrik appear on some of my shows. But you could see he wasn't the same fighter. It was like something was bottled up inside, but just couldn't come out."

Holmes offers no alibis.

"It was mostly a mental thing," he said. "I didn't see the light until it was too late. I didn't have definite goals, and just didn't fight Mooney hard enough."

It took more than 14 months to get over his frustration and return to the ring.

"I let everything go after 1976," he said. "I was retreating from boxing, not acting like a man.

"I'd ride around Washington talking to a lot of people. First, I'd ask them if they knew Sugar Ray, and, of course, they all did because he'd won his gold medal. Then I'd ask them if they knew Derrik Holmes, and I'd draw only blanks. I decided I had to make myself known again."

His lifestyle already was changing dramatically. Roger Leonard, Ray's older brother who won a number of amateur titles but enjoyed only moderate success as a pro, was one of Derrik's regular companions.

"I was with Ray and Derrik from the start," said Roger, now helping another brother, Kenny, promote professional boxing in the Washington area. "In 1972, I was on the Air Force team fighting in the National AAU tournament. Derrik and Ray came down to San Antonio to live with me. They wanted to go to the 1972 Olympics, but they were both under age.

"When we started fighting at Palmer Park, I outweighed Derrik by some 20 pounds, but I still couldn't get the best of him. He was special.

"But when we turned pro, we didn't have that same blind dedication like Ray did. And when Derrik got knocked out by Gomez, he was devastated. Guys from the neighborhood kept mocking him. It hurt his pride and ego.

"After that, he was never the same. We used to gamble and party together. But Derrick got into . . . trying to be slick with fast cars and dice. He put the street ahead of the gym. You can't have it both ways."

When Sugar Ray Leonard made his professional debut in Baltimore on February 5, 1977, he received $42,000 for a six-round fight with Luis "The Bull" Vegas. Sixteen months later, Holmes made his professional debut in Washington in a four-rounder against Jimmy Jones. He received $500.

While Leonard was padding his bank account quickly, Holmes was bringing home $350 every other week by working as a data processor at the Goddard Space Center. His brother, John, earned $155 as a bellboy at the Hyatt Regency Hotel.

"I need the extra money from fighting to help my mother," Derrik said. "She had high blood pressure and had to quit her job with the (AFL-CIO) union. We didn't know how long she'd be with us."

Clarissa Holmes says she tried to dissuade her son from turning pro. "I wanted him to remain an amateur and try for the 1980 Olympic team," she said. "If he'd won a gold medal like Leonard, he'd be able to get top management people like Angelo Dundee working with him.

"The stakes in boxing are too high for Derrik to be fighting for small purses. If he were illiterate or didn't have a good education, it would be different. But $500 barely pays the rent."

Holmes persevered, however, scoring quick knockouts over obscure rivals named Rodell Stevenson, Ronnie Newby and Felix Rodriquez while earning just enough to keep out of debt until the next fight.

Adrian Davis, a ranking welterweight in the '60s, remembered those bittersweet days when Holmes was trying to fight his way back into the limelight.

"I took Derrik under my wing like a child," he said. "He was the first good fighter I had. While I was training him, he lived with me and I fed him and clothed him like part of the family.

"I tried to keep him an amateur, and paid his way to the 1977 Nationals in Biloxi, Miss. When he decided to turn pro, I stuck with him. He was a great fighter, and I know how much it hurt him watching Leonard and Leon Spinks fighting on TV and making all that money.

"But Derrik was much better as an amateur than a pro. In 1978, he won all his amateur fights until he lost to Bernard Taylor, a real good fighter. Derrik was disgusted, and laid off a whole year.

"Trouble was, he could never fight his way through obstacles. If he had family or personal problems, he'd just give up fighting. I remember one time he came into my gym, saw someone he didn't like, and walked right out."

Davis and Holmes remained together until the Gomez fight, when Bret Molivinsky, a Maryland insurance man, became his manager and sent Derrik to Philadelphia to be tutored by Benton, who had trained a number of champions.

The Gomez fight . . . so many different versions of what happened. So many people pointing fingers. So many tragic repercussions.

"My gut reaction was that the Gomez fight was a rush job," said Janks Morton, one of the original supervisors at Palmer Park and the man who trained Leonard after he won the welterweight title from Wilfredo Benitez. "Molivinsky invested some money in Derrik and saw a chance to get some back."

Molivinsky had purchased Holmes' contract in 1979 from his original manager, Nathaniel Williams, for a reported $100,000, after Williams went bankrupt.

"We thought long and hard about spending the money," Molivinsky said, "but with Derrik's background, we thought it was a sure thing. I wasn't in it for a tax loss. I saw Derrik, with his talent and exciting style, making a pocketful of money."

For the August 22, 1980 title date with Gomez, Holmes was guaranteed $30,000 by promoter Don King. It was meant to be a down payment on a three-fight option by King worth $375,000 if Holmes upset the champion from Puerto Rico.

Then the facts start to get fuzzy.

"Derrik had all the money spent before the fight," Molivinsky said. "He had borrowed money from the Riggs Bank, and I had to pay $10,000 to square it. But he didn't want to deduct that from his end of the purse. He wanted it all."

"I paid the loan back myself," Holmes contends. "I found out that Molivinsky took advantage of me. I could have gotten a $30,000 purse talking for myself. Anybody could've done it. They got me cheap."

What happened before and after the fight also is hotly debated. According to ringsiders, including Leonard, who was working as a TV analyst, Holmes clearly outboxed Gomez in the first two rounds, then suddenly began falling apart like a punch-drunk fighter.

He would have his jaw shattered, get knocked down eight times and finish the fight on the seat of his pants in the fifth round, shards of bone protruding from his mouth and a molar hanging loose.

"I got so emotionally involved and upset, I got in trouble with the network after the Gomez fight," Leonard said. "I just felt so helpless sitting there, not able to help Derrik."

Holmes would look back on the fight and wonder how he lasted that long. "After my jaw was broken, every time I moved, I felt a terrible shooting pain," he said. "The last time I went down, the pain was so bad, I crossed my legs, looked up at the referee and said, 'Just count me out!' "

Molivinsky said Holmes' trouble started long before the fight.

"Derrik just got caught up with a real bad crowd back home," he said. "Guys who were doing drugs, robbing homes and the rest of it. I can't say for certain he was on drugs, but all the symptoms were certainly there.

"Two hours before the fight, I couldn't find him anywhere in the hotel. Then he shows up in the dressing room looking shaky and glassy-eyed. He gets in the ring and starts jumping around like a frog, doing deep knee-bends, stuff I'd never seen him do before.

"And then he fought like he was on something, throwing a lot of wild punches and going down when he wasn't even hit by Gomez. After the fight, he was in such bad physical shape that they didn't even bother to give him a urine test.

"We split up after that, but I heard he became a desperate person, doing anything for drugs. That's why I don't think the shooting was an accident. I think he did it out of rage, and he deserves whatever he got."

Holmes disputed Molivinsky's story. "I didn't disappear before the Gomez fight," he said. "I was in my room, just me and my bodyguard. I didn't want to be bothered by anybody."

George Benton, who worked Holmes' corner in the Gomez fight, said the title was there for the taking.

"Holmes had Gomez on the verge of a knockout in the first two rounds, but didn't go after him," said Benton, now training four of the 1984 Olympic champions. "Then, he just fell apart. The last time he went down, I screamed at him to get up, but he didn't even move. He just sat there staring.

"Yeah, he was a hell of a prospect, with just as much ability as Leonard. But he got messing with drugs, and then he needed money to support his habit. A 'high' doesn't last long, so it gets expensive.

"It's a shame because I always admired intelligent fighters, and he had real smarts. He boxed beautifully, but he was also a tremendous puncher for his weight. Most of all, he was a thinker. He fought like it was a chess match, always a move ahead.

"But Derrik just wasn't enough of a man. He listened to his friends and was too weak to resist taking drugs. Just not man enough."

After he was knocked out in the fourth round by Paul DeVorce on September 15, 1982, Holmes quit fighting. His life became aimless and he was unable to find steady employment.

★   ★   ★

Jerry Gray sits in his Mexican-style restaurant in New Carrolton and wonders how Holmes' world turned topsy-turvy in a matter of years. He had befriended him as an admirer of his boxing talents, and, ironically, brought Holmes together with Roswell Howard, hiring them to work on his Christmas tree lot in 1983. At the time, Holmes was unemployed, but had told Gray he had been promised a job at a Washington-area car dealership.

"I feel like I've lost a real good friend," Gray said. "I first met Derrik on the boardwalk in Atlantic City in 1979 when he was fighting at one of the casinos. He was such a beautiful fighter. He could throw a left jab, hook to the body and come back to the head before you could blink an eye.

"I'd go to all his fights, and he'd introduce me as his 'white uncle.' I felt he had a lot of character, high moral standards and truly cared about his family and friends.

"I could see a real change after the Gomez fight. I remember writing him a letter that was like a pep talk, trying to cheer him up. Then I started hearing about his using drugs and doing strange things to people he knew.

"I saw his last few fights, but he didn't have the heart for fighting anymore. And he wouldn't train. He just wouldn't pay the price."

In his own heart, though, Gray says he could not believe Holmes was capable of attempted murder.

"The facts were hard to reconcile," Gray said. "Derrik had been working at the lot long enough to know I'd already taken several thousand dollars to the bank and there wasn't much money left in the office. But people at the restaurant across the street said they saw Derrik running away after the shooting.

"The funny thing was, Derrik showed up at the lot the next morning. Then he must have heard the police were looking for him, and disappeared.

"Still, I went to question Howard in the hospital. He was all torn up. I don't know how he survived. I asked him if it was Derrik Holmes, the fighter, who shot him, and he nodded his head. I kept trying to crack his story, but I couldn't. His story was just too consistent.

"It's funny, but I remember Derrik once telling me, 'You don't really know me. I've got a mean streak in me.' I didn't think about it 'til much later."

Sugar Ray Leonard sits in a restaurant in Bethesda, trying to make sense of it all.

"You know, I haven't gone to see Derrik since he's been in jail," he said softly. "There just so much emotion, pain and hurt. I'm not used to seeing someone I loved in such a predicament. But I still care. I still love him."

Derrik Holmes sits in a guarded interview room, remembering a boyhood friend.

"At first, all the fuss over Leonard bothered me," he said. "But I never really envied him. He worked for it and became a great champion. His success only helped to motivate me."

Then Derrik began talking about the fellow inmates he is training. "We've got some real boxing talent in here," he said. "They just need a chance to show the public."

Then, after a long pause, he added, "I still know there's a world out there, and I want my freedom. I'll let the Lord take care of it."

He waved good-bye, and the steel door clanged shut.

'The Natural'—Live!

BASEBALL

By *Glenn Dickey*

From Inside Sports
Copyright © 1986, Inside Sports

"With a sob Roy fell back and swung. . . . The ball shot through Toomey's astounded legs and began to climb. The second baseman, laying back on the grass on a hunch, stabbed high for it, but it leaped over his straining fingers, sailed through the light and up into the dark, like a white star seeking an old constellation."

—From "The Natural,"
by Bernard Malamud.

It was the Oakland A's training camp, and a young man named Jose Canseco seemed the second coming of Roy Hobbs. When he walked—strutted would be the better word—into the batting cage, all eyes turned to watch him. Showing a flair for the dramatic, manager Jackie Moore saved him for last in batting practice. "That's a good way to end it," said Moore. "He's the fireworks show."

Canseco put ball after ball against the fences or over them, even clearing the 50-foot sign behind the center-field fence, 450 feet from home plate. Fans cheered his batting practice, and after one such performance, A's second baseman Donnie Hill yelled out, "Hey, Jose, how can we play catch if we don't have any balls left?"

And a writer commented, "He might as well have a P for 'Phenom' on his chest."

Now, there are phenoms and there are phenoms. The term was apparently invented in 1947 by Garry Schumacher, baseball's first public relations man (for the then-New York Giants), to describe rookie Clint Hartung in spring training of that year.

The only question about Hartung seemed to be whether he'd go into the Hall of Fame as a pitcher or as an outfielder. He was hitting 400-foot home runs in spring training games and striking out hitters with great frequency when he pitched.

If you visit Cooperstown, don't bother looking for Hartung's plaque. The pressure ruined Clint. Used primarily as a pitcher for four years, he was 29-29. Switched to the outfield on a part-time basis for two years, he hit .238. By 1953 he was gone.

In 1951 the second kind of phenom appeared. The New York Yankees had a young shortstop who had led a Class C league in errors but could run like the wind and hit the ball 500 feet. The Yankees switched him to the outfield. His name: Mickey Mantle.

Meanwhile, the Giants had a young prospect they had signed out of the Negro League. Manager Leo Durocher said he was already the best defensive center fielder in baseball and that he had as much power as Ralph Kiner, who had averaged 48 homers for the previous four seasons. His name: Willie Mays.

And, yes, you can find Mantle and Mays at Cooperstown.

Thirty-five years later, Canseco was being compared to both Mantle and Mays, a comparison that increased after his second home run of the spring, coming against the San Francisco Giants, cleared a line of trees beyond the left-field fence at Phoenix Stadium, a good 500 feet from home plate.

"I don't think it's fair to compare him to players like Mickey Mantle, who had great careers," said Moore, "but I don't know what else you can do. Truthfully, in my years in baseball I've never seen anybody who compares to him coming up. He creates such excitement because he hits the ball so far."

"He reminds me of Mays when he came up for his first game in Philadelphia," said A's executive Bill Rigney. "Willie popped up his first swing, then hit a liner to left. On his third swing he hit one that rattled off the scoreboard and everybody stopped and watched him. It's the same way with this kid. Everything stops cold when he's up there. He puts on a show."

The cover of the A's media guide, drawn up like an old-time movie poster, reads, "Filmed on location in cities across the country, and introducing Jose Canseco as 'The Natural.' "

Nobody was talking about Clint Hartung.

★   ★   ★

Canseco got so much early attention that Moore fretted that he'd feel too much pressure. "I just hope people can let him be Jose Canseco and not expect too much at the start," Moore said. He tried to take pressure off his phenom by batting him seventh.

You wanted to say to Moore, an eminently decent man: "Don't worry, Jackie. The kid belongs, and he knows it." Nothing fazes Canseco, not even striking out 14 times in his first 28 major league at-bats last September.

Let's talk about pressure. As most people do, Moore was confusing pressure with attention. Attention is what other people give you; pressure is self-inflicted. Canseco was getting a ton of attention, but he reveled in it. Though he pretended that he didn't notice how everything stopped when he took batting practice—"I'm concentrating on working on different things when I'm in the cage"—in fact, you could see the smile on his face as he stepped in. This is one cool cat, confident to the point of cockiness. He takes the extravagant accolades as his due.

When asked about pressure, he just shrugged his massive shoulders. "I don't feel any pressure," he said. "When I came up last year I was nervous. I was just a 21-year-old kid, in the big leagues for the first time. But not now. I just go out and do my job."

Those aren't just brave words masking insecurity. Observing Canseco around the clubhouse, you could see that he had the confidence of a true believer. Moore even assigned veteran Dusty Baker to the job of trying to keep Canseco from becoming too cocky. "I try to tell him to keep cool," said Dusty. "He knows how good he is. I just try to tell him that he will have bad days. Everybody does. He just has to realize it won't all come easy. But he'll do it."

The players accepted Canseco early as part of the team, not pretending that he had to prove himself. He was subjected to the kind of rough clubhouse kidding that is an important part of baseball.

One day in the clubhouse Canseco put on a T-shirt that was stretched to the bursting point over his rippling muscles. "You must be wearing a medium," said outfielder Mike Davis. "You've got to quit shopping in the boys' department." Canseco protested that the shirt was an extra-large. Baker said, "You must have washed it in hot water then," and looked inside to see the size—extra-large. "You shrunk the bitch," he exclaimed. "We have to kid him to bring him down to earth sometimes," said outfielder Dwayne Murphy.

Jose Canseco is his own man. He designed a weightlifting program that added 40 pounds of muscle and transformed him from a fair prospect into a phenom. He designed his own batting stance, a peculiar, open-stanced crouch in which his left foot is aimed at third base. When the pitch comes, he strides toward the pitcher. "I can see the ball better from that stance," he said.

And, though the A's hitting instructor, Bob Watson, has tried to get him to realize "he doesn't have to hit every pitch 800 feet," Canseco isn't going to change his swing. Hitting instructors are for the mortals on the team; Jose Canseco marches to his own drummer. "It may look like I'm trying to hit every pitch a long way," he said, "but that's just the way I swing. I've just got a big swing. I'm comfortable with that swing." So was Babe Ruth.

Confidence sometimes comes easy when people are talking and writing about you in extravagant terms, but Canseco seems always to have had it. Baseball people who knew him early in his career talk of his frustration because his expectations exceeded his performance. He says himself that he thought in high school he would be a major league player, and though he didn't hit .300 in the minors until last season, "I always knew I could do it. I always knew I had the ability. My trouble was that I struck out too much, but I knew I could lick that."

What gives the young man this extraordinary confidence? In part, it's because of a maturity that was forced on him when his mother died of a brain tumor early in the 1984 season. Her loss shattered Canseco, and he wasn't the same for several months.

"I couldn't concentrate on what I was doing," he said. "That was all I could think of. My mind wasn't in the game at all. It's a wonder I did as well as I did (league-leading 15 homers and 73 RBIs at Class A Modesto).

"But that did a lot to mature me. I realized that there was a lot more to life than baseball. It put everything into better perspective for me. I'm religious (Catholic) and I believe we're predestined to do what we're going to do in life. I could break a leg tomorrow, and my career could be over. If that happened, I'd just have to do something else with my life. I can't worry about it."

He has a single-minded devotion to the game, comfortable only when he's talking about baseball. If he has any other interests, he keeps them well-hidden. An inquiry about books he's read draws a blank, puzzled stare. What does he do in the offseason? "I go fishing some," he said. "And I lift weights."

He likes girls and they like him. But questions about a steady girlfriend are met with a laugh. "There's nothing to talk about," he said. His best friend on the club, pitcher Tim Birtsas, said Canseco's idea of a good time is "dragging the main," and added, "He goes to parties sometimes, but he's not a party boy. He's pretty quiet, really. He's real serious about his baseball."

Canseco was born in Havana, but his family moved to Miami when he was 1. Sounds like an interesting story, but not to Jose. The circumstances don't interest him. "I don't know if it was political. There were a lot of people moving." His twin brother, Ozzie, is a pitcher in the New York Yankees chain, but that doesn't seem to strike him as unusual, either.

Except on the battlefield, he is a passive young man, the opposite of the stereotype of the emotional Latin. You won't get sparkling dinner conversation from him, but he has the perfect emotional makeup for the game he plays so well. All he wants to do is play ball. That's fine with the A's.

★   ★   ★

A natural? He didn't seem like it as a 15th-round draft choice out of high school in Miami in 1982, seemingly one of those faceless players who struggle through a couple of minor league seasons and wind up pumping gas in their hometowns.

Even Canseco isn't sure what the A's saw in him, though he'd had a good year as a high school senior. "I hit .400, and I remember I hit some home runs," he said, but that was the only year he'd even made the team.

"Camilo Pascual (a former major league pitcher) scouted him for us," said Walt Jocketty, the A's director of baseball administration, "and he thought Canseco might grow a little. He was 6'3", but only 170 pounds, so he had room to put on some weight. But, frankly, we weren't even sure what position he would play."

Canseco had been a third baseman in high school, but it was quickly obvious that wouldn't be his position in the pros. "I met Jose for the first time in the instructional league in Arizona that fall," recalls Brad Fisher, who later managed Canseco. "He was just a horrible offensive player and a horrible defensive player. There really wasn't a whole lot to impress you, except that I remember he hit a couple of balls that really got out of the yard in a hurry."

The first change for Canseco was from third base to the outfield. "I feel much more comfortable in the outfield," he says now. "I enjoy playing defense. When I'm in the outfield I'm not thinking about my next time at bat, I'm trying to do my best. I think I'm a pretty good defensive player."

Canseco hit only two home runs in 66 at-bats his first season. The next season in Class A (splitting the season between Madison and Modesto) he had 14 in 285 at-bats, but Fischer, his manager at Madison, wasn't impressed. "When I managed him at Madison, he had to be watched constantly," Fischer said. "I was worried about him getting into trouble on the field and off"—though Fischer adds that he wasn't talking about any serious trouble, "just the normal growing up kids that age go through."

The next year, Canseco's mother died in May. He hit 15 homers at Modesto, but also fanned 127 times in 410 at-bats. His frustration was obvious. But his transformation started in that offseason, and Fisher says he was amazed at Canseco's maturity by 1985.

"I decided that I was going to work hard with the weights," said Canseco. "I worked out six days a week for four straight months. I'd spend two and a half hours at a time in the weight room. One day I would work on my upper torso and the next day I would work on my legs.

"I also started concentrating more on my diet. The first thing is to stay off junk food. If I played basketball, when we got done, I'd have orange juice or apple juice. I try to eat good, balanced meals, making sure I get the right amounts of protein, carbohydrates, and fat."

Those changes effected a miracle. Canseco added 30 pounds of muscle and reported in at 215 pounds, surprising the A's; he was listed at 185 pounds in a preseason organizational chart. And he was on his way to a 1985 season so good it seemed almost fictitous.

He started the season in Double A Huntsville in a setting as ideal as a minor league team can be. "They'd never had baseball before in Huntsville," said Canseco, "and you can't believe how excited they were about our team. The people were just great to us. They really made us feel welcome. I think they knew right away what a good team we had. You can't get a better team in the minor leagues, and they knew a lot of us will be playing in the major leagues."

The A's had stocked the Huntsville team with most of their top prospects—pitchers Tim Belcher, Eric Plunk, and Darrell Akerfelds, outfielders Stan Javier and Luis Polonia, and first baseman Rob

Nelson. The A's expect all to make the majors eventually, but even on that team Canseco stood out.

He hit a home run in his first at-bat and went 5-for-5, including three 400-foot-plus home runs, in his last game at Huntsville. Despite a three-week layoff because of a broken finger in May, he batted .318 with 25 homers and 80 RBIs in just 58 games. Though he played less than half a season, he was named the Southern League's most valuable player. In a poll of managers he was named the best hitting prospect and the outfielder with the best arm.

Another indication of Canseco's "season": Huntsville fans dubbed him "Jose Parkway" because so many of his home runs landed on a highway beyond the park. "They talk about him in whispered tones in Huntsville," said A's assistant director of scouting Jay Alves. "Anybody who ever goes there from now on will be compared to him."

A's director of player development Karl Kuehl had insisted early in the season that Canseco would be left for the full year at Huntsville to give him the experience the A's thought he needed. But in midseason Canseco was at AAA Tacoma. "What could we do?" wondered Kuehl. "He'd had a full season statistically."

Canseco was nearly as impressive in the Pacific Coast League, hitting .348 with 11 homers and 47 RBIs in 60 games. He'd only been in the league one week when managers voted him the best hitting prospect and the outfielder with the best arm—and Tacoma had to open the gates early because so many people were showing up just to watch Canseco take batting practice.

Overall, he had a .333 batting average, 36 homers, and 127 RBIs in 118 games, enough to win him the selection as Minor League Player of the Year.

Promoted to the A's at the end of the PCL season, Canseco was distracted by the media attention. "I was trying to show off in batting practice," he admits. "I didn't get my concentration back until the last couple of weeks."

But when he got into the groove, he awed major league fans as he had those in the minor leagues. His first home run was to dead center in Oakland, and he later hit a home run onto the roof at Comiskey Park, only the 40th time that had been done in nearly 50 years. In late September he was named American League Player of the Week after he hit .481 with a slugging percentage of .852 in that stretch. He wound up at .302 with five homers and 17 RBIs in 29 games.

More than sheer statistics, though, are the impressions Canseco left with baseball people. Some sample comments:

• "Canseco is the best player I've seen in any league I've been in. He's got all the tools. I've never seen anybody with Canseco's power. He has a good eye at the plate and knows what pitches to lay off. He's not the type of batter you want to pitch to when you're behind in the count."—*Portland manager Bill Dancy.*

• "He's awesome. I haven't seen a guy hit the ball like that in a long, long time. He hits 'em into orbit. He doesn't believe in chea-pies."—*Former Birmingham Barons manager Gordy MacKenzie, who saw Canseco at Huntsville.*

• "Not since 1971, when Burt Hooton struck out 19 in his Tacoma debut, was there so much interest in a Tacoma player. People I'd never seen before made special trips to the park to buy tickets, say-ing they wanted to see Jose."—*Betty Howes, Tacoma ticket manag-er.*

• "Canseco's physical power is in the class of a Mickey Mantle or Frank Howard."—*Tacoma pitching coach Chuck Estrada, a former major league pitcher.*

• "He's got the power of a Jim Rice and the arm of a Dwight Evans. We were struggling before he showed up and he turned us around."—*Tacoma manager Keith Lieppman.*

And, from A's second baseman Tony Phillips, who played with Canseco at Tacoma: "One day it was clouding up and he took a big swing and knocked the rain back two days."

★   ★   ★

The first thing you notice about Jose Canseco is his muscles. For a change, when baseball people say, "Look at that build," they're not talking about a big-breasted blonde in the stands.

His weightlifting routine bulked him up to 228 pounds for the '86 season. He looks like he should be playing tight end or linebacker for the Chicago Bears, not outfielder for the Oakland A's. When he grips the bat tightly, his muscles leap out at you and you can almost see sawdust coming out of the bat. He seems almost a cartoon character —Ozark Ike, perhaps.

Going against the norm of lighter, whippier bats, he uses a 35-inch, 35-ouncer ("When two masses meet," he says, "the heavier mass is going to have the advantage."), but gets it through the strike zone faster than anybody.

"I don't think any player in the last 50, 60 years has had his kind of bat speed," said Bob Watson. "He's in a class by himself. I had the chance to hit behind Cesar Cedeno, Jim Rice, Fred Lynn, Reggie Jackson and Dale Murphy, and all of those guys had bat speed. His is quicker."

One last point: Though his gargantuan home runs get all the at-tention, Canseco is much more than just another Dave Kingman. "He reminds me some of Harmon Killebrew or Willie McCovey, the way he rips the ball through the infield," said Rigney. "He can hit a ball that's just two feet from an infielder, but it gets out there so fast the guy doesn't have a chance to get it."

"I admit I'm as impressed as everybody else with the long balls," said manager Moore, "but the thing I really liked about him last September was a ball he hit over the right-field fence in Oakland that just got into the stands. He had to go down to get a curveball, but he adjusted perfectly. He's going to get a lot of those pitches, so he's got to hit them."

"With my power," says Canseco, simply, "I can hit the ball over any fence, so I don't have to pull everything."

In "The Natural," Roy Hobbs strikes out the first batter he faces in organized baseball on three pitches. He hits the first three pitches in batting practice over the right-field fence, the left-field fence, and into the center-field bleachers. In his first game he literally knocks the cover off the baseball.

Perhaps Malamud was remembering Clint Hartung.

But he might have been anticipating Jose Canseco.

Great Scott!

by Terry Bochatey of United Press International. What goes up must come down. That's the hard lesson learned by Houston Astros righthander Mike Scott while trying to make a putout at first base in a 1986 game against the Cincinnati Reds. Trying to get out of the way is umpire Fred Brocklander. Copyright © 1986, Terry Bochatey, United Press International.

Who's Listening?

by John William Coniglio of the Chattanooga Times. Coaching youngsters, especially 6-year-olds, can be as frustrating as it is rewarding. Most young superstars would rather make faces than listen to coaching advice. Copyright © 1986, John William Coniglio.

PRIZE-WINNING WRITERS IN BEST SPORTS STORIES 1987

Ron Cook (Alcohol: Sports' Deadliest Drug) is a special-assignments sportswriter for the *Pittsburgh Press*. The 30-year-old Cook, a 1978 graduate of Northwestern University's Medill School of Journalism, worked as a sportswriter for five years with the *Beaver County (Pa.) Times* before going to Pittsburgh in 1983. He covered West Virginia University football for one season, the Pittsburgh Maulers of the United States Football League for one season and the Pittsburgh Steelers of the National Football League for a year before accepting his current position. Cook has won two Golden Quill Awards and was a top 10 finisher in the Associated Press Sports Editors Contest for best sports stories in 1984.

David DeVoss (Edwin Tapia Gets His Chance With the Dodgers) is a staff writer for *Los Angeles Times Magazine*. DeVoss, a 1968 University of Texas graduate with a degree in political science, began his journalism career in 1968 in Houston as a correspondent for *Time* magazine. He performed the same function in Montreal in 1970, Detroit in 1971, Saigon in South Vietnam in 1972, Los Angeles from 1973 to '77, Hong Kong from 1977 to '81 and Bangkok from 1981 to '83 before serving two years as a bureau chief in Mexico. The Dallas native, who joined the Times staff in 1985, is making his first appearance in *Best Sports Stories*.

John Feinstein (For Driesell, a Sad Farewell and The Odd Couple) grew up in New York City and received a history degree from Duke University in 1977. After working as a summer intern at the *Washington Post*, he was hired as a metro staff reporter before moving to the sports department. During his 10 years in Washington, he has covered police, courts and state politics on the news side and pro soccer, college football and basketball, major league baseball and tennis on the sports side. He currently covers college basketball and tennis. Feinstein, who is making his fourth appearance in *Best Sports Stories*, has contributed to such publications as *Sports Illustrated, The Sporting News, Inside Sports*, the *Washington Post Sunday Magazine* and *Outlook*. His first book, *A Season on the Brink—One Year With Bob Knight and the Indiana Hoosiers*, was published last fall and reached *The New York Times* bestseller list six weeks later.

William Gildea (Donovan Still Casts a Big Shadow) is a member of the *Washington Post* sports department. The 1960 Georgetown University graduate attended graduate school at Columbia University in 1961 and then worked two years for the *Baltimore Sun* before taking a job with the Post. Gildea also has worked as a sports columnist and feature writer after spending six years as an assignment editor for the Post's style section. The 1978 Nieman Fellow also won the feature competition in *Best Sports Stories 1985* and is making his fourth appearance in the anthology.

OTHER WRITERS IN BEST SPORTS STORIES 1987

Paul Attner (Bird Gift-Wrapped Celtics' Title) has been a national correspondent for *The Sporting News* since 1984. The former *Washington Post* staff writer is a 1969 graduate of California State University at Fullerton, where he earned a Bachelor of Arts degree in Communications. Attner, the author of three books, has won numerous sportswriting awards, including three first places in the annual Pro Football Writers Association of America writing contests and a first-place award in the U.S. Pro Basketball Writers annual contest. He is an active member of the Society of Professional Journalists, Pro Football Writers Association of America and Pro Basketball Writers of America.

Doug Bedell (SMU Lets Collins, Hitch Quit) writes special-assignment sports features for the *Dallas Morning News*. The 35-year-old New York City native was raised in Houston and majored in biology for four years at Northwestern University before transferring to Baylor and graduating with a journalism degree. Bedell began his career with the *Beaumont Enterprise and Journal* as an assistant state editor before becoming a news reporter in the paper's Orange, Lake Charles and Port Arthur bureaus. He accepted a job as a general assignment reporter for the *Dallas Times Herald* in 1976 and moved four years later to the *Louisville Courier Journal and Times* to cover state and federal courts. Bedell returned to Dallas in 1986 as a general assignment reporter with the Morning News and recently moved to sports. He is making his first appearance in *Best Sports Stories*.

Bill Brubaker (Taylor: A Troubled Giant) is a sportswriter for the *Washington Post*, specializing in investigative stories. Brubaker, who was born in New York City and raised in Miami, Fla., was previously employed by the *Hollywood (Fla.) Sun-Tattler*, the *Miami News*, the *New York Daily News* and *Sports Illustrated*. The four-time winner of the New York Newspaper Guild's Page One Award is making his first appearance in *Best Sports Stories*.

John Capouya (Jerry Falwell's Team) is a contributing editor for *Sport* magazine. He is a graduate of Grinnell College who received a master's degree from the Columbia University School of Journalism. Capouya, formerly a senior editor at *Sport*, has been a frequent contributor to the *Village Voice*. He is making his first appearance in *Best Sports Stories*.

Dan Daly (Lehigh's Sad Story of Human Isolation) is a sportswriter for the *Washington Times*. The Williams College graduate began his journalism career with the *Worcester (Mass.) Telegram* in 1976 and later worked for the *Arizona Republic* in Phoenix and the *Daily Oklahoman* in Oklahoma City. He joined the Times' sports department in 1982. Daly, who has received several writing awards, is making his first appearance in *Best Sports Stories*.

Ken Denlinger (Verdict Raises No Cheers in NFL Camps) has been a sports columnist for the *Washington Post* since 1975. Denlinger, a 1964 graduate of Penn State University, worked two years for the *Pittsburgh Press* before joining the Post. He has co-authored two books, *Athletes for Sale* and *Redskin Country/From Baugh to the Super Bowl*. Denlinger, who lives with his wife in Rockville, Md., is included in *Who's Who in America*.

Glenn Dickey ('The Natural'—Live!) has been a daily sports columnist for the *San Francisco Chronicle* since 1971. The University of California at Berkeley graduate, who began his career at the Chronicle in 1963, also is a frequent contributor to magazines and has written nine non-fiction books, the latest of which is titled *The History of the World Series*. Dickey lives across the bay in Oakland with his wife, Nancy, and son, Scott.

Ray Didinger (All-Pro's Last Fight) has been a sports columnist for the *Philadelphia Daily News* since 1980. The 1968 Temple University graduate began his career as a news reporter for the *Delaware County Daily Times* in Chester, Pa., before joining the *Philadelphia Bulletin* as a sportswriter. Didinger has won three Associated Press Sports Editors Awards and four Keystone Press Awards for writing. He was the 1974 feature category award winner in *Best Sports Stories* and is making his seventh appearance in the anthology.

Mike Downey (Unite, Fans of Boston Strugglers) is a syndicated sports columnist for the *Los Angeles Times* whose column appears weekly in *The Sporting News*. The 35-year-old Downey began his career as a sportswriter in Chicago for both the *Chicago Daily News* and *Chicago Sun-Times*. He also wrote about show-business personalities for the entertainment pages and authored a one-hour NBC-TV special on Comiskey Park and Wrigley Field. He became a columnist for the *Detroit Free Press* in 1982 and twice was voted Michigan Sportswriter of the Year by the National Sportscasters and Sportswriters Association. He served as a columnist for the Knight-Ridder News Syndicate at the Summer and Winter Olympic Games as well as the Democratic and Republican national conventions. This is Downey's first appearance in *Best Sports Stories*.

Glen Duffy (The Silence) is a contributing editor to *Philadelphia* magazine. The 32-year-old graduate of Ohio State University is a former columnist for the *Atlantic City Press*. Duffy is making his first appearance in *Best Sports Stories*.

Molly Dunham (Master of the Mount) covers college sports for the *Baltimore Evening Sun*, with an emphasis on the University of Maryland. The 1978 graduate of Towson State University began her journalism career with the *Frederick (Md.) News-Post* and the late *Baltimore News American* before joining the Evening Sun 2½ years ago. Dunham is making her first appearance in *Best Sports Stories*.

Randy Giancaterino (Belated MVP) is an editor for the South Philadelphia *Review-Chronicle*. The Temple University graduate has spent most of his six years with the weekly publication covering sports, but recently has been assigned to spot news and general-interest features. The 24-year-old Giancaterino, who writes a bi-monthly column that deals with sports personalities and local trends, was a first-place winner in the Philadelphia Press Association competition in 1983 and '85. Giancaterino, who is making his first appearance in *Best Sports Stories*, also coaches high school baseball and soccer.

Alan Goldstein (One Who Didn't Make It) is a sportswriter for the *Baltimore Sun*. The New York University graduate began working at the Sun in 1959, covering the old Baltimore Bullets. The 54-year-old Goldstein, who lives in Baltimore with his wife and two children, now writes general features while covering pro football, pro basketball and boxing.

Jerry Green (Mauch's Eyes, Not Words, Say It All) has been a sports columnist for the *Detroit News* since 1973. Prior to '73, Green covered football for the paper after working seven years with the Associated Press, two of those years as AP's Michigan sports editor. His other newspaper experience came from the *New York Journal-American* and *Long Island Star-Journal*. He also is the author of two books, *Year of the Tiger* and *The Detroit Lions—Great Years, Great Teams*.

Lee Green (The Race That Had It All) is a free-lance writer out of Ojai, Calif., whose work has appeared in such publications as *Sports Illustrated, Esquire, Playboy* and *TV Guide*. He also is a contributing editor and columnist for *Outside* magazine. Green, a 1972 UCLA graduate who worked as publicity director for women's athletics at the university from 1974 to '78 after a stint as a television news and sportswriter for Metromedia in Los Angeles, has written one book, *Sportswit*, and is working on a novel about the American Old West. He is making his second appearance in *Best Sports Stories*.

Randy Harvey (LeMond Packs Up Tour de France and Fighting the System) has been a sports feature writer for the *Los Angeles Times* since 1981. Harvey, born, raised and educated in Texas, worked at the *Tyler Morning Telegraph, Austin American Statesman* and the *Dallas Times Herald* before moving to the *Chicago Sun-Times* in 1976. He went to the *New York Daily News* in 1980 and moved to Los Angeles in 1981. Harvey, who holds a journalism degree from the University of Texas at Austin, is making his fourth appearance in *Best Sports Stories.*

Phil Hersh (The McMahon Mystique) handles special assignments for the *Chicago Tribune,* which in 1985 presented him an Outstanding Professional Performance award for "his compelling writing in regularly bringing to life the fascinating characters and personalities that lurk behind the box scores in sports." Hersh, a 1968 graduate of Yale University, previously worked for the *Gloucester (Mass.) Daily Times, Baltimore Evening Sun, Chicago Daily News* and the *Chicago Sun-Times.* Hersh, the 1986 winner in the commentary category of *Best Sports Stores,* is making his fifth appearance in the anthology.

Stan Hochman (Shoemaker Wins Kentucky Derby) has worked as a baseball writer, sports editor and columnist during his 27 years with the *Philadelphia Daily News.* Hochman began his career as a high school history teacher before turning to journalism as a writer for newspapers in Georgia, Texas and California. The Brooklyn native, who holds a master's degree from New York University, is not the only member of the Hochman family with a flair for journalism. His wife, Gloria, is an award-winning medical writer and his daughter, Anndee, is a reporter for the *Washington Post.*

Richard Hoffer (The Black Pioneers) has been writing features and covering a variety of sports for the *Los Angeles Times* for the last eight years. The Miami (Ohio) University graduate previously worked for the *Massillon (Ohio) Evening Independent, Riverside (Calif.) Press-Enterprise* and the *Cincinnati Post.* Hoffer, who also holds a master's degree from Stanford University, was the 1985 winner in the *Best Sports Stories* reporting category and is appearing in the anthology for the fifth straight year.

Jan Hubbard (The Sad Odyssey of Jason Burleson) has been a sportswriter for the *Dallas Morning News* for the past 3½ years. The Southern Methodist University graduate previously worked four years for the *Fort Worth Star-Telegram* and is in his seventh year of covering the Dallas Mavericks of the National Basketball Association. The 38-year-old Dallas native has contributed an NBA column to the pages of *The Sporting News* for five years.

Stan Isaacs (Cosell Leaves 'Em Fascinated) is a television sports columnist for Long Island-based *Newsday.* The Brooklyn College graduate has worked as a general sports columnist, a feature columnist and a sports editor in his 30-plus years with the publication and has won a National Headliners Award for sports column writing. His journalism career began on the *Chelm (Neb.) Avenger* and he went on to become a National Endowment for the Humanities Fellow at Stanford University. He lives in Roslyn Heights, N.Y., with his wife, Natalie, and three daughters.

Armen Keteyian (A Straight-Arrow Addict) is a writer-reporter for *Sports Illustrated.* The 1976 San Diego State University graduate began his career as a writer for the *Times Advocate* in Escondido, Calif., and later worked for two years as a free-lancer in San Diego. His 1982 contribution to the *San Diego Union* on triathlete Julie Moss captured first prize in the feature category of *Best Sports Stories.* Keteyian moved to New York in 1982 after being hired by Sports Illustrated and currently specializes in investigations, special projects and offbeat features.

Dave Krieger (Proposition 48 Teaches Athletes a Lesson) has been a general assignment and special projects sports reporter for the *Rocky Mountain News* since January 1986. He covered the city hall beat when he joined the publication in 1981 and later covered the 1983 Denver mayoral race and the Denver Broncos before taking his current assignment. Krieger was born in New Haven, Conn., and raised in Chicago before attending Columbia University and Amherst College. Before coming to Denver, he worked for the *Cincinnati Enquirer,* the *Burlington (Vt.) Free Press* and the *Claremont (N.H.) Eagle-Times.* Krieger also served as press secretary to U.S. Sen. Patrick J. Leahy of Vermont. The Colorado chapter of the Society of Professional Journalists presented Krieger with its Award of Excellence in 1984 for his investigative series on prescription drug abuse.

Kevin Lamb (Three Seconds) has covered the Chicago Bears and the National Football League since 1975 for the *Chicago Daily News* and the *Chicago Sun-Times.* He is a frequent contributor to magazines and has written three books, one of which was titled, *Quarterbacks, Nickelbacks & Other Loose Change: A Fan's Guide to the Changing Game of Pro Football.* The 34-year-old Lamb also has worked at the *Milwaukee Journal* and *Newsday* and has covered major league baseball and pro and college basketball as well as football. He is a 1973 graduate of Northwestern University.

David Levine (The Knee) is an articles editor at *Sport* magazine. He has written numerous stories for the magazine in his five years on the staff and has contributed to other publications such as the *New York Daily News.* Levine is making his first appearance in *Best Sports Stories.*

Franz Lidz (Mixing It Up With the Guys) is a staff writer for *Sports Illustrated* based in Philadelphia. Lidz, a graduate of Antioch College, effectively mixes the off-beat with sports and approaches life in much the same manner. Lidz has been a disc jockey, a soda jerk, an improvisational actor, a South American wanderer, a Boston cabbie and a bus driver near Baltimore. He is making his second appearance in *Best Sports Stories.*

Barry Lorge (The Most Majestic Rivalry Ever) is sports editor of the *San Diego Union* and a contributing editor to *Tennis* magazine. The 1970 Harvard College graduate moved to San Diego in 1971 after five years as a staff writer for the *Washington Post.* Lorge is making his first appearance in *Best Sports Stories.*

Judy Mills (Cracking Up) is a free-lance writer based in Missoula, Mont. Her stories have appeared in such publications as *Outside, Sunset* and *Women's Sports & Fitness,* in which this selection was included. Mills is making her first appearance in *Best Sports Stories.*

Malcolm Moran (Feller Still Pitches Coast to Coast and The Revolution Started With the Shot He Fired) has been covering a variety of sports for *The New York Times* since 1979. The 1975 Fordham University graduate worked for three years at Long Island-based *Newsday* before joining the Times. He lives with his wife Karla in Stamford, Conn., and is making his second appearance in *Best Sports Stories.*

Scott Ostler (If Athletes Abuse Drugs, It's Their Problem) is a sports columnist for the *Los Angeles Times.* Prior to becoming a columnist in 1981, Ostler's assignments included the Los Angeles Dodgers, California Angels, Los Angeles Lakers and a variety of other feature stories. He has been voted California's Sportswriter of the Year each of the past five years.

Mark Purdy (Jack Nicklaus Recaptures Mastery) has been sports editor of the *San Jose Mercury News* for the last three years. Before moving to San Jose, Purdy worked for the *Cincinnati Enquirer, Los Angeles Times* and the *Dayton Journal Herald.* The Celina, Ohio, native is making his second appearance in *Best Sports Stories.*

Rick Reilly (King of the Sports Page) has been writing about sports for nine years, the last two with *Sports Illustrated.* The Boulder, Colo., native began his career with the *Boulder Daily Camera* after graduation from the University of Colorado and later worked for the *Denver Post* and *Los Angeles Times.* Reilly won two national awards at the Associated Press Sports Editors convention in 1984 and won the top feature award at the Associated Press Editors convention the same year. He is making his third appearance in *Best Sports Stories.*

Jerry Zgoda (The Americanization of Frantisek Musil) covers the Minnesota North Stars of the National Hockey League for the *Minneapolis Star and Tribune.* The 1984 University of Minnesota graduate began his career as a sports reporting intern at the *Boston Globe* and *Miami Herald* before landing a job upon graduation with his hometown paper. Zgoda is making his first appearance in *Best Sports Stories.*

PRIZE-WINNING PHOTOGRAPHERS IN BEST SPORTS STORIES 1987

Louis DeLuca (Autograph Seekers and Now, Touch Your Toes) is a staff photographer for the *Dallas Times Herald.* He began his career with the *Shreveport (La.) Journal,* moved to the *Chicago Sun-Times* in 1983 and to Dallas a year later. The 30-year-old DeLuca was named 1982 Photographer of the Year in Louisiana, Texas and New Mexico and has won numerous other awards, including first places in the 1984 and 1986 *Best Sports Stories* black-and-white action categories.

Ken Geiger (Look Out Below) has been a staff photographer for the *Dallas Morning News* for the last four years. Geiger was born in Bremerton, Wash., and attended high school in Singapore before attending college at Rochester Institute of Technology. The 29-year-old Geiger is making a successful debut in *Best Sports Stories.*

William Johnson (A Situation Well in Hand) is a staff photographer for the *Bucks County (Pa.) Courier Times.* After graduating from high school, Johnson attended the Middle Bucks Area Vocational Tech School where he studied commercial art and photography and later studied at Bucks County Community College and Tyler School of Art. Johnson, who lives in Hatboro, Pa., with his wife and three daughters, has won more than 50 regional and national awards in his nine-year journalism career. He is making his first appearance in *Best Sports Stories.*

OTHER PHOTOGRAPHERS IN BEST SPORTS STORIES 1987

David Bauman (No. 1 on the Hit Parade) has been a staff photographer with the *Riverside (Calif.) Press-Enterprise* since 1976. David's father, Fred, has been Photo Editor at the Press-Enterprise since the younger Bauman's birth in 1954. David began taking photos at age 9 and was stringing for the Associated Press and United Press International while attending high school. After a brief stint as lab technician at the *Antioch (Calif.) Ledger,* Bauman attended Riverside City College and eventually joined his father at the Press-Enterprise. He is making his first appearance in *Best Sports Stories.*

Terry Bochatey (Great Scott!) has worked for *United Press International Newspictures* since his graduation from Colorado State University in 1972. He began his career in New York and was transferred to Columbus, O., a year later to take over as bureau manager. He moved to Cincinnati in 1980 to become Newspictures manager for the Ohio-Kentucky region. Bochatey is making his fourth appearance in *Best Sports Stories.*

Bernard Brault (Full Cycle) is a staff photographer for *La Presse* newspaper who also does free-lance work out of Canada. Brault, who lives in Longueuil, Quebec, began his career in 1976 as a staff photographer for a local newspaper before taking the free-lance trail four years later. His work has appeared in several Quebec sports magazines and he has contributed to such wire services as *United Press Canada, Reuters* and *Canadian Press.* Brault, who began contributing to La Presse in 1984, has earned numerous citations for his work and is making his second appearance in *Best Sports Stories.*

John William Coniglio (Who's Listening?) is a staff photographer for the *Chattanooga Times.* Coniglio, who was born in Oak Ridge, Tenn., and lived in Nashville, London, England, and Memphis, received a bachelor of science degree from the University of Tennessee at Chattanooga. He was previously employed as a social worker and a laborer before turning to free-lance photography. Coniglio, who was hired by the Times in 1979, is making his first appearance in *Best Sports Stories.*

Karl M. Ferron (Rain, Rain Go Away) is a staff photographer for the *Baltimore Sun.* The Rochester, N.Y., native was chosen for the Smithsonian Internship program in 1981, launching his professional career. Six months of free-lance work for the *Baltimore News American* prepared Ferron for his current position. He is making his first appearance in *Best Sports Stories.*

J.B. Forbes (Passing Fancy) has been a staff photographer for the *St. Louis Post-Dispatch* since 1975. As a general-assignment photographer, Forbes has covered a lot of sporting events, but assignments also have taken him to shoot the fighting in El Salvador and Nicaragua, unrest in Haiti, an earthquake in Mexico and fashions in New York. Forbes was born in Kansas City and received a photojournalism degree from the University of Kansas. While attending school, he worked as a lab assistant in the photo department of the *Topeka Capital Journal.* Forbes later worked for the *Parsons (Kan.) Sun* and the *Miami (Fla.) News* before joining the Post-Dispatch. Forbes, who has won numerous awards for his photography, lives with his wife and four children in south St. Louis County, where they run a horse boarding and breeding operation.

Sam Forencich (Double Trouble) is a staff photographer for the *Palo Alto (Calif.) Times Tribune.* Forencich, a graduate of Stanford University, has covered a variety of sports events since beginning his career with the Tribune four years ago. He is making his first appearance in *Best Sports Stories.*

Adrian Keating (A Shady Shot) is a staff photographer for the *Journal Inquirer* in Manchester, Conn. Keating began his professional career as an English teacher in the Connecticut public school system before deciding that a change was in order. He hit the free-lance photography trail in 1977, doing work for both the *Associated Press* and *United Press International.* He became a staff photographer for the *Bristol Press* in 1983 but was part of a company-wide layoff that resulted in his move to Manchester. Keating, who won the 1985 black-and-white action category in the *Best Sports Stories* competition, is making his third appearance in the anthology.

Paula Nelson (Read My Lips) is a staff photographer for the *Dallas Morning News.* The 1982 University of Missouri School of Journalism graduate started her professional career as a free-lancer before spending 10 months as editor of a cruise-ship newspaper. Nelson is making her first appearance in *Best Sports Stories.*

Smiley N. Pool (Down and Out) is a staff photographer for the *Austin (Tex.) American-Statesman.* Born and raised in Texas, Pool spent two years in St. Louis where he began his photography career with the *St. Louis Suburban Newspapers.* He returned to Austin in 1986 to take his current job at age 19 while continuing his education at Austin Community College. Pool is making his first appearance in *Best Sports Stories.*

Steven Wayne Rotsch (Tension Personified) is a free-lance photographer based in West Virginia whose primary client is the Associated Press. After obtaining a journalism degree from Southern Illinois University at Edwardsville, Rotsch worked on a free-lance basis from 1980 to '83 for the *Post-Dispatch* and *Globe Democrat* in St. Louis. He is making his first appearance in *Best Sports Stories.*

Boris Spremo (Getting His Kicks) is an internationally acclaimed photographer based in Canada. Spremo was born in Yugoslavia and educated at Belgrade's Cinematographic Institute before emigrating to Canada. After free-lancing for five years, he joined the *Toronto Globe & Mail* staff in 1962 and moved to the *Toronto Star* in '66. Spremo has won more than 200 major national and international awards and has collaborated on two books, *Toronto by Boris Spremo* and *20 Years of Photo Journalism.* Two of his most noteworthy achievements occurred in 1966 when he became the first Canadian to capture a first-prize gold medal in the World Press Photo competition in The Hague and when he was awarded the official title of Master of Photographic Arts by the Professional Photographers of Canada Inc. He was honored that same year as Canadian Photographer of the Year and was commissioned in 1967 by the Canadian federal government to compile a photographic essay for the Canadian Pavilion at Expo '67. In addition to his numerous awards, Spremo has had his photographs published in major publications throughout the world and he has traveled extensively with Canadian Prime Minister Pierre Trudeau. He has shot everything from drought and famine to such distinguished dignitaries as Pope John Paul II and England's Royal Family. Sports assignments include several Olympics and World Cup Soccer in Mexico. Spremo has exhibited his photographs at numerous one-man shows and is a sought-after speaker for photography seminars at colleges throughout Canada and the United States.

John Walker (Crunch!) is a staff photographer for the *Fresno (Calif.) Bee.* The California State University graduate began his professional career with the *Mesa (Ariz.) Tribune* in 1980 and moved to Fresno five years later. Walker, who has won several awards in his six-year career, is making his first appearance in *Best Sports Stories.*

Billy Weeks (Follow the Bouncing Ball) has been a staff photographer for the *Chattanooga Times* for 2½ years. He took that job after graduation from the University of Tennessee at Chattanooga. Weeks, who enjoys photographing nature and wildlife as well as sporting events, is making his first appearance in *Best Sports Stories.*

THE PANEL OF JUDGES FOR BEST SPORTS STORIES 1987

Brian Brooks is the *St. Louis Post-Dispatch* Distinguished Professor of Journalism at the University of Missouri and managing editor of the *Columbia Missourian*. The former reporter and editor at the *Memphis Press-Scimitar* is co-author of *News Reporting and Writing* and *The Art of Editing*, best-selling textbooks in their fields.

George Kennedy is an associate dean at the University of Missouri and an associate professor in the university's School of Journalism. Before moving to Columbia, Kennedy spent 7½ years as a reporter and editor with the *Miami Herald* and two summers as a writing coach for the *San Jose Mercury*. He is co-author of *News Reporting and Writing* and *The Writing Book*, two college and professional textbooks.

Bill Kuykendall is an associate professor and director of the photojournalism sequence at the Missouri School of Journalism. He formerly was director of photography at the *Seattle Times* and a frequent speaker on photojournalism and photo department management. Kuykendall also directs the international Pictures of the Year Competition.

Daryl Moen is a professor at the University of Missouri and director of mid-career programs at the university's School of Journalism. He is the former managing editor of the *Columbia Missourian* and two other dailies. Moen also is co-author of *News Reporting and Writing* and *The Writing Book* and author of *Newspaper Layout and Design*.

Byron Scott is the Meredith Professor of Magazine Journalism and director of the service journalism program at the University of Missouri. He has worked as a newspaper reporter and magazine editor in Miami, Chicago, New York, Washington and Long Beach. Scott formerly headed the magazine sequence at Ohio University's Scripps Journalism School.